Keys to the Japanese Heart and Soul

装丁 ● 菊地信義
装画 ● 野村俊夫

編集 ● 鈴木節子
翻訳 ● 一場慎司

挿画 ● 水木しげる
　　　尾竹国観（兎）
　　　石井滴水（狸）
　　　鴨下晃湖（雀）
　　　井川洗涯（蟹）
　　　米内穂豊（鼠）

Published by Kodansha International Ltd.,
17-14 Otowa 1-chome, Bunkyo-ku, Tokyo 112-8652.

First Edition 1996

ISBN 4-7700-2082-1
　00 01　15 14 13 12

英語で話す「日本の心」

和英辞典では引けないキーワード197

Keys to the Japanese Heart and Soul

「英文日本大事典」［編］

まえがき

本書は『英文日本大事典』(講談社刊)から、日本文化を理解するためのキーワードを集め、和訳をつけて対訳本にしたものです。

　『英文日本大事典』は日本の全体像を12000にものぼる項目で解説した百科事典です。この百科事典の前身の『エンサイクロペディア・オブ・ジャパン』では企画のスタートに際して、内外で2つの編集参与会を組織しました。故E.O.ライシャワー元駐日米国大使をチェアマンとする外国人参与会が項目選定にあたって、とりわけ強く主張したことの一つが、日本的な社会構造、人間関係、慣習、心理構造を解説する項目を立てることでした。その結果「あきらめ」、「遠慮」、「頑張る」、「腹」、「顔」、「生きがい」等々の日本固有の言葉や日本語的な使われ方が、日本人の思想や行動を理解するうえで必須であるとして項目になりました。これらは、他の事典類には見当たらない、非常にユニークな項目でした。

　本書ではこれらの項目のほかに、美意識、宗教観、哲学思想、社会概念、民間信仰、俗信、動物、植物などの分野から日本文化の基盤となっている約200項目を選び、1冊の本にしたものです。海外のジャパノロジスト(日本研究家)によって執筆された項目も多く、外国人の目を通して見た日本の記述には、われわれ日本人が気がつかなかった視点も見られます。

　本書は、国際交流に携わる人々やビジネスマンの異文化コミュニケーションに、また英語を学習中の人に、必携の書となるものと期待しています。

講談社バイリンガル・ブックス編集部

Foreword

The present volume is a bilingual collection of articles explaining certain words and phrases selected from *Japan: An Illustrated Encyclopedia* (also published by Kodansha) that are crucially important to an understanding of Japanese culture.

An extensive collection consisting of twelve thousand entries on every aspect of Japan, *Japan: An Illustrated Encyclopedia* was the work of two editorial committees, one in Japan and the other in the United States, originally set up for the production of a much longer precursor, the nine volume *Encyclopedia of Japan*. The contents were decided by a foreign editorial board headed by the former U.S. ambassador to Japan, the late Edwin O. Reischauer, and articles on the structure of Japanese society, how human relations work, as well as the customs and psychology of Japanese people, received a special emphasis, with the result that it included explanations of particular Japanese words, as well as their connotations, vital to an understanding of Japanese thought and behavior—words such as *akirame* (renunciation), *enryo* (deference, reserve), *gambaru* (stout persistence), *hara* (abdomen, true intention), *kao* (face, honor), and *ikigai* (purpose in living).

The present volume is comprised both of those and other words and phrases necessary for a fundamental knowledge of Japanese culture, arranged under the eight topic heading of Aesthetics, Religious Concepts, Philosophy and Thoughts, Social Concepts, Folk Religion, Folk Beliefs, Animals, and Plants. Many entries were written by specialists in Japanese studies abroad, providing insights from their unique vantage point that might easily be missed by Japanese people themselves.

This text will be essential for businesspeople and others whose work involves exchange and communication with other cultures, and for Japanese people eager to improve their English language abilities.

Editorial Department for Kodansha Bilingual Books

CONTRIBUTORS

Allan A. ANDREWS
Harumi BEFU
Carmen BLACKER
Robert BORGEN
Martin C. COLLCUTT
H. Byron EARHART
EJIMA Yasunori
FUJITA Tomio
FUKUDA Hideichi
Allan G. GRAPARD
Money HICKMAN
HOSHINO Eiki
IMAMICHI Tomonobu
INAGAKI Shisei
INOKUCHI Shōji
IWAI Hiroaki
Whalen LAI
Takie Sugiyama LEBRA
MATSUDA Osamu
MATSUNAMI Yoshihiro
MISUMI Haruo
MIYAKE Hitoshi
MIYAKE Masahiko
HELMUT Morsbach
Kyōko Motomochi NAKAMURA
NAKANE Chie
NAKAZATO Michiko

NOGUCHI Takenori
ŌNISHI Harutaka
ŌTŌ Tokihiko
ŌUCHI Eishin
Stuart D.B. PICKEN
Robert RHODES
Thomas P. ROHLEN
SAITŌ Shōji
Hiroshi SAKAMOTO
SANEYOSHI Tatsuo
James H. SANFORD
SEIKE Kiyosi
Jack SEWARD
SHIMBORI Michiya
Robert J. SMITH
SONODA Minoru
SUCHI Tokuhei
SUZUKI Eiichi
TSUCHIDA Mitsufumi
TSUCHIDA Tomoaki
William J. TYLER
UEDA Kenji
Makoto UEDA
Hiroshi WAGATSUMA
Stanley WEINSTEIN
YAMAZAKI Yukio

目次

Contents

第6章　俗信

第7章　日本文化と動物

第8章　日本文化と植物

Chapter 6   Folk Beliefs

Chapter 7   Animals in Japanese Culture

Chapter 8   Plants in Japanese Culture

第一章

美学
Aesthetics

美学

日本の伝統的美意識の大きな特徴は、象徴的表現を写実的描写より重視することである。もう一つの特徴は、真の芸術とは、美しいものを選択的に表現し、粗末、卑俗なものを排除することを当然としていたことである。したがって、画家たちは、民衆の日常生活の描写よりも、自然を主題に選ぶことが多かった。平安貴族の優雅と洗練の趣味が後世の文化の伝統に影響を与えて、「優雅」が美の重要な規準の一つとなった。「おかし」「風流」「幽玄」「粋(いき)」という重要な概念は、すべて「優雅」の意味を内包している。もう一つの重要な規準は「はかなさ」であり、至上の美も、もろくはかないものと考えられるところから、これも「優雅」の一変形と考えられた。人生の無常を強調する仏教は、この「はかなさ」の思想を吸収して、哲学的な深さをもたらした。「あわれ（後に、もののあわれに発展する）」「幽玄」「侘(わび)」「寂(さび)」などという美的理念は、すべてその意味に「ほろび」を内包している。

芸術的に作り出された時間的、空間的余白は、重要な美学的要素の一つになった。簡素は、内在する本質を如実に表現しようとする模倣の概念にとって必然的結果であり、象徴的表現を強調するものであった。「侘(わび)」「寂(さび)」「間(ま)」「余情」「渋い」などという概念は、その基本的含蓄に、簡素への指向が見られ、お

aesthetics

(*bigaku*). A distinctive feature of traditional aesthetic thought in Japan was the tendency to value symbolic representation more highly than realistic delineation. Another characteristic was the assumption that true art involves a selective presentation of the beautiful and avoidance of the humble and vulgar. Consequently artists tended to choose nature for their subjects, avoiding the depiction of everyday life for the common people. The Heian court taste for grace and refinement had exerted a lasting impact on the later cultural tradition, establishing elegance as one of the main criteria for beauty. Such important concepts as *okashi*, *fūryū*, *yūgen*, and *iki* all carried a connotation of elegance. Another highly valued quality was impermanence, which could be considered a variation of elegance, for exquisite beauty was considered fragile and fleeting. Buddhism, with its emphasis on life's mutability, merged with this ideal and provided philosophical depth. Such aesthetic principles as *aware* (and its later elaboration, *mono no aware*), *yūgen*, *wabi*, and *sabi* all implied transience perishability.

An artistically created void, either in time or in space, became an important idea in aesthetic speculations. Simplicity was a corollary to the concept of mimesis, which stressed symbolic representation. Concepts like *wabi*, *sabi*, *ma*, *yojō*, and *shibui* were all inclined toward simplicity in their basic implications, uniformly showing distaste for ornate beauty. Simplicity also

しなべて華美を嫌う。簡素は、芸術的表現では、自然さ、ないしは技巧に欠けることを意味する。日本伝統の美学では、芸術と自然の距離は、西欧の美学と比べて、きわめて近いのである。自然の神秘は、描写では表現できない。ただ暗示によってのみ表現されるのであって、その暗示が簡潔であればあるほど効果的なのである。

日本人の自然観

英語の nature を訳した日本語の「自然」の語源的な意味は、「おのずからなる生成発展とそれによって生じた状態」である。漢字の文字どおりの意味は「あるがままのさま」であり、自然の秩序の存在よりも、存在の様相を表している。自然界に対する一般的表現である「自然」という言葉は日本語の古語には見当たらない。古代の日本人はあらゆる現象を神の顕示と考えていた。「天地」、「生きとし生けるもの」が自然を表す包括的な言葉に最も近かった。

『日本書紀』（720年成立）の神話に出てくる原初の夫婦神伊弉諾と伊弉冉の最初の子供たちは、神でも人間でもなく、島であり陸塊であった。このように、日本では、西欧思想と異なって、人間は自然に勝るもの、あるいは自然に対立するものとは考えなかった。

meant naturalness, or lack of artifice, in artistic expression. In traditional Japanese aesthetics the distance between art and nature was considerably shorter than in its Western counterpart. The mystery of nature could never be presented through description, however: it could only be suggested, and the terser the suggestion, the greater its effectiveness.

concept of nature

(*nihonjin no shizenkan*). The basic, etymological meaning of the Japanese word *shizen*, which is used to translate the English word "nature," "is the power of spontaneous self-development and what results from that power." The Chinese characters for the Japanese term *shizen* literally mean "from itself thus it is," expressing a mode of being rather than the existence of a natural order. Indeed, the term *shizen* as a general expression for nature is not found in ancient Japanese. The ancient Japanese people recognized every phenomenon as a manifestation of the *kami* (god or gods). Such terms as *ametsuchi* (heaven and earth) and *ikitoshi ikerumono* (living things) were the closest to a comprehensive word for nature in their language.

In the mythology of the *Nihon shoki* (720), the first offspring of the primordial couple Izanagi and Izanami were neither *kami* nor human but islands and landmasses. Thus human beings were not considered to be superior or opposed to nature, as in Western thought; their lives were embedded in it. This classical idea may be

人間の生命は、自然に抱え込まれていたのである。この古典的思想は、さまざまな日本文化、たとえば禅画、文人画、茶道、生け花などに散見される。自然の中で主体と客体は溶け合って一つの現実となるが、この事実が、詩の中に季節の花や動物や風景が多用される理由である。「自然」という語に自然界の秩序という西欧の概念が入り込むのは、明治時代になってからである。

芸術と植物

絵画その他の日本の芸術は、伝統的に作者の自然観に負うところが大きく、一般に簡潔で、こぢんまりとしていて、控え目に優雅である。伝統的な日本の風景描写は、西洋の油絵のように、多彩な色使いをしない。彫刻も、多くは繊細で、規模も小さい。

織物や塗り物、および焼き物には、植物、花、鳥や、その文様が、写実的な色で再現されることも多い。自然の形を愛し、それを理想的に表現しようとする熱意が、日本の伝統芸術、たとえば、生け花、茶の湯、盆景、盆栽、造園、の発展の最大の原動力であった。これらの表現手段によって、日本人は、自然の美を日常生活と精神的価値にとりこんだのである。茶室の飾りには、「花は野にあるようにいけよ」という理論にかなうように、控えめの花を選んだ。日本人は、自然の大きさと簡潔性を表現するために、ぽつんと置いた

seen expressed in various Japanese cultural forms such as
Zen painting, literati art works, the tea ceremony, and
flower arrangement. In nature, subject and object
become fused into one reality, a fact that explains the
frequent use in poetry of the various seasonal flowers,
animals, and sights. It was only after the beginning of
the Meiji period that the Western concept of nature, sig-
nifying the natural order, came to be attached to *shizen*.

plants in the visual arts

(*geijutsu to shokubutsu*). Pictorial and other arts in Japan
have traditionally relied heavily on the artist's sensitivity
to nature and have generally tended toward the simple,
compact, spare and graceful. Traditional Japanese ren-
ditions of landscapes do not display the wide range of
color seen in Western oil paintings. In sculpture, too,
works are in general delicately carved and small in scale.

Plants, flowers, and birds or their patterns are frequently reproduced in lifelike colors on fabric, lacquer
ware, and ceramic ware. This love of natural form and an
eagerness to express it ideally have been primary motives
in the development of traditional Japanese arts such as
flower arrangement, the tea ceremony, tray landscapes
(*bonkei*), *bonsai*, and landscape gardening. By means of
these arts, the Japanese people have tried to integrate the
beauty of nature into their daily lives and spiritual values. For decorating a teahouse, an unassuming flower
was selected to conform with the principle that "flowers should always look as if they were in the wild." The

花瓶に野の花を一輪だけ活けたのである。

風流

教養ある洗練された人の上品な趣味、あるいはそのような人が関わっている芸術作品や事物を表す。中国語が語源で、「良い振る舞いと物腰」という意味であった。8世紀に日本に伝わると、より審美的意味に用いられ、都会人の洗練されたふるまいを表すようになり、後には、優雅で、風趣に富み、芸術的とされるあらゆるものに適用された。

　12世紀には、「風流」の意味は、大きく二つに分かれる。一方で、大衆芸術における世俗的で、はでな美を風流と称したのに対し、他方では、庭園、生け花、建築、漢詩に「風流」を求めた。後者の流れが、室町時代に茶の湯を生んだのである。

　江戸時代には、世俗的な意味の「風流」は、浮世草子などに明らかである。対照的に茶の湯を生んだ「風流」は、俳諧、漢詩、文人画に見られ、人生の重荷から逃れた隠者の生き方を唱道した。芭蕉は、『奥の細道』で、後者の意味でこの語を用いている。

　　　　　風流の
　　　　　はじめや奥の
　　　　　田植歌

Japanese sought to express the vastness and simplicity of nature with a single wild flower in a solitary vase.

fūryū

Refers to the refined taste of a cultivated person and to works of art and other things associated with such persons. The word was derived from the Chinese term *fengliu*, which literally meant "good deportment and manners." After reaching Japan around the eighth century, it was employed in a more aesthetic sense, referring to the refined manners of an urbane person and later to all things regarded as elegant, tasteful, or artistic.

In the twelfth century, *fūryū* began to follow two separate lines of semantic evolution. In one, the word was applied to the more earthy, showy beauty manifest in popular arts. In the other, men attempted to discover *fūryū* in the beauty of landscape gardens, flower arrangement, architecture, and Chinese nature poetry. This gave birth to the tea ceremony in the Muromachi period.

In the Edo period, popular *fūryū* manifested itself in the type of fiction known as *ukiyo-zōshi*. By contrast, the second type of *fūryū* as seen in *haikai* verse, Chinese poetry, and the *nanga* style of painting (*bunjinga*), advocated the lifestyle of a hermit who withdraws from the conflict-laden activities of human life. The term was employed in this sense by Bashō in a *haiku* he wrote during his famous journey to the far north:

> The beginning of *fūryū*:
> This rice-planting
> Song of the north.

現代の「風流」は、意味の歴史的な変遷を内にとどめながらも、おもに、洗練された趣味を表す説明的な語として残っている。

粋
（いき）

江戸時代の町人の美的、道徳的理念。もとの意味は、「心意気」「心もち」である。後に「一段上の心意気」「高い心もち」といった意味になり、洗練された人の話しぶり、身のこなし、あるいは身なりなどもさすようになった。19世紀になると、江戸町人の理想を表す語となり、大坂の「粋」（すい）に影響されて意味も似てきた。「すい」と同じ意味で使われることもよくある。しかし、通常はその意味が微妙に異なる。美的概念として、「いき」は「すい」より地味な傾向がある。「いき」な人は、灰色、焦げ茶、濃紺などを好み、明るい色や色彩豊かなデザインを敬遠する。また、「すい」よりも、多少官能や色っぽさの意味合いが濃いように思われる。「いき」は女性、とりわけ、品良く色っぽさを見せる限界を知っている花街の女性を描写するときによく用いられた。「すい」な女性と比べたとき、「いき」な女性は、意気盛んで、その振る舞いには男勝りのところがあり、好きな男のためならみずからを犠牲にすることも辞さなかった。他方、その振る舞いはあきらめを示すことでもあり、その結果、悲しみと孤独に陥ることもあった。「いき」は、人情本にもっと

Today, *fūryū* remains in the Japanese language largely as a descriptive term denoting refinement of taste, though its past semantic vicissitudes are still latent underneath its surface meaning.

iki

Aesthetic and moral ideals of urban commoners in the Edo period. *Iki* originally denoted "spirit" or "heart." It later came to mean "high spirit" or "high heart" and referred to the way in which a high-spirited person talked, behaved, or dressed. As it became expressive of the Edo commoners' ideal during the nineteenth century, its connotations moved closer to those of the Ōsakan concept of *sui*. Indeed, *iki* was sometimes used as an equivalent of *sui*. Yet normally it carried a slightly different shade of meaning. As an aesthetic concept, *iki* leaned toward a beauty somewhat less colorful than *sui*. Many male adherents of *iki* liked such colors as gray, dark brown, and navy blue, showing a distaste for bright colors and multicolored designs. Also, *iki* seems to have had a slightly more sensual and coquettish connotation than *sui*. It was often applied to the description of a woman, especially a professional entertainer, who knew exactly how much a display of eroticism was desirable by the highest standard of taste. Compared with a woman of *sui*, a lady with plenty of *iki* in her heart seems to have been more high-spirited—almost manly—in her conduct, always willing to make sacrifices for the man she loved. On the other hand, her behavior sometimes indicated resignation, and conse-

もよく表現されている。為永春水の人情本
『春色梅児誉美』は、「いき」を貫いて生きた
人々の良い例が示されている。端唄、清元、
新内などにも「いき」はかかせない。

粋

江戸時代の町人の美的、道徳的理念。「粋」
の概念は、17世紀後半、初めは大坂で発展
した。「粋」は、世の中のすいもからいもか
みわけて、他人の苦労を思いやり、自分をい
ろいろな境遇に適応させることができ、同時
代人の趣味や流行のリーダーになる人の振る
舞いをあらわしたものである。大坂や京都の
商人で、40歳をこえていて、裕福な人物が、
その典型であった。彼らは、働き盛りに富を
追求し、財をなしては、現世のあらゆる楽し
み、とりわけ遊里での楽しみを求めた。人間
の二大欲望（富と性的充足）の権威である彼
らは、現世の男の「鑑」であった。「すい」
は、浮世草子、とくに井原西鶴の作品の人物
によく表現されている。

quently a sense of sadness and loneliness emerged. *Iki* had its best literary expression in works of the *ninjōbon* genre. *Shunshoku umegoyomi* (Spring Love: A Plum-Blossom Almanac) by Tamenaga Shunsui presents fine examples of people who conducted themselves in accordance with the ideal of *iki*. *Hauta*, *kiyomoto-bushi*, and *shinnai*, are also permeated with *iki*.

sui

Aesthetic and moral ideals of urban commoners in the Edo period. The concept of *sui* was initially cultivated in the Ōsaka area during the late seventeenth century. It described deportment of a person who fully knew the sour taste of this life, was able to infer other people's suffering, adapt himself to various human situations, and become a leader in taste and fashion for his contemporaries. Typically he was a person of the merchant class in Ōsaka or Kyōto, over forty, and financially well off. He had spent his prime years in pursuit of wealth; having attained it, he now sought out all the pleasures on this earth, especially in the licensed pleasure quarters. An expert in two of the greatest human passions (wealth and sexual gratification), he represented the "pure essence" of the man of the world. *Sui* is frequently manifest in the characters of the genre of fiction called *ukiyo-zōshi*, particularly in those of Ihara Saikaku.

通
<small>つう</small>

江戸時代の美学。「通」とは、ある物事、とりわけ、吉原の遊廓事情に通じていた人をさす。その豊かな蘊蓄で自らも楽しむとともに、傍観者としての立場からくる自由をも持っていた。通の上っ面をまねる人を半可通といい、通の全くわからない人を野暮といった。三者とも、江戸時代の大衆小説本、黄表紙と洒落本に描かれている。明治時代以後になると、通は、花柳界に通じているという意味だけに限られず、もっと広い、機転の利いた、というような意味に用いられるようになった。

間
<small>ま</small>

日本の伝統芸術、特に音楽、舞踊、芝居で広く用いられる言葉で、芸術的に配置した時間的、空間的余白を意味する。音や色がないことによって、間は全体のリズムやデザインにアクセントを与えてくれる。日本の演奏家は、伝統的に、自分の解釈によって休符を自由にのばしたり縮めたりする。舞踊や芝居でも、かなり自由に、歌やせりふや所作に休みを入れたり引き伸ばしたりする。能では、演技中に一瞬動きを止めたとき、高度の劇的表現に達することが期待される。歌舞伎でも、せり

tsū

An aesthetic ideal of the Edo period. A *tsū* was a man who was well informed about something, usually the Yoshiwara licensed pleasure quarters. He was able to enjoy himself by putting to use his copious knowledge and experience, while always retaining the freedom assured by his status as a bystander. Those who were mercly superficial imitations of *tsū* were called *hankatsū*, while those who had no understanding whatsoever of the *tsū* concept were referred to as *yabo*. All three types were portrayed in *kibyōshi* and *sharebon*, two genres of Edo-period popular fiction. After the Edo period, the term *tsū* was no longer restricted to familiarity with the pleasure quarters and assumed a broader meaning, akin to that of "savoir faire."

ma

Term widely used in traditional Japanese arts—especially music, dance, and the theater—to designate an artistically placed interval in time or space. By its very absence of sound or color, *ma* helps accentuate the overall rhythm or design. Traditionally, Japanese musicians have had a greater liberty in lengthening or shortening a rest according to their interpretation of a given composition. In dance and drama also, performers have considerable freedom to insert or extend a pause in their singing, speech, and bodily movement. In Nō drama, an actor is expected to attain highly dramatic

ふや所作のあいだに、静止の効果が最大になるように演技をしなければならない。そのような「間」の一つが見得（みえ）に集大成されている。落語と漫才では、「間」は、滑稽の効果をあげるのに、重要な役割をする。

「間」の概念は、舞台芸術以外でも用いられる。日本画家は、空間を意図的に使って、「意味ある余白」を創造する。造園では、全体のデザイン効果を高めるために、空間を計画的に用いる。和歌における余情や幽玄は「間」の概念の一つと見なすことができる。

もののあわれ

平安時代に発達した、文学的、美学的理念。この中心には、自然や人生の諸相に現れるはかない美に対する深く強烈な理解があり、したがってふつうは一種悲しみの色をたたえているが、場合によっては、賞賛と畏敬と、時には喜びを伴うこともある。

この語は、本居宣長（もとおりのりなが）の著述を通して復活した。宣長によれば、「あわれ」は二つの感嘆詞「あ」と「はれ」を組み合わせたもので、両者とも、心を強く動かされたときに、自然に出てくる言葉である。平安朝の貴族は、感情的激しさを弱めて、「あわれ」の意味を、優雅な美、静かな憂鬱、それに仏教の無常を強調するように限定した。しかしながらこの語は、しだいに言外にあった幸せの意味を失

expression when he stops all motion momentarily during an act. In *kabuki*, too, intervals between words or gestures are acted out in such a way that the effect of stillness may be maximized. (One such interval has been codified as *mie*.) In *rakugo* and *manzai*, *ma* plays an important role in achieving the intended comic effect.

The concept of *ma* is also utilized outside the performing arts. Traditional Japanese painters try to create a "meaningful void" by the deliberate use of blank space. In landscape gardening, open space is used strategically to enhance the effect of the whole design. In poetry, ideas like *yojō* ("overtones") and *yūgen* ("mystery and depth") can be seen as variations of the same concept.

mono no aware

A literary and aesthetic ideal cultivated during the Heian period. At its core is a deep, empathetic appreciation of the ephemeral beauty manifest in nature and human life, and it is therefore usually tinged with a hint of sadness; under certain circumstances it can be accompanied by admiration, awe, or even joy.

The word was revived through the writings of Motoori Norinaga. According to Norinaga, the word *aware* is a combination of two interjections, *a* and *hare*, each of which was uttered spontaneously when one's heart was profoundly moved. The Heian court nobility toned down the emotional intensity and limited the meaning of *aware* so as to stress elegant beauty, gentle melancholy, and the Buddhist sense of ephemerality. The word gradually lost its happier connotations, how-

って、宣長の時代には、「あわれ」は哀れみ、悲しみ、嘆きだけを表すようになった。

　宣長は『源氏物語』研究によって、「あわれ」は、散文、韻文をとわず、平安文学全般に見られる重要な美学的理念であることに気づいた最初の学者であった。この理念を、当時よく使われていた哀れ、悲しみ、嘆きを表す「あわれ」と区別するために、宣長は「もののあわれ」、という句をあてた。その意味するところは、「ものごとにかかわる深い感情」であった。いかなる教養と育ちの人にも、悲しいことは悲しいのであり、もし悲しいと感じることのできない人がいるなら、その人は心のない人で、「もののあわれ」を知らない人である。宣長の考えでは、「もののあわれ」は、自然と人間の心の奥底に近い、純化され、高められた感情である。それは、はかない美と、その美を理解することのできる感性に富んだ心が主眼となる。

無常

生あるものは死に、あらゆるものが変転するという意味の仏教用語を語源とする。「諸行無常（万物は、はかないもの）」という句は、仏教の根本教理の三法印の第一である。日本人は、伝統的に、ものごとのはかなさを理解しているので、無常感は文学の重要なテーマの一つになっている。『方丈記』『徒然草』『平家物語』といった中世の文学作品は、この仏教的人生観によってよく知られている。

ever, and by Norinaga's time *aware* referred almost exclusively to pathos, sorrow, or grief.

From his study of the *Tale of Genji*, Norinaga was the first scholar to notice that *aware* was an important aesthetic ideal pervading all Heian literature, prose and poetry alike. In order to distinguish this ideal from the ordinary *aware* of pathos or grief used in his own time, he called it *mono no aware*—literally, "a deep feeling over things." A sad thing is sad to any man of cultivation and breeding; if there is anyone who fails to feel sad, he is heartless or he does not know *mono no aware*. In Norinaga's view, *mono no aware* is a purified and exalted feeling, close to the innermost heart of man and nature. It tends to focus on the beauty of impermanence and on the sensitive heart capable of appreciating that beauty.

mujō

(impermanence, transience, mutability). Originally a Buddhist term expressing the doctrine that everything that is born must die and that nothing remains unchanged. The phrase *shogyō mujō* (all the various realms of being are transient) is the first of the Three Laws of Buddhism. Japanese have traditionally been keenly aware of the impermanence of things, and the sense of *mujō* has been a major theme in literature. Works of the medieval period, such as the *Hōjōki* (*The Ten-Foot-*

おかし

基本的な意味は「愉快な」あるいは「魅力的な」で、「あわれ」よりも、場面や出来事に対し、客観的で陽気な反応を示すものである。この語の表すおかしさには幅があり、優雅な宮廷的美しさの楽しみから、滑稽に対する笑いにまでにわたっている。

　平安朝の文学では、「おかし」の意味は、一般的には優雅な美の鑑賞に重心があった。清少納言の『枕草子』では、この語が四百六十六回出てきて、春のあけぼの、芽吹く柳、秋の虫の声、祭り、月夜に浅瀬を渡る牛車などの描写に用いられている。鎌倉時代以降になると、「おかし」は滑稽なおかしさの意味に急速に移っていく。能役者世阿弥は、「おかし」を「人が笑うもの」と広い意味に定義した。必然的に、この語は、狂言や川柳のような滑稽文学と結びついた。一般的に使われるようになると、「おかし」は美学的意味を失い、現代使われている「滑稽な」「楽しい・面白い」という意味の単純な形容詞となった。

Square Hut), the *Tsurezuregusa* (*Essays in Idleness*), and *Heike monogatari* (*The Tale of the Heike*), are especially noted for this essentially Buddhist view of life.

okashi

The basic meaning of the term is "delightful" or "charming," referring to a more detached, light-hearted response to scenes and events than *aware*. The delight it designates encompassed several different types, ranging from enjoyment of graceful, courtly beauty to laughter at the ludicrous.

In general the meaning of *okashi* leaned toward an appreciation of elegant beauty in the literature of the Heian period. In Sei Shōnagon's *Makura no sōshi* (*Pillow Book*) the word appears 466 times and is used to describe such scenes as a spring dawn, pussy willows in bud, chirping autumn insects, a Shintō festival, and an ox-drawn cart crossing a shallow stream on a moonlit night. From the Kamakura period onward the meaning of *okashi* steadily shifted toward amusement with the ludicrous. The Nō actor Zeami broadly defined *okashi* as "that which people laugh at." Inevitably the term came to be associated with comic literature, such as *kyōgen* and *senryū*. With the popularization of the term, *okashi* in time lost its aesthetic implications and became a plain adjective meaning "laughable" or "amusing," the sense in which it is used in modern Japanese.

寂 ^{さび}

Bashō

芭蕉とその門下によってうちたてられた詩的
理念。「寂」は、老年、孤独、あきらめ、静
穏などを結合した中世の美意識を指向する
が、同時に、多彩で庶民的な江戸時代の文化
をも内包している。時には茶の湯の美的理念
である「侘」の同義語として、また、「侘」
と組み合わせて使われる。

　藤原俊成は、「寂」の関連語「さぶ」をは
じめて使った高名な歌人であるが、海辺の霜
枯れの葦といったイメージをひいて、内包す
る孤独と荒涼の意味を強調した。その後、中
世の芸術家世阿弥や心敬は、「寂」の意味と
して荒涼に比重を置いたので、そこから生ま
れる美は、かなり冷え冷えとしていた。この
理念の底に流れるのは、中世仏教徒に典型的
な宇宙観で、人間の実存的孤独を認識し、自
らその孤独に身をまかせ、孤独の中に美を見
出そうとした。

　芭蕉自身は、「寂」についてほとんど書い
ていないが、弟子たちの俳論から推し量ると、
芭蕉の「寂」は中世の理念をかなり変えたも
のであったらしい。芭蕉は向井去来の次の句
に「寂」を認めたという。

　　　　花守や

　　　　白きかしらを

　　　　つき合せ

このように、白い桜の豪華な美と、白髪の老

sabi

Poetic ideal fostered by Bashō and his followers. *Sabi* points toward a medieval aesthetic combining elements of old age, loneliness, resignation, and tranquillity, yet the colorful and plebeian qualities of Edo-period culture are also present. At times *sabi* is used synonymously or in conjunction with *wabi*, an aesthetic ideal of the tea ceremony.

Fujiwara no Toshinari, the first major poet to employ a *sabi*-related word (the verb *sabu*), stressed its connotations of loneliness and desolation by, pointing to such images as frost-withered reeds on the seashore. With later medieval artists such as Zeami and Shinkei, the implications of *sabi* focused so heavily on desolation that the emerging beauty seemed almost cold. Underlying this aesthetic was the cosmic view typical of medieval Buddhists, who recognized the existential loneliness of all men and tried to resign themselves to, or even find beauty in, that loneliness.

Bashō himself wrote little on *sabi*, but from his disciples' writings it can be inferred that his concept of *sabi* was a considerably modified version of the medieval ideal. Bashō is said to have found *sabi* in this *haiku* by his disciple, Mukai Kyorai:

> Two blossom-watchmen
> With their white heads together
> Having a chat.

Such a synthesis of conflicting aesthetic values—the

人の無彩色の美という、美的に対立する価値を組み合わせることによって、孤独の意味をいっそう高めているのである。人生の無常に目覚めた人は、肉体の衰えや孤独をおそれない。それより、その事実を、静かなあきらめをもって受け入れ、そこに喜びの源泉さえも発見するのである。

渋い

微妙で控えめながら、深く感動させる美しさを表す形容詞で、室町時代の芸術家や目利きが用いはじめた。色彩、意匠、趣味、声などを表現するのはもちろんのこと、人のふるまい全般を表現するのに用いられる。中世の美意識に端を発するこの理念は、「侘（わび）」「寂（さび）」「粋（いき）」などと関係があり、時には重なる。

　江戸時代に町人が控え目な魅力を好むようになると「渋（しぶ）い」は広く用いられるようになった。小唄の師匠のやわらかい声、練達の役者の抑制のきいた芝居、名陶工の簡潔な絵付けなどは、その抑えの効いた美しさが、「渋い」と賞賛された。極彩色の美は洗練されていない人のもので、「渋い」は、まばゆい見かけにまどわされない目利きのものであった。

　渋好みは、現代にも生き続けて基本的な美意識の一部を成し、建築、室内装飾、陶芸その他の芸術作品に生かされている。

gorgeous beauty of the white cherry blossoms and the "colorless" beauty of white-haired old men—elevates loneliness to a higher level of meaning. A person awakened to the essential mutability of life does not dread physical waning or loneliness; rather, he or she accepts these sad facts with quiet resignation and even finds in them a source of enjoyment.

shibui

An adjective designating a subtle, unobtrusive, and deeply moving beauty, cherished by artists and connoisseurs since the Muromachi period. The term is applied to color, design, taste, and voice as well as to human behavior in general. Originating in the medieval aesthetic sensibility, it is related to and sometimes overlaps such concepts as *wabi*, *sabi*, and *iki*.

The use of *shibui* became widespread when urban commoners of the Edo period asserted their preference for a quietly appealing ambience. The subdued voice of a master singer, the disciplined performance of a seasoned actor, or the simple pattern designed by an expert ceramic artist had an understated beauty and as such was praised as *shibui*. Colorful beauty was for the unsophisticated, but *shibui* was for connoisseurs who were not to be misled by the dazzling surface.

The penchant for *shibui* still survives in Japan, forming part of the basic aesthetic taste and manifesting itself in architecture, interior design, ceramic art, and other artistic forms.

敬

中国の儒者朱子 (1130〜1200年) のとなえた
哲学理念で、本心を存し養い尊厳を保つこと
を意味する「存心自敬」のような句に表され
る。江戸時代の思想家の間には、「敬」の解
釈で基本的には二つの派があった。山崎闇斎
は、これを日常のあらゆる行動を規制する儒
教の重要な道徳律ととらえたが、伊藤仁斎は
厳格な道徳からの解放を唱え、「敬」を道徳
の手続きにすぎないと考えた。日常生活では、
「敬」という言葉は、「謙遜」「分別」「自制」
など、さまざまな意味を表す。

有心
うしん

鎌倉時代に始まる美学理念を表す用語で、特
に、厳粛で優美な和歌や連歌を無心（心や深
い思いがないこと）の狂歌から区別するため
に用いた。以前は分別や洞察力を表していた
この言葉は、次第に洗練された趣味と美的感
受性を意味するようになった。仏教では、
「有心」はまったく異なった意味を表し、こ
の世からの離脱ないしは空（悟り）を表す
「無心」に対し、この世への執着を意味する。

tsutsushimi

(seriousness of mind). Philosophical concept elaborated by the Chinese Confucian philosopher Zhu Xi (1130–1200), as in the phrase *cunxin chijing* (*sonshin jikei*); "preserving one's mind/heart and maintaining seriousness,"). Among Japanese thinkers of the Edo period, there were essentially two views concerning *tsutsushimi*. The school of Yamazaki Ansai regarded it as the cardinal moral principle of Confucianism that regulated every aspect of daily conduct, while the school of Itō Jinsai insisted on liberation from moral rigor and regarded *tsutsushimi* as only a moral method. In everyday parlance the word *tsutsushimi* has a range of other meanings, including "modesty," "discretion," and "self-restraint."

ushin

(literally, "having heart or feeling"). Aesthetic term used from about the Kamakura period, particularly to distinguish serious, elegant *waka* or *renga* from *kyōka* , for which the term *mushin* ("lacking heart or depth of feeling") was used. Formerly referring to discretion or discernment, the word gradually came to mean having refined taste and aesthetic sensitivity. In Buddhism *ushin* takes on a radically different meaning, referring to worldly attachment as opposed to *mushin*, which means detachment or emptiness (enlightenment).

侘
_{わび}

Sen no Rikyū

俗世間を離れ、閑寂でゆったりとした人生の
よさを唱道する、美学的、道徳的理念。中世
の隠者にその端を発し、簡素で質素な美と、
静穏で高遠な精神を強調する。「侘」は茶の
湯の美学の中心をなすもので、和歌、連歌、
俳句にもしばしば見られ、その精神は「寂」
「風流」に通じる。

　「侘」という語は、動詞「わぶ（気落ちす
る）」、形容詞「わびしい（孤独の、味気ない）」
からきたもので、もとは、困難な環境に陥っ
た人の痛みを表した。しかし、鎌倉時代と室
町時代の修行者的な知識層は、貧困と孤独を、
物心両面からの解放ととらえ、表面上の美の
欠如をより新しく高度の美に転換することに
よって、「侘」を肯定的な概念へと発展させ
た。「侘」の新しい理念は特に茶人によって
発展した。中でも千利休は茶の湯に禅の精神
を取り入れ、貧しさに豊かさを、簡素に美を
求めることの重要性を強調して、茶の湯の芸
術性を高めようとした。藤原定家の次の和歌
は、「侘」の極致としてしばしば引き合いに
出される。

　　　　　見わたせば
　　　　　花も紅葉も
　　　　　なかりけり
　　　　　浦の苦屋の
　　　　　秋の夕暮れ

wabi

An aesthetic and moral principle advocating the enjoyment of a quiet, leisurely life free from worldly concerns. Originating with medieval hermits, it emphasizes a simple, austere type of beauty and a serene, transcendental frame of mind. It is a central concept in the aesthetics of the tea ceremony and is also manifest in some works of *waka*, *renga*, and *haiku*. Its implications partly coincide with those of *sabi* and *fūryū*.

The *wabi* was derived from the verb *wabu* (to languish) and the adjective *wabishi* (lonely, comfortless), which initially denoted the pain of a person in difficult circumstances. But ascetic literati of the Kamakura and Muromachi periods developed it into a more positive concept by making poverty and loneliness synonymous with liberation from material and emotional worries and by turning the absence of apparent beauty into a new and a higher form of beauty. These new connotations of *wabi* were cultivated especially by masters of the tea ceremony, such as Sen no Rikyū, who sought to elevate their art by associating it with the spirit of Zen and stressed the importance of seeking richness in poverty and beauty in simplicity. The following poem by Fujiwara no Sadaie has been cited as suggesting the essence of *wabi*:

As I look afar
I see neither cherry blossoms
Nor tinted leaves:
Only a modest hut on the coast
In the dusk of autumn nightfall.

余情

歌人に尊重された美的理念。漢字の文字通りの意味は「有り余る情意」であるが、普通はovertones（含み）と翻訳される。和歌における「余情」は、文字上の意味に加えて、言外に表現された意味をさす。近世以前は「よせい」と読まれ、11世紀から13世紀の歌論でよく用いられた。時にその意味するところが、「幽玄」と重なることもあった。藤原俊成、その子定家、鴨長明などの歌人によって、「余情」は微妙な引喩、巧みな比喩、なぞのような言い回しを特徴とする象徴性豊かな和歌を評価する複合的な文学上の美学となった。

　「余情」の理念は、歌論以外にも見られる。金春禅竹は能の芸術を語るとき、役者の演技には「表面に出さない感情を感じさせる何か」が必要であると主張している。この理念は、「空白は絵の一部である」と言った画家土佐光信や、芭蕉の句にも潜んでいる。その後「幽玄」の影に隠れがちになるが、「余情」は、日本の文学と美術の底流をなす、もっとも重要な理念の一つである。

幽玄

12世紀から15世紀にかけて、歌人や能作者によってうちたてられた美学的理念。「幽玄」

yojō

An aesthetic ideal fostered by *waka* poets. Written with Chinese characters that literally mean "excess feeling," but usually translated as "overtones," *yojō* refers to the meanings a poem obliquely implies in addition to its overtly stated message. The term, pronounced *yosei* in premodern times, was most frequently used in *waka* criticism from the eleventh to the thirteenth centuries. At times, its connotations overlapped those of *yūgen*. With such poets as Fujiwara no Toshinari, his son Fujiwara no Sadaie, and Kamo no Chōmei, *yojō* became part of a complex literary aesthetic that valued poetry of rich symbolism, featuring subtle allusions, exquisite imagery, and cryptic diction.

The concept of *yojō* can also be observed outside *waka* criticism. Komparu Zenchiku, in discussing the art of the Nō drama, insisted that an actor's performance should "have an aura of unstated sentiment." The concept is also latent in the aesthetics of the painter Tosa Mitsuoki, who observed that "blank space is also part of a painting," and in the poetics of Bashō. Though somewhat overshadowed by *yūgen* in later centuries, the term remains one of the most pervasive concepts in Japanese literature and art.

yūgen

Aesthetic ideal cultivated by poets and dramatists from the twelfth through the fifteenth centuries. The term

という言葉は、神秘、暗さ、深み、優美、曖昧さ、静けさ、移ろいやすさ、悲しみなどの雰囲気を、幅広く意味した。本来、中国で見たり理解したりできないほど深いところの物を描写するために用いられた。この語は仏教でもよく使われ、知性ではとらえられない究極の真実を表すものだった。

　「幽玄」は、12世紀には和歌に欠かせない理念になり、「余情」の理念と一体になった。この変化の底流には、和歌はきわめて繊細で微妙な感情を表現する必要があるので、「余情」を通して、婉曲にしか表現できないという美学的認識があった。藤原俊成は、「優れた和歌は、言葉や形で過剰に表現しなくても、暗示的意味を喚起する」と説明している。そこで引いている例は、秋の月の和歌で、そこに描写していないのに、読者には鹿の鳴き声が聞こえてくる。13〜14世紀には、「幽玄」は、「余情」の含みを持たせながら、優雅でこの世のものとは思えない美を表すようになる。この変化は、主に俊成の息子、藤原定家がもたらしたものであった。能作者世阿弥は、この意味の「幽玄」の体現者であった。15世紀には、「幽玄」のもろもろの要素のうち、静かな諦念が中心的位置を占めるようになる。

　中世の美学の中核を占める「幽玄」は、後の時代にも相当の影響力を及ぼした。「侘」「寂」などの理念の発展は、「幽玄」をはぐくんだ精神に負うところが大きかった。

yūgen broadly designated an ambience of mystery, darkness, depth, elegance, ambiguity, calm, transience, and sadness. It originated in China to describe an object lying too deep to be seen or understood. It often appeared in a Buddhist context, referring to ultimate truth that could not be grasped through intellect.

Yūgen developed into a poetic principle in the twelfth century, when it was integrated with the concept of *yojō*. Underlying this development was the aesthetic notion that *waka* should embody emotion so delicate or subtle that it could be suggested only obliquely, through overtones. Fujiwara no Toshinari commented that "a fine poem often evokes associations not overtly expressed in word or form." An example he cited was a poem on the autumn moon that made the reader hear a deer's cry not described therein. In the thirteenth and fourteenth centuries, *yūgen* came to imply a more elegant, ethereal beauty, although connotations of "overtones" persisted. This shift in emphasis was due largely to the influence of Toshinari's son, Fujiwara no Sadaie. The Nō playwright Zeami was an ardent exponent of this type of *yūgen*. In the fifteenth century, calm resignation came into greater prominence among the components of *yūgen*.

As the central concept in medieval aesthetics, *yūgen* exerted considerable influence on artists of the succeeding centuries. The development of concepts such as *wabi* and *sabi* were both greatly idebted to the spirit that had fostered *yūgen*.

哲学思想

Philosophy and Thoughts

東洋と西洋の倫理学

東洋では、倫理学は間主観性の研究、すなわち共同体の研究であるが、西洋では、個体性ないしは主観性の研究として出発したので、倫理観は互いに異なっている。たとえば、社会的責任の概念にその違いを見ることができる。英語の responsibility が個人の行動に対する道義的責任の意味を表すようになるのは18世紀末であるが、古代ローマの時代から行動の主体としての個人という概念は存在した。したがって、すべての人間は、個人として神の前で平等であるという存在論的認識があった。それに対して、日本では、古代から責任という概念は存在したが、個人は共同体での身分と分かちがたい関係にあった。個人は天と共同体に対して責任があるのであり、その責任を果たすことが善行であった。この概念は、中世には、「義理」という語で表現された。「人情」に対する「義理」の優越性は、江戸時代の文学の多くのテーマとなった。

　古代日本では、宣命や祝詞は「あかき、きよき、なおきこころ」を理想として列挙した。神社で着る白い着物は清浄の重要性を立証するものであった。『延喜式』には「水無月の晦日の御祓」という祝詞があり、これによってあらゆる罪は風に払われて海の底に沈むとされた。これが罪に対する考え方であり、個

ethics, Eastern and Western

In the East, ethics is the study of intersubjectivity—the study of the community—while in the West, it emerges as the study of individuality or subjectivity, thus giving rise to different perceptions on ethical thinking. The contrast can be observed, for example, in the concept of social responsibility. The English word "responsibility" was not used in the sense of moral accountability for one's actions until the late eighteenth century, but from the time of ancient Rome there has existed the concept of the person as the subject of action. Thus there was the ontological idea that all human beings were equal as persons before God. In Japan, on the other hand, the concept of responsibility already existed in the classic period, but the individual was inseparable from his status in the community. Each individual had a responsibility toward heaven and the community, and virtue lay in carrying out this responsibility. This concept made its appearance in medieval Japan under the Japanese term *giri*. The superiority of *giri* as opposed to *ninjō* formed the theme of much of the literature of the Edo period.

In ancient Japan, the *semmyō* and the *norito* cited a clear, pure, and upright heart (*akaki, kiyoki, naoki koko-ro*) as ideal. The white clothes worn at Shintō shrines attest to the importance placed on purity. The Engi Shiki contains the ritual prayers known as *Minazuki no tsugomori no ōharae,* by which all sins (*tsumi*) are said to be blown away with the wind and carried to the bot-

人の道義心は欠落している。しかし、このことは、古代日本人に倫理観がなかったことを意味するものではない。汚れた不純な精神を心から追い出すことにより、人間の最高の状態としての、純粋で美しい精神という理想を保ったのである。この精神は、どのような形をとるにせよ、日本人の倫理感の中核を成している。菅原道真は、この精神を表す和歌を残している。〈心だに誠の道にかなひなば祈らずとても神やまもらむ〉この和歌が示すように、日本人は、「誠」を中核として、内面化された非宗教的倫理に向かったのである。

武士道

江戸時代に支配階級の武士の道徳律に対して一般的に用いられた言葉。武士道は、武術の心構えや技術だけではなく、主君への絶対的服従、強い名誉心、義務への献身、ことある時は、戦に命をかけたり、切腹する勇気までを含んでいる。

宮本武蔵の『五輪書』（1643年ごろ）は、武士とその主君が侍の真の栄誉を得るために兵法の奥義を適用することを強調した。しかし、その当時でさえ、武士は城下町に集められて、武力の行使は極端に少なくなっていた。武士道が完成するのは、比較的安定して知的になった徳川時代であった。絶対忠誠と、主君のために命をささげるという理想化された

tom of the ocean. In this approach to sin, the concept of individual conscience is lacking. This, however, does not mean that the ancient Japanese lacked ethical ideas. By banishing from the stained and impure heart they held to the ideal of a pure and beautiful heart as the highest state for humanity. This spirit is at the very core of Japanese ethical concepts, no matter what form they take. Sugawara no Michizane left a poem that captures this spirit: "If my heart but follow the Way, the gods will watch over me though I neglect to pray to them." As this verse suggests, the Japanese were moving toward an internalized nonreligious ethic with sincerity (*makoto*) as its axis.

bushidō

(literally, "the Way of the warrior"). A term that came into common use during the Edo period to designate the ethical code of the ruling *samurai* class. *Bushidō* involved not only martial spirit and skill with weapons, but also absolute loyalty to one's lord, a strong sense of personal honor, devotion to duty, and the courage, if required, to sacrifice one's life in battle or in ritual suicide.

Miyamoto Musashi's *Gorin no sho* (ca. 1643; *The Book of Five Rings*) emphasized the application of military strategy to gain glory for the samurai and his lord as the true distinction of a warrior. But even then, military adventuring was being sharply curtailed as warriors were gathered in castle towns. It was in the relatively stable social and intellectual climate of the ensuing Tokugawa regime that *bushidō* came to fruition. The idealized

中世の伝統が、儒教倫理と結びついたのである。その下にある伝統的思想がもっとも雄弁に述べられているのが山本常朝の武士道の古典『葉隠』（はがくれ）（1716年）である。『葉隠』によると、武士の理想と武士道の本質は、主君への自己犠牲にあるという。山鹿素行は、戦にも生産にも貢献していない徳川の社会における武士の存在を正当化するためには、武士は道徳および政治の指導に献身する義務があることを強調した。

　伝統的武士道は儒教と結びついて、江戸時代武士階級の道徳行為と知的要求を大きく規制した。武士道に内在する行動力、動機付けの純粋さ、忠義、政治的知的指導力が、明治維新への推進力として、武士階級が貢献できたこと、および、その結果、日本の近代化で強い影響力を持ち得たことの理由である。明治時代初期の近代化と西洋化のうねりの中で、武士道は一時影がうすくなったが、日清戦争の後、愛国心、天皇への忠誠という形でよみがえった。新渡戸稲造は『武士道』（1899年）で、武士道こそ、日本の伝統と社会の中でもっとも賞賛すべきものであると述べている。1930年代には、軍国主義者によって、武力的側面が強調されたが、第二次世界大戦後は退けられた。多くの日本人が、武士道は、戦後民主主義社会と相容れないとして拒んだのである。

medieval tradition of absolute loyalty and willingness to die for one's lord came to be overlaid with Confucian ethics. The underlying native tradition found its most eloquent expression in Yamamoto Tsunetomo's *bushidō* classic, *Hagakure* (1716). According to the *Hagakure,* the samurai ideal and essence of *bushidō* are expressed in self-effacing service to one's lord. Confucian scholar Yamaga Soko stressed that to justify their existence in Tokugawa society, where they had neither to fight nor to contribute to production, samurai, had a duty to devote themselves to moral and political leadership.

The composite of indigenous and Confucianized *bushidō* regulated much of the ethical behavior and intellectual inquiry of the samurai class in the Edo period. The emphasis on action, purity of motivation, loyal service, and political and intellectual leadership inherent in *bushidō* helps to explain why the samurai class could serve as the moving force of the movement that led to the Meiji Restoration and ultimately play an influential role in the modernization of Japan. Although *bushidō* was temporarily submerged in the early Meiji surge of modernization and Westernization, after the Sino-Japanese War it found new expressions in patriotism and devotion to the emperor. It was also later interpreted by Nitobe Inazō in his *Bushido: The Soul of Japan* (1899) as all that was most admirable in Japanese tradition and society. The more martial aspects of *bushidō* came into vogue in the militarist 1930s, but again fell into disfavor in the aftermath of World War II. Most Japanese then disowned *bushidō* as incompatible with their postwar democratic society.

腹切り

自分で自分の腹を切る日本の儀礼的自殺。日本では「切腹」という言葉の方が好まれる。昔から、腹は魂が宿る場所で、行動を生み出す心気の源であると考えられていたので、切る部位に選ばれたのである。加えて、身体の中央にあたる腹からは、人の意志、勇気、精神、怒り、雅量が生まれると考えられていた。

封建時代初期に、切腹は徐々に儀式化され、江戸時代には、武士階級の罪人に対する五階級の刑罰の一つになった。切腹の作法には細かい規定が作られた。装束、場所、時、立会人、検視役、介錯人である。場所がしつらえられ、立会人、護衛、検視役がそろうと、切腹する人は着物の前をはだけ、右手を伸ばして刀をとり、左から右に腹を切る。この場合、死ぬほど深く大きくは切らず、あとは介錯人に任せる。本人から介錯人にあらかじめ打ち合わせてある合図があり、そこで介錯人が刀を振り下ろして首を切り落とす。

集団切腹の有名な例が、四十七士で、吉良上野介を殺害した後、切腹を命じられた。現代史のページにも腹切りは点在するが、もっとも有名なのが、1912年、明治天皇に殉死した陸軍大将乃木希典である。1945年に日

harakiri

Japanese ritual suicide by self-disembowelment. *Seppuku* is the preferred term in Japan. The abdomen (*hara*) was chosen as the target of the suicidal knife because ancient Japanese regarded it as the place where the soul resides and the source of action-derived tension. Additionally, the abdomen, at the physical center of the body, was regarded as the cradle of the individual's will, boldness, spirit, anger, and generosity.

During Japan's early feudal period, suicide by self-disembowelment gradually became more ritualized, and by the time of the Edo period it had become one of the five grades of punishment for wrongdoers among the *samurai* class. All aspects of the *seppuku* ritual were prescribed with precision: apparel, site, time, witnesses, inspectors, and assistant. When the site had been readied and the witnesses, guards, and inspectors assembled, the doomed man would open his *kimono*, stretch out his right hand to grasp his knife, and cut into his abdomen from left to right. Often this wound was neither deep nor intended to bring on death: that task fell to the assistant. Upon the man's making a prearranged signal to his *kaishakunin* (assistant), the *kaishakunin*'s sword would slash down, severing the head.

A famous instance of mass *seppuku* is that of the forty-seven *rōnin*, who were ordered to commit *seppuku* after they had murdered Kira Yoshinaka. Instances of *harakiri* have continued to dot the pages of the modern history of Japan, the most famous being that of General

本が連合軍に降伏した直後、多くの人が、皇居の前で腹を切った。1970年11月、小説家三島由紀夫は、センセーショナルで劇的な腹切りをとげた。

道徳

西洋では、道徳の概念は慣習と伝統に基づいている。中国と日本はこれと異なる。この意味を表す日本語は漢字二字でできていて、最初の文字は「道」を表す。孔子は「道」を次のように解釈している。「朝に『道』を聞かば、夕に死すとも可なり」（『論語』）。ロゴスの理念と聖人の道は、ともにこの「道」の理念に表される。老子の言葉に「『道』の『道』とすべきは常の『道』にあらず」とあるように、道徳は普遍的原理であり、人の内面に隠されていて、その思想と行動を律する。東洋の道徳は、単なる倫理体系でなく、人間社会の法ないしは生きるための規範である。これは、絶対的存在に対する人間の態度（宗教）、他人に対する態度（道徳）、人間以外の生き物と物質に対する態度（技術）からなっている。

　現代日本の道徳は、環境、性、安楽死など人命に関わる技術の衝撃が引き起こすさまざ

Nogi Maresuke, who, in 1912, chose to follow the emperor Meiji in death. A considerable number of persons committed *harakiri* in front of the Imperial Palace shortly after the announcement of Japan's surrender to the Allied Forces in 1945. In November 1970, the novelist Mishima Yukio committed *harakiri* in a sensational and theatrical manner.

morality

(*dōtoku*). In the West, the concept of morality is based on custom and tradition. This is not the case in China and Japan. The word corresponding in meaning to "morality," pronounced *dōtoku* in Japanese, is written with two Chinese characters, the first of which means "the Way." Confucius expounded the Way thus: "In the morning hear the Way; in the evening die without regrets" (*Analects* 4:8). The idea of *logos* and the Way of sainthood are both represented in this idea of the Way. As is implied in Lao Tzu's saying that "the Way which can be named is not the true Way," morality is held to be a universal principle, concealed in the inner part of man, that governs his thought and action. Morality in the East is thus not merely a system of ethics, that is, an act of human society or a model for living. It consists of the attitude of man toward absolute being (religion), other human beings (ethics), and other creatures and things (technology).

Japanese morality at present is going through a process of transition similar to other societies as it seeks

まな問題に折り合いをつける道をさがして、
ほかの社会と同じく、変化の時期にさしかか
っている。

誠

中国の哲学では、「誠」は基本的な徳であり、
儒教の五徳の基礎をなす形而上的原理であ
る。儒教の古典『中庸』の中心的概念と解さ
れる「誠」は、人道の本質と天の「道」を意
味するようになった。中国の朱子学では、
「誠」を正直と解釈して強調した。

　日本では、伊藤仁斎など異端の朱子学者は、
「誠」を、人と人の関係を支配する心や精神
の誠実さと解釈した。同時に、神道の伝統で
は、「誠」（「ま」は真、「こと」は言葉または
行為）は、心や精神の純粋性や誠実を理解す
る不可欠の徳であると考えられ、江戸時代の
神道学者や国学者にしばしば用いられた。

道

思想、信仰、芸術、技能などの体系の基礎を
なす原理を表す。また、広い意味で、一つの
思想体系や信仰全体、あるいは一つの芸術を
成り立たせる理論と技術の総体を表す。後者
の意味では、茶道や武士道等各種の伝統的技

to come to terms with problems occasioned by the impact of technology on human life, relating to areas such as the environment, sexuality, and euthanasia.

makoto

(Chinese: *cheng*; sincerity). In Chinese philosophy, *cheng* is the cardinal virtue and metaphysical principle underlying the Five Virtues of Confucian teaching. Expounded as a central concept in the Confucian classic *Doctrine of the Mean* (*Chūyō*), it came to mean both the essence of humanity and the Way of Heaven. The school of the Chinese Neo-Confucian philosopher Zhu Xi (Shushi) emphasized *cheng,* interpreting it as truthfulness.

In Japan, Itō Jinsai and other nonorthodox Confucian thinkers interpreted *makoto* as the sincerity of mind or heart that should rule relationships between individuals. At the same time, in the native Shintō tradition, *makoto* (*ma,* true or genuine; *koto,* words or conduct) was considered an essential virtue that underscored purity and honesty of mind or heart, and the term was often used by Shintoists and Kokugaku (National Learning) scholars of the Edo period.

michi

(Chinese: *dao* or *tao*; literally, "the Path," "the Way"). A term used to denote the fundamental principle underlying a system of thought or belief, an art, or a skill, it is also used by extension to refer to a system of thought or belief in its entirety or to the entire body of

術や行動規範の名称の一部となっていることが多い。

古代中国では、「道」は、人間行動の規範という意味で、儒教の重要な概念であったが、より神秘的な意味で、道教で知られる哲学の名称に用いられた。江戸時代の日本では「みち」と発音され、古学という日本の儒教の中心的概念となったが、今日の真理に近い意味を持っていた。古学の伊藤仁斎は、「道」は人が従うべき道、または倫理の基準であると主張した。

名誉

昔から、いろいろな面で、日本の社会を規制している基本的概念。日本人は、たとえそれが自分の行動を規制するにしても、自分の「名」をいちばん大切にしてきた。

12世紀に武士階級が台頭してくると、「名を惜しむ」という思想が日本人の心理構造の中核を占めるようになった。軍記物語には、「名」と「恥」がしばしば出てくるが、これは、個人の「名誉」に限らず、家族や先祖の「名誉」に関わることであった。自分の恥は、先祖の恥であり、ひいては、子孫の恥でもある。

principles and skills that constitutes an art. In this latter sense, it is used in Japan as part of the name of a number of traditional skills or codes of behavior, as in *chadō* (the Way of Tea) and *bushidō* (the Way of the Warrior).

In ancient China, *dao* or *tao*, in the sense of a norm for human action, was an important concept in Confucianism, and in a more mystical sense it gave its name to the philosophy known as Taoism. In Edo-period Japan the term, pronounced *michi*, became one of the central concepts of the school of Japanese Confucianism known as Kogaku (Ancient Learning), with a meaning close to the present-day word *shinri* (truth). Such thinkers of the school as Itō Jinsai asserted that *michi* was a road or ethical standard that human beings must follow.

honor

(*meiyo*). A fundamental concept that has regulated Japanese society in various ways since ancient times. The Japanese traditionally attached overwhelming importance to one's "name," even to the point where it regulated one's actions.

With the rise of the warrior class in the twelfth century, the idea of "valuing one's name" (*na o oshimu*) came to occupy a central place in the psychological makeup of the Japanese. It is highly significant that the constant references to "name" (*na*) and "shame" (*haji*) in warrior tales are not limited to the honor of an individual but also encompass that of one's family and ancestors. Thus, shame to oneself is at the same time loss of honor to one's ancestors as well as descendants.

　江戸時代の町人階級は、「名誉」の概念を武士階級から借りて、「分が立たぬ」とか「男が立たぬ」という表現を使った。

　明治時代になり、国が一つの家長制家族の形を呈すると、歴史的君臣関係が模範とされ、「名誉」の重要性が強調されるようになった。第二次世界大戦で破れてはじめて、日本人は、「名誉」をより個人の問題と考え直すようになった。

忠

儒教の「忠」の思想は、早い時期に中国から取り入れられ、封建時代には、武士と主君の関係を成立させる思想的基礎であった。忠は、主君から受ける恩寵に対して、命を賭しても主君に仕えることを求めた。直属の上司がまず「忠」の対象であり、鎌倉幕府や徳川幕府のような何百何千の人々が構成する大組織では、「忠」の関係で結ばれた小さなグループがピラミッド形を作る構造になった。明治時代になると、「忠」の概念は、天皇や非個人的な組織である国家にまで拡大され、国民国家という現代的世界に封建的関係をとりこむことになった。

In the Edo period, the merchant class (*chōnin*) appropriated the idea of honor from the warrior class and expressed it in such phrases as "*bun ga tatanu*" (I will lose my honor) or "*otoko ga tatanu*" (I will lose honor as a man).

In the Meiji period, when the state was presented as a patriarchal family, the historic lord–vassal relationship was held up as the model, and a renewed emphasis was given to the importance of honor. It was only with defeat in World War II that the Japanese began to reconsider the nature of honor in more personal terms.

loyalty

(*chū*). The Confucian concept of loyalty was introduced to Japan from China early in the historical period. In the feudal period it provided an ideological basis for the relationship of a warrior to his lord. Loyalty required service to one's lord, even at the risk of death, in return for the rewards that the lord gave. One's immediate superior was the primary object of loyalty, so that large-scale organizations involving hundreds or thousands of people, such as the Kamakura or Tokugawa governments, were actually constructed from smaller groups tied together through an ascending series of loyalty relationships. In the Meiji period the concept of loyalty was extended to apply to the emperor and to the state as a nonpersonal entity, in an attempt to adapt feudal relationships to the modern world of nation-states.

恩

大きな好意や贈り物を受けて負う社会的、心理的債務。「恩」は日本の社会的秩序を保つ価値観の中心を占め、この中で人間関係は互いに義理の網にからまれる。

　封建時代の日本では、「恩」は、武士が主君より土地と庇護を受け取ったことにより生じる恩義を意味し、戦いで尽くす義務を伴った。同様に、命を与えてくれた両親や先祖から「恩」を受けるが、これに応えるのが孝である。先生、雇い主、あるいは命を救ってくれた人なども恩人である。「恩」は、人の好意にお返しをするという思想、義理と深く結びついている。「恩」にお返しをしない者は、恩知らずと呼ばれ、日本人の受ける最悪の非難である。また、「恩」は返しきれないほど深いものであり、したがって恩人には一生頭が上がらない。

孝

孝行または親孝行ともいう。子は親に従い、年老いたら面倒を見、死んだ後は崇拝しなければならないという、儒教の教えは、5世紀から6世紀に中国から日本にもたらされた。中国の儒学者は、孝行こそ家族の要であり、

on

(favor; indebtedness). The social and psychological debt one incurs upon receiving a favor or gift of major proportions. *On* occupies a central place among the values that maintain the Japanese social order, in which human relations are bound in a network of reciprocal obligations.

In feudal Japan, *on* referred to the debt a warrior incurred in receiving land and protection from his lord and carried the obligation to serve in battle. Similarly, one receives *on* from one's parents and ancestors; this is repaid with filial piety (*kō*). Others who may be *onjin* (a person to whom one owes *on*) include a teacher, an employer, or someone who has saved one's life. *On* is intimately linked to *giri*, the Japanese concept that one is required to return a favor, and a person who fails to repay *on* is called *on shirazu* (one who does not know *on*), one of the worst insults a Japanese can receive. At the same time, *on* is so profound that one can never fully repay it, which puts the *on*-receiver in a relationship of permanent subordination to the *on*-giver.

filial piety

(*kō*; also known as *kōkō* or *oyakōkō*). The notion that children owe an obligation to their parents to be obedient, to care for them in their old age, and to venerate them after their death was a basic tenet of Confucianism, which was introduced to Japan from China in the

ついで、家族こそ社会の要であると考えた。日本の支配層は、「忠」とともに、「孝」を社会の基本的理想とした。

江戸時代、「孝」は武士階級に浸透し、主君への忠義と密接に関係すると考えられた。明治維新後、「孝」はあらゆる層に徐々に広がり、国民道徳となった。実際、政府は「孝」を、愛国主義と国家主義育成に利用した。天皇への「忠」は、「孝」を拡大したものとされた。第二次世界大戦後、「孝」の教育は、公式に廃止された。親に従う習慣がなくなりつつあるのは、公（おおやけ）に「孝」を奨励しなくなったせいだけではなく、核家族化を促し、年長者の社会的地位を低くした、技術的、経済的、社会的変化によるところが大きい。

罪

現代日本語の「罪」は、英語の sin（宗教上の罪）、offense（規則違反）、crime（犯罪）の同義語である。古代には、生命力を低下させたり妨げる行為や状況を表す広い意味に使われた。「罪」の理念は、儀礼的不浄を表す「穢れ（けがれ）」と深い関係にあった。現存するもっとも古い用例は、10世紀の『延喜式』にあ

fifth or sixth century. The Chinese Confucians saw filial piety as the cornerstone of the family, and the family in turn as the cornerstone of society. The upper stratum of Japanese society took this notion, along with that of loyalty (*chū*), as its primary ideal.

During the Edo period, the concept of filial piety spread through the warrior class and was considered closely related to loyalty to one's lord. After the Meiji Restoration, filial piety was deliberately propagated among all classes of Japanese and became part of the national ethic. Indeed, it was used by the government to foster the ideals of patriotism and nationhood; loyalty to the emperor, it was argued, was simply filial piety writ large. Since World War II, the inculcation of filial piety has been officially abandoned. The decline in the custom of paying deference to one's parents is not due merely to the lack of official encouragement; it can be ascribed equally to the changing technological, economic, and social circumstances that have fostered the nuclear family and reduced the status of the elderly in society.

tsumi

In modern Japanese the word *tsumi* is the equivalent of such English words as sin, offense, or crime. In ancient times it was a broad term applied to actions or conditions that debase or obstruct the development of the life force; the concept of *tsumi* was closely related to the notion of *kegare*, or ritual impurity. The oldest extant enumeration of *tsumi* is the "Ōharae no Kotoba," found

る「大祓詞」である。そこにあげる例は、田
の畔をとり放すこと、清浄な場所を排泄物で
穢すこと、いぼや腫れ物のような皮膚病、近
親相姦や獣姦などの行為、鳥や虫や稲妻など
の災いなどである。罪は個人の責任の及ばな
い外部の力によって起こされるという考え
が、神道の大祓の儀式の重要性の根底にある。
したがって、宗教の役割には、(1) 清浄を保
ち、祈り通じてこの世を再生し、創造する神
の行為に参加し、(2) 罪や穢れを償うことが
含まれる。

悪

日本人の道徳的、律法的意味での「悪」の理
解は、5世紀半ばと6世紀半ばに中国の儒教
と仏教の影響のもとに形成され、7世紀の律
令制で制度化されたと一般的に考えられてい
る。大陸からの影響を受ける前の「善し」、
「悪し」の理解は、道徳的というより存在論
的であった。

　善と悪は、元来宗教的感情と結びついてい
た。したがって、「善し」と「悪し」は、は
っきりした道徳上の両極端を表すものではな
く、「清し（きれい、きよらか）」とか「穢し
（悪い、正しくない）」という精神状態を描写
するものであった。悪神は、おそれ、敬い、
鎮めなければならない強大な霊的存在とされ
た。「悪」は、恐れられはしたが、畏敬の念

in the tenth-century Engi Shiki. Examples include destroying ridges between rice paddies, polluting pure places with excrement, skin eruptions such as warts and tumors, actions such as incest and bestiality, and calamities caused by birds, insects, or lightning. The belief that *tsumi* may be brought on by powers outside the realm of individual responsibility underlies the importance of purification rites in Shintō ceremony. Hence, religious responsibility includes: (1) maintaining one's purity and participating through worship in the god's activities aimed at regenerating and creating this world, and (2) atoning for crimes or impurities.

evil

(*aku*). The Japanese understanding of evil in the ethical and legalistic sense was formulated under the influence of Confucianism and Buddhism between the mid-fifth and mid-sixth centuries and was institutionalized in the *ritsuryo* system in the seventh century. Prior to this time, the indigenous understanding of the adjective *yoshi* (good) and *ashi* (evil) had been more ontological than ethical.

Good and evil were originally associated with religious sentiments. Thus, *yoshi* and *ashi* do not represent defined moral extremes, but rather describe a spiritual state that is either *kiyoshi* (clean, pure) or *kitanashi* (foul, unfair). Evil gods were espoused as great spiritual influences to be feared, worshiped, and allayed. While evil was generally abhorred, it was also accompanied by a feeling of awe, and the term *aku* was even made part of

も伴い、「悪」という言葉は、恐れを知らない武士悪源太（源義平）のようにほめ言葉にさえ使われた。

大和魂

第二次世界大戦の終わりまでは、日本人特有の精神を表す言葉として用いられた。その意味する範囲は、肉体的、道徳的不屈の精神、勇気、誠意、献身から、ドイツ人が「国民精神」と呼ぶものまでにわたっていた。

「大和魂」の意味の変遷は、文学作品にうかがえる。平安時代の「大和魂」は、日本古来の思想や行動様式を、中国のものと区別するために用いられた。江戸時代後期になると、国学者が再発見し、別の意味に使った。本居宣長は、「大和魂」を平安時代の王朝文学の精髄である「おんなごころ」と同じ意味に解し、中国にへつらう儒学者の態度に対立させた。しかし、平田篤胤などは、時代の情勢を反映して、「大和魂」を尊皇攘夷と同義に用いた。

近代になると、「大和魂」は、この意味で軍部や超国家主義者に熱烈に支持され、公教育の思想的要とされた。1930年代はじめから第二次世界大戦終結までの軍国主義時代に

eulogistic names like that of the fearless warrior Aku Genta (Minamoto no Yoshihira).

yamato-damashii

(Japanese spirit). Phrase used until the end of World War II to describe spiritual qualities supposedly unique to the Japanese people. These range from physical and moral fortitude and courage, sincerity, and devotion, to what the Germans called *Volksgeist*.

Literary works reveal how the definition of *yamato-damashii* has changed over time. In the Heian period, *yamato-damashii* was used to distinguish native ideas and patterns of behavior from those of China. In the late Edo period, when it was rediscovered by Kokugaku (National Learning) scholars, the term took on different meanings: Motoori Norinaga equated *yamato-damashii* with the feminine spirit (*onnagokoro*) that was the essence of the courtly literature of the Heian period and held that it should counter the sycophantic attitude of pro-Chinese Japanese Confucianists. Hirata Atsutane and others, however, reflecting the conditions of the time, made *yamato-damashii* synonymous with the militant idea of *sonnō jōi* (Revere the Emperor, Expel the Barbarians).

It was in this last sense that *yamato-damashii* was taken up enthusiastically by militarists and ultranationalists in the modern era and made the ideological cornerstone of public education. During the militaristic period from

は、「大和魂」は、天皇と国家に対する絶対
的忠誠とみなされた。

和魂洋才

西洋の学問や知識を取り入れ、日本の伝統文
化に適用すること。この言葉は、かつての
「和魂漢才」の変形である。「和魂漢才」は、
9世紀に古来の日本文化の伝統と独特の精神
に注意を向けるために作られたという。同じ
ように、「和魂洋才」は、西洋の知識や技術
が日本で大規模に取り入れられた明治時代に
広がった。このことは、佐久間象山の「東洋
の精神と西洋の技術」という表現にも通ずる。
「和魂洋才」の言葉は、近代日本文明で、伝
統文化と西洋の技術が組み合わされた過程を
示している。

the early 1930s to the end of World War II *yamato-damashii* was equated with unquestioning loyalty to emperor and nation.

wakon yōsai

(Japanese spirit, Western knowledge). The ideal of adopting and applying Western learning and knowledge in conformity with native Japanese cultural traditions. The phrase was a modification of an earlier, similar sounding slogan, *wakon kansai* (Japanese spirit, Chinese knowledge), said traditionally to have been coined in the ninth century to call attention to the importance of the native cultural heritage and the unique spirit inherent in Japanese civilization. In like fashion, the phrase *wakon yōsai* gained currency in the Meiji period as Western knowledge and technology began to be adopted on a large scale in Japan. It also echoed the expression "oriental ethics (spirit), Western technique (science and technology)" of the *samurai* thinker Sakuma Shōzan. The term *wakon yōsai* exemplifies the process by which traditional Japanese culture and Western technology were woven together in modern Japanese civilization.

Chapter

3

第三章

社会概念・観念
Social Concepts

タテ社会

人類学者中根千枝の1967年出版のベストセラー『タテ社会の人間関係』で一般的になったこの言葉は、日本の社会、人間関係の特色をあらわすものとしてよく使われる。中根は、日本の社会を構成する基本単位は「場」を共通にする集団であり、集団内の人間関係はタテにつながる二者の関係が何よりも優先していると論じて説得的である。

　タテの関係としては、上役と部下、先輩・後輩、親と子などに典型的にみられるが、夫と妻の関係なども往々にしてヨコの関係というよりタテの関係になりやすい。このタテの関係は親会社と子会社というように、集団と集団の関係にもみられるものである。「系列」などはこのタテ関係の連続したものである。このようにして、タテの関係は集団内の個々人、集団と集団の間を結んで、全体として序列を形成する。実際この序列意識は日本人にとって大きな意味をもっているし、社会の秩序を保つ上に重要な役割をもっている。

　このタテの上下関係は、能力差などよりも

vertical society

A phrase that became widely known with anthropologist Nakane Chie's 1967 best-selling book *Tateshakai no ningen kankei* (English version: *Japanese Society*, 1970) is commonly used to refer to distinguishing features in Japanese society and interpersonal relations. Nakane argued persuasively that the basic principle of Japanese society is any group that shares a common *ba*, or "frame," and that the internal organization of such groups is a marked preference for relationships in which the constituent members tied vertically.

Typical examples of vertically tied relationships might be those between superior and subordinate, senior and junior, or parent and child—but in Japanese society, Nakane argues, other relationships too, such as that between husband and wife, often become vertically rather than horizontally oriented. Such vertical structure can also be seen in relationships between group organizations, as is shown by the terms *oya-gaisha* and *ko-gaisha*, "parent company" and "child company." The formation of *keiretsu*, or linked companies on the basis of linear relationship, is a successive extension of this vertical relationship. Vertical relationships link individual members within the group, and groups with other groups—and altogether constitute an entire system of ranking. It is a fact that a consciousness of rank holds great significance for Japanese people, and plays an important part in the maintenance of the social order.

This vertical relationships is thought to be based on

順番によるものと考えられており、この序列意識の背後には人々は全て平等であるという価値観がある。従って、全体として序列によって構築されているタテ社会は、階級社会などとは異なる構造をもっているのである。

家

日本における社会組織の伝統的な基本単位。「家」は family（家族）と英訳されることが多いが、household のほうが日本語の「家」の概念により近い。ふつう「家」は基本となる家族を核として形成されるが、親類や非血縁者さえもその成員となりうるのであり、一度成立すると世代を超えて永続するものとみなされる。

　日本の社会は「家」を基礎とし構成されている。多くの地方で、名家は他の「家」とも同じ苗字とは別に、その「家」だけの屋号を持つのが常である。「家」は現存の家成員ばかりでなく、すでに亡くなった祖先たちもしてこれから生まれる子孫をも含む連続体である。「家」の成員は誕生、結婚、死亡によって入れ替わるが「家」は存続していく。

[継承の規則]

家長の継承には二つの重要な規則がある。まず第一に家長は「息子」が継承しなければな

seniority, rather than innate differences in ability: behind the consciousness of rank lies a belief in the equal potential of individuals. A vertical society, which structured by rankings as a whole, has a different structure from that of a class society.

ie

(household). Traditional primary unit of social organization in Japan. *Ie* is often translated as "family," but the term "household" comes closer to conveying the Japanese concept of *ie*. Usually formed around an elementary family as its nucleus, it will often include other relatives and even nonrelatives. Once established, a household is expected to exist through generations.

In Japan, communities are built on the basis of households. It is the common practice in many areas for a well-established household to have an exclusive house-name apart from a family surname often shared by others. The *ie* is seen not simply as a contemporary household but as a continuum, embracing not only current living members but also their deceased predecessors and successors yet unborn. Members come and go, through birth, marriage, and death, but the *ie* persists.

Rules of Succession

Two important rules of succession to the headship of an *ie* are common throughout Japan. The first is that the

らない。男性であれば血縁、非血縁をとわず法的に養子または婿養子になることで「息子」になることができる。たとえ家長に自分の息子がいても家長の継承に適さないとみなせば、家業を持つ「家」ではよく行われる事であるが、養子をとることもある。

日本では家長の継承を目的とする養子が多く見られる。養子、婿養子は実の息子と同等の継承、相続の権利を持つと同時に、養父母の老後や他の成員の面倒を見る義務を負う。

第二に「家」の継承は一子に限られ、決して共同では行われない。息子が二人いる場合、「家」の継承者と非継承者は明確に区別され、非継承者ならびにその妻や子は「家」の正式な成員とはみなされない。実際には結婚した二人の息子が一つの「家」に住むことはほとんどなく、非継承者は結婚と同時に「家」を離れるものとされている。非継承者が新たに「家」を創立すれば、別個の財産保有単位となり、そこにも同じ原則が働く。

継承の慣例によって新たに家長になった者は父親の家と財産の大部分を受け取る。1947年の新民法はすべての子供（男子も女子も）に父親の財産の平等な相続権を定めたが、農家ではほとんど例外なく非継承者はその権利を放棄し、農業を継いで親の面倒を見る兄（弟）に家と土地を譲る。

head must be succeeded by a "son." Any male, related or not, can be the son provided he has been legally adopted into the family as its adopted son (*yōshi*) or adopted son-in-law (*muko-yōshi*). Even if the head already has a son of his own, if he considers him unfit to be his successor, he may adopt another, as is occasionally done among *ie* that maintain family businesses.

Adoption to ensure succession to a headship has been very common in Japan. An adopted son or adopted son-in-law has the same rights in succession and inheritance as a real son and assumes the reciprocal obligation of caring for his adoptive parents in their old age and for other household members.

The second rule of succession is that it is by only one son never joint. In a household occupied by two brothers there is a sharp distinction in status between the successor and the nonsuccessor, with the wife and children of the latter being considered less than "full members" of the household. In fact, it is rare for two married brothers to reside in the same household, since nonsuccessors are supposed to leave upon marriage. Once they have established their own independent households, these become separate property-holding units in which the same principles operate.

The customs of succession ensure that the new head receives the father's house and the lion's share of the father's property. Although the 1947 Civil Code gives equal inheritance rights in the father's property to all sons and daughters, among agricultural families nonsuccessors almost invariably sign over their rights and leave the house and land intact for the brother who succeeds

伝統的な「家」集団内部の人間関係は、単なる血縁関係より重要視される。異なる「家」の成員間に血縁関係があっても、経済的、社会的にとくに密接な関係がなければ特別な意味は持たない。「家」を別に創設した兄弟は、異なる社会単位に属するとみなされ、一方、かつてはまったく外部の人間であった義理の息子は継承者となることによって別居する兄弟より重要な存在となる。

管理すべき財産や家業のある人にとって、「家」の継続は非常に重要な意味を持っていたので、都市でも農村でも「家」の意味は顕著なものであった。江戸時代、「家」は武士社会においても基本単位であった。武士の身分は「家」に割り当てられ、一つの「家」に一人の男子が原則であったので、家長のみがその特権を享受し、継承者にそれを伝えていくことができた。

第二次世界大戦後、経済的条件の変化により「家」制度は次第に衰えてきた。都市部の人口が急増し、「家」の財産管理よりも給与所得で生計を立てる者が増えた。管理、世襲する財産のない「家」の継承は意味がなくなった。給与労働者の増加、農村部からの若年人口の流失、また女性が夫の家族との同居を嫌うようになったことも「家」の衰退につながった。

and assumes responsibility for their parents.

Human relationships within the traditional household group are seen as more important than relationships based merely upon consanguinity; the kinship relation between individual members of different households have no specific importance unless the households are involved in a specific economic or social relationship. A brother who has established his own household is thought of as belonging to another social unit, whereas a son-in-law, once a complete outsider, assumes more importance as the successor than a brother living apart.

The concept of *ie* was manifested in both rural and urban areas, as family continuity was greatly valued by those with property or businesses to manage. It was also the basic unit of the *samurai* community in the Edo period (1600–1868); the status of samurai was assigned to the household so that the household head alone could enjoy its privileges and transmit them to his successor alone, one man to one household being the rule of the *ie* system.

The decline of the *ie* institution came about because of changing economic conditions following World War II. The population of urban areas burgeoned, increasing the numbers of those who lived on salaries rather than from the management of household property. Ensuring the continuity of the household became meaningless when the household had no significant property to manage and conserve. The growth of salaried workers, the exodus of the younger population from rural areas, and the growing reluctance of women to submit to living

[現代の家]

今日、「家」制度は農業や芸術、工芸など技の継承が求められる伝統的職業、また医者や僧侶のような一定の範囲の人々を顧客とする職業に残っている。現代の日本では、家族の多くが核家族である。老夫婦は別に住んだり、娘家族と同居するなど必ずしも長男家族と同居しない。

　家族制度としての「家」は衰えているものの、その基本概念は現代の日本で集団の構造基盤として今も生き続けている。例えば、会社は経営者を家長、全従業員をその構成員とする一つの「家」とみなすことができる。会社は従業員の家族も包含し、彼らの社会的、経済的責任を引き受け、従業員家族にとって会社は第一の関心事となっている。この意味で企業、その他のいかなる職場単位にも集団として「家」の投影を見ることができる。「家」の概念は日本の社会構造の基盤として集団認識の中に生き続けている。

非言語コミュニケーション

きわめて同質的日本社会では、意識的、無意識的に身につけた礼儀や動作が、個人間のコミュニケーションで重要な役割を果たしてい

with in-laws all contributed to the decline of the *ie*.

The Modern Ie

Today the institution is found mostly among farmers and men of traditional occupations (such as traditional arts and crafts), where techniques are handed down to the next generation, or in professions with fairly fixed clientele, such as medical practitioners or temple priests. The majority of contemporary Japanese households are nuclear families. Older parents may live by themselves or with their married daughters, not necessarily with their eldest son's families.

Despite the decline of the *ie* system as a family institution, the basic concept has in fact survived as a structural basis for contemporary Japanese groups. For example a company is conceived of an *ie*, all its employees qualifying as members of the household, with the employer as its head. The company envelopes the employee's personal family, taking social and economic responsibility for it, and the employee's family in turn considers the company its primary concern. In this sense the role of the *ie* institution is now played by the enterprise, or any unit of work organization, and the concept of the *ie* persists in group identity as the basis of Japanese social structure.

nonverbal communication

(*higengo komyunikēshon*). In the highly homogeneous society of Japan, consciously learned and unconsciously absorbed etiquette and gestures account for a significant

る。それは非言語的合図として働き、言語コミュニケーションを左右する。日本人として文化を共有していることを始めとして、仕事や職場や家庭にまでいたる広い人間関係を通じて、会話を理解するに必要な情報は、個人の言葉の合間の沈黙と省略で提供される。

沈黙をコミュニケーションの一手段とする教育は、母子の関係から出発する。日本の母親は子供との非言語コミュニケーションを重要視し、素直の美徳をはぐくむ。もっと広い社会関係では、「恩」と「義理」といった複雑で入り組んだ行動様式が、個人間のコミュニケーションを成り立たせる。公と私で意見の対立があるときは、対決を回避するために、口を閉じたり、本当の気持ちを抑えて同意することがある。あることに沈黙を守ることは、それに対する関心と、外見上は快活に見えて、実は深い感情を伝えることになる。会話の中の沈黙は、共通の雰囲気を味わう喜ばしい幕間となることがよくある。

日本では、おじぎが握手と同じ役割をするが、さらに、おじぎの深さによって、相手との社会的地位の上下を表現するのである。ほほえみは、喜びを表現するほかに、敵対感情や深い悲しみを隠すときにも用いられる。西洋と比べて、会話中に目を合わせることが少なく、目を合わせすぎると、脅かしていると思われる。

portion of the communication between individuals. Functioning as nonverbal cues, they set the context for verbal communication. Across a broad range of human relationships, beginning with that implied by the shared culture of Japan and extending to that of members of a profession, workplace, or family, essential information for the interpretation of a conversation is supplied by the silences and ellipses that link individual utterances.

Inculcation of silence as a means of communication begins with the relationship of mother and child. Japanese mothers place great importance on nonverbal communication with their children and foster the virtue of *sunao*. In the larger social framework, complex and interacting behavioral patterns such as the concepts of *on* and *giri* condition communication between individuals. The social convention of avoiding of confrontation, manifested in the radical bifurcation of public and personal opinion, encourages silence or even concurrence in opinions contrary to one's true feelings. Silence concerning a matter may convey concern about it, and apparently blithe remarks, deep feeling. Silences during a conversation are often felt to be a pleasant interval during which a shared atmosphere is savored.

In Japan, the bow (*ojigi*) serves the same purpose as a handshake, but it can also, depending on its depth, signify a hierarchy between two or more persons. The smile, besides displaying pleasure, is also used to hide feelings of antagonism or deep unhappiness. Eye contact during a conversation is much less frequent than in Western countries and, if excessive, may be construed as threatening.

義理と人情

「義理」とは、他人との関係において、社会の命ずるように行動しなければならない義務のことである。しかし、それは、社会的つながりを持つ特定の人にだけに関わることで、普遍的というよりは個別的な基準による。「人情」は、広い意味では、愛、好意、哀れみ、同情、悲しみなど、一般的人間感情のことで、親子関係とか恋人関係に見られるような、人に対していだく「自然の」感情である。

「義理」とは、互恵関係を守ることを義務づける規範で、助けてもらった人を助けたり、親切にしてもらった人に親切にすることである。この概念は、社会の構成員に、たとえ「人情」に背いても、社会的に当然とされる互恵関係を強制する道徳的な力を意味する。封建時代の武士にとって「義理」とは、まず、命を賭しても主君に奉仕する義務であり、主君から受けた「恩」に報いることであった。日本では、「義理」を守ることは道徳的に高い価値がある。お返しの義務を怠ることは、人の信用を失うことであり、結果、その支持を失うことである。

一般に、人間の感情は、社会の規範と矛盾しないものであり、「義理」を守ることは、「人情」を否定することではない。しかし、ときには、社会的義務と自然の気持ちのはざまで悩むこともある。「義理」と「人情」という言葉は、現代日本でははやらなくなった

giri and ninjō

Giri refers to the obligation to act according to the dictates of society in relation to other persons. It applies, however, only to particular persons with whom one has certain social relations and is therefore a particular rather than a universal norm. *Ninjō* broadly refers to universal human feelings of love, affection, pity, sympathy, sorrow, and the like, which one "naturally" feels toward others, as in relations between parent and child or between lovers.

Giri is a norm that obliges the observance of reciprocal relations—to help those who have helped you, to do favors for those from whom you have received favors, and so forth. The concept implies a moral force that compels members of society to engage in reciprocal activities even when their natural inclination (*ninjō*) may be to do otherwise. To feudal warriors, *giri* referred foremost to their obligation to serve their lord, even at the cost of their lives, and to repay *on* received from the lord. In Japan, to be observant of *giri* is an indication of high moral worth. To neglect the obligation to reciprocate is to lose the trust of others and, eventually, to lose their support.

Generally, human feelings do not conflict with social norms, and observance of *giri* does not contradict *ninjō*. However, conflicts sometimes do arise between social obligation and natural inclination. Though *giri* and *ninjō* as terms have outmoded connotations in modern Japan, the concepts are still important in guiding conduct. In

が、その概念は、今なお日本人の行動指針として重要である。「義理」を欠くと人付き合いがうまくいかなくなるし、仕事上の昇進も望めない。

建て前と本音

申し立てられた理由（建て前）と現実の意図や動機（本音）が異なることを表す対語。これは、公的性格や行動が私的な関係と対立することを表す「表」と「裏」という表現に似ている。伝統的社会規範はむつまじい人間関係と集団の団結を強調してきた。自己主張は強く押さえられ、個人は、集団内の対立を避けるために、自分の欲求と感情を犠牲にしなければならないことがしばしばある。社会規範は絶対に必要なものであると考えられ、日本人は、早いうちから自分の目標を守るよう教えられるが、建て前に公然と逆らってはいけないことも教えられる。その結果、社会状況によっては、人の真の意図を見分けるのが難しくなる。主人は礼儀の形式に合わせて客を歓待するが、並外れた丁寧さは、帰ってもらうためのサインだと客が理解することも望んでいるのである。

諦め

日本の伝統的行動概念。最近まで日本人は、痛みや死別にじっと耐えるのが美徳であるとしてきた。これは儒教の武士の掟の一つであ

neglecting these obligations, a Japanese will find it difficult to get along with others, let alone advance in a career.

tatemae and honne

Pair of words used to describe a situation in which a person's stated reason (*tatemae*) differs from his real intention or motive (*honne*). It is analogous to the expressions *omote* and *ura* (front and back), which describe public character or behavior as opposed to private interactions. Traditional Japanese social norms have greatly emphasized harmonious interpersonal relations and group solidarity. Self-assertion is strongly discouraged, and the individual often finds that he must sacrifice personal needs and emotions so as to avoid confrontation in the group. Social norms are considered indispensable: Japanese people are taught early to follow their personal aims but not to defy *tatemae* openly. The result is that in certain social situations it becomes difficult to discern the person's real intentions. A host may offer hospitality to conform with the formalities of etiquette, yet hope that the guest will interpret the excessive cordiality as a sign to leave.

akiramc

(renunciation, resignation). An important behavioral concept in traditional Japanese popular psychology. Until recently the Japanese have tended to emphasize

り、自己規制と忍耐の大切なことを教えるものであった。「諦め」の気持ちで自ら進んで耐え、避けられないことを甘受することは、仏教思想（および道教）から得た運命論を反映している。この運命論には、「苦あれば楽あり」という俗言に見る楽観主義を含んでいた。あらゆる自然と同じく、人間の運命は、痛みと困難を伴い、はかないものであると考えていた。このほとんど禁欲的とも言える「諦め」のため、多くの日本人は、困難に逆らわず、厳しい階級社会の中で、「諦め」の精神で自らの位置を受け入れた。

甘え

「甘え」とは「よりかかりたい願望」で、「甘える」の名詞形。「甘える」の同義語は英語になく、他人の愛や忍耐や寛容に寄りかかりたい願望を意味する。

　「甘え」は、無力感と愛されたい欲求から生ずる。日本社会では、親子関係が、夫婦、教師と生徒、指導者と被指導者など成人関係にも多く反映されているので、「甘え」は成人の一生を通じてそこここに見られる。土居健郎は、「甘える」を「他人の愛につけ込みたい」「他人の甘やかしに浴したい」「他人の親切に身を任せたい」欲望と定義づけている。また、「甘え」は、依頼心や依存関係に比較的寛大な日本文化の精神力学を理解するため

the virtue of enduring pain and deprivation with patience. This was a part of the warrior's code (reflecting the influence of Confucian ethics), that taught the importance of self-control and perseverance. The willingness to endure and suffer the unavoidable in a spirit of resignation also reflected a kind of fatalism derived in part from Buddhist thought (and perhaps Taoism). This fatalism contained a certain optimism as expressed in the popular saying, "Pain is followed by pleasure." Like all of nature, human life, with its pain and hardships, was accepted as transient. Because of this almost stoic resignation, many Japanese endured hardships without protest and accepted their place in a rigidly hierarchical society with a sense of *akirame*.

amae

Amae, which can be translated as "dependency wishes," is the noun form of *amaeru,* a verb that has no true equivalent in English but refers to the desire to depend upon the love, patience, and tolerance of others.

Amae arises from feelings of helplessness and the need to be loved. Since the parent–child relationship is reflected in Japanese society in many adult relationships, including those of husband and wife, teacher and pupil, and leader and follower, *amae* tends to be prolonged and diffused throughout adult life. Doi Takeo defines *amaeru* as the desire "to presume upon another's love," "to bask in another's indulgence," or "to indulge in another's kindness." He holds that *amae* is a key to understanding the psychodynamics of Japanese culture,

の鍵としている。土居は、その著書、とりわけベストセラーになった『「甘え」の構造』で、「甘え」を関連語や関連する感情の中核にすえ、日本伝統の「義理」と「人情」のジレンマを理解する鍵ととらえている。

　土居の定義によれば、日本式人情とは、どのように甘えるか、他人の「甘え」にどう応えるかを知る技術である。社会的義務である「義理」は、「人情」にどっぷりつかって存在する。「甘え」はまた、日本の社会においては母子関係が中心的役割を果たすこと、他人にとけ込む能力の重要性、あいまいな主体と客体あるいは自他の認識、プライバシーと個人の権利の認識が異なること、型にはまった論理と事務的関係を嫌うこと、高度の非言語コミュニケーション、美的指向の強い文化などを解く鍵である。

遠慮

日本におけるきわめて重要な個人の行動の基本的原理。英語に直訳するのは難しいが、説明は可能。

　客がうっかりして人の家に食事時まで止まった場合、主人が食事に誘うと、客は「遠慮」して断るが、主人は、「どうぞ、『遠慮』なさらないで」と言う。客は、主人を前にしてどの程度「遠慮」するかによって、その誘いを受けるか受けないかを決める。また、「遠慮」

which is relatively tolerant of dependency feelings and relations. In his writings, especially his bestselling *Amae no kōzō* (1971; translated as *Anatomy of Dependence,* 1973), he sees *amae* as the core of a constellation of related words and feelings and as the key to understanding the traditional Japanese dilemma between *giri* and *ninjō*.

In Doi's definition, Japanese-style *ninjō* is the art of knowing how to *amaeru* and how to respond to the call of *amae* in others; *giri,* or social obligations, exists to be pervaded by *ninjō*. *Amae* also explains for Doi the centrality of the mother-child relationship in Japanese society; the importance attached to the ability to "merge" (*tokekomu*) with others; the somewhat vague notions of subject and object, self and other; differently defined concepts of privacy and individual rights; a dislike for cut-and-dried logic and businesslike relationships; the high degree of nonverbal communication; and the strong aesthetic orientation of the culture.

enryo

(reserve, constraint). A cardinal principle of personal conduct in Japan. Though a difficult word to translate, it can be illustrated.

When a guest unwittingly stays at someone's home until mealtime and the host invites him to a meal, the guest declines out of *enryo*, but the host insists, saying, "Please, *enryo* is unnecessary!" The guest may or may not accept the invitation, depending upon how much *enryo* he decides to maintain vis-à-vis the host. Again,

から、特定の人の間で沈黙を守ったり、特定の人から距離を保つこともある。特定の集まりで腹蔵なく発言したり、他人の所有物を勝手に使ったりした場合、「遠慮」がないといって非難されることもある。「遠慮」しないと、自分の必要と要求を他人に押しつけすぎることになる。遠慮が過ぎると、他人と近づきになれない。

いちばん「遠慮」が少ないのは親と子の間で、その次が近い親族と友人である。しかし、近い親戚でもなく、まったくの他人でもない人には「遠慮」が必要である。「甘え」との釣り合いで、「遠慮」は、出しゃばったり立ち入りすぎたりするのを防いでくれる。日本人の対人関係では、「遠慮」と「甘え」のほどよい釣り合いを保つために、かなりの社交的機転が必要とされる。

恥

文化を「罪の文化」と「恥の文化」に二分するとき、人類学者ルース・ベネディクトは、日本文化を典型的恥の文化とした。彼女の定義によれば、「罪の文化」には道徳の絶対的基準を説いて個人の自覚の成長に待つが、「恥の文化」では、絶対的な意味で罪を感じるのではなく、行為をとがめられたときだけ悪いと感じるのである。言いかえれば、「恥の文化」は、良い行いに対する表面的拘束力に立脚するのであって、内面的罪の自覚に立つのではない。

one may keep silent among certain people or keep one's distance toward a specific person out of *enryo*. If one speaks without reserve in a given circle or helps himself uninvited to another person's material possessions, he may be blamed for not having *enryo*. Without *enryo*, one imposes too much of one's needs and demands upon others. With too much *enryo*, one can never become close to others.

Enryo is least expected between parents and children, and then between other close kin and friends. But it is expected between those who are neither close relatives nor total strangers. As a counterbalance to *amae*, it prevents people from imposing on or presuming too much of one another. A considerable degree of social tact is required to maintain an appropriate balance between *enryo* and *amae* in Japanese interpersonal relationships.

haji

(shame). In classifying cultures into "guilt cultures" and "shame cultures," the anthropologist Ruth Benedict described Japanese culture as a typical shame culture. According to her definition, a guilt culture inculcates absolute standards of morality and relies on the development of a personal conscience, while in a shame culture people feel bad only when caught in the act, rather than feeling guilty in an absolute sense. In other words, a shame culture relies on external sanctions for good behavior, not on an internalized conviction of sin.

ベネディクトの「恥」と「罪」の文化の区分けは、あまりにも単純な二極化である。実際、日本の文化は、公衆の目にさらされようがさらされまいが、行動基準の個人的内面化と、自らの行為についての深い道義心に負うところが大きい。「旅の恥はかきすて」という表現もあるが、日本人の「恥」の概念は、「君子は独りを慎む」という表現により正確に表されている。日本人は自分自身の内面的理想に生きようとするが、それに失敗すると、自分と他人の目で自分自身を恥じるのである。「恥」は、ベネディクトが言うほど他人の批判に対する反応ではなく、また追放への恐怖でもなく、自分自身の理想的イメージを傷つけたことの自覚に対する反応なのである。

腹

日本の伝統的大衆心理学と人間関係の重要な概念。「腹」という語は、身体の部分を意味するとともに、感情、思想、意向、性格と関係のある成句でいろいろに使われる。たとえば、怒ったときは、「腹が立つ」という。言葉のコミュニケーションによらず、他人の計画、意図、考えなどを探るときは、「腹を探る」という。人と率直に話し合うことを、「腹を割る」という。悪い人の腹は「黒い」。「腹芸」とは、言葉による直接のコミュニケー

Benedict's classification of shame and guilt cultures creates an oversimplistic dichotomy. In actuality, Japanese culture depends heavily upon individual internalization of behavioral standards and on a deep sense of conscience with regard to personal conduct, whether exposed to public scrutiny or not. Although there is an expression, *Tabi no haji wa kakisute* (While on a trip shame can be thrown away), a more accurate sense of the Japanese notion of shame is reflected in the expression *Kunshi wa hitori o tsutsushimu* (When alone, the superior man is watchful of himself). The Japanese try to live up to an internalized ideal image of themselves and when they fail, they feel ashamed of themselves in their own eyes and in the eyes of others. Shame (*haji*) is not so much a reaction to other people's criticism—as Benedict understood it—or fear of ostracism, as it is a reaction to the realization that one has tarnished one's ideal self-image.

hara

(abdomen, stomach, belly, viscera, womb). An important concept in Japanese traditional popular psychology and interpersonal relationships. In addition to referring to actual body parts, the word *hara* is used in a number of Japanese idioms having to do with emotions, thoughts, intentions, or character. For example, when a person is angry, it is said that his "*hara* stands up" (*hara ga tatsu*). When one tries to probe another's plans, intentions, or thoughts without verbal communication, one "gropes around," "reads," or "gauges" the other's

ションなしで、相互に理解する方法である。

　これらの「腹」を使った表現は、腹部が感情、思想、意向などの中心と考えられてきたことを示している。

　座禅や武道では、臍下丹田に力を集めて、緊張を解くとともに精神を集中する。腹切りは、腹こそ生命と人格の中心であることを証明している。

勘

直感的認識の方法を表す重要な概念。「勘」は、直感、いわゆる第六感、予感、事をなすこつ、霊感、一瞬の理解など、いろいろの属性を包んでいる。「勘」は、武道や美術工芸などの伝統的技術を含む日本人の生活のいろいろな局面に欠くことができないと考えられる。

　「勘」には明確な二つの様相がある。一つは、認識と判断に示される直感的力である。「勘」のこの面は、西洋の直感の概念に似ている。もう一つはこつで、これは物の扱いやその他の自発的行動に現れている。日本の芸術家や職人が、作品や仕事で獲得しようとつとめてきたのが、このこつである。これは努

hara (*hara o saguru*). A person having a frank talk with another "cuts his *hara* open" (*hara o waru*). A wicked man's *hara* is "black" (*haraguroi*). *Haragei,* or "belly play," is supposed to be a way to reach mutual understanding without direct verbal communication.

These and other expressions using *hara* indicate that the abdominal region has traditionally been considered the focus of emotions, thoughts, and intentions.

In the practice of Zen meditation and the martial arts, the student concentrates on the center of the abdominal region (*seika tanden*) to become at the same time relaxed and alert. *Harakiri* testifies to their belief that *hara* is the locus of life and character.

kan

An important Japanese concept referring to a form of intuitional cognition. *Kan* encompasses a number of attributes including intuition, the so-called sixth sense, premonition, a knack for doing things, inspiration, and sudden realization. *Kan* is considered essential in many spheres of Japanese life that involve traditional skills or techniques, such as the martial arts and artistic endeavors.

There are two distinct aspects of *kan*. The first is an intuitive power revealed in cognition and judgment. This aspect of *kan* resembles the Western notion of intuition. A second aspect is *kotsu* (a knack or physical skill), which manifests itself in the handling of objects or in other voluntary acts. It is *kotsu* that Japanese artists and artisans have traditionally sought to attain in their

力と経験の積み重ねの産物で、勤勉と訓練なしには実現不可能である。

礼

中国儒教の重要な倫理社会概念。『礼記(らいき)』によると、「礼」は儀式での正しいふるまい、礼儀作法であると同時に、国家の法や規則である。荀子は、「礼」を、人間と社会を治めるための、人間が作った規則と解釈した。日本では荻生徂徠が荀子に近い立場にたち、社会秩序と「礼」は、人間の作ったものであるとした。その思想が、1868年の明治維新後、西洋の政治、社会制度をスムーズに受け入れる下地になったと言う人もいる。多くの日本人にとって、「礼」あるいは礼儀とは、伝統、とりわけ行儀作法を守るための、社会的に確立された行動様式である。

顔

日本の対人関係における重要な概念。「顔」という語は、多くの成句で用いられる。知人の範囲が広い人を、「顔が広い」と言うし、影響力が大きければ、「顔がきく」という。「顔を汚す」と「顔をつぶされる」ということは、はずかしめられることである。メンツが保た

works and performances; this is a product of cumulative effort and experience which does not come about without hard work and discipline.

rei

(Chinese: *li*; rites, propriety, decorum). An important ethical and social concept in Chinese Confucianism. Its classical formulation is found in the *Li ji* (Japanese: *Raiki*), which describes *li* as proper conduct in rituals and ceremonies, etiquette, and the laws and regulations of the state. Xunzi (Japanese: Junshi) interpreted it as man-made rules that guided man and society. In Japan, Ogyū Sorai took a position similar to Xunzi's, viewing the social order and *li* or *rei* as man-made. His ideas are considered by some to have prepared the way for the ready acceptance of Western political and social institutions by the Japanese after the Meiji Restoration of 1868. To most Japanese, *rei,* or its compound form *reigi,* means a socially established pattern of conduct conforming to tradition, especially in the sense of proper manners and etiquette.

kao

(literally, "face"). An important concept in Japanese interpersonal relationships. The word *kao* is used in a number of idioms. If a person has a wide circle of acquaintances, his *kao* is "broad" (*kao ga hiroi*); if he is influential, his *kao* "works" (*kao ga kiku*). When a person "smears his *kao* with dirt" (*kao o yogosu*) or his *kao* is

れた時は「顔を立てる」と言う。「顔」はほとんど面目と同義である。面目も汚されたり、壊されたり、灰を塗られたりする。これらの言葉で表現される「顔」は、個人の社会的一面、あるいは世間に公表している自己の一面である。日本では、名声を保ち、名を汚さないことが、処身の基本原理となっている。

虫

「虫」という言葉は、感情や感覚を表す成句に使われる。気落ちしている人は、「ふさぎの虫にとりつかれ」ているという。機嫌の悪いときは、「虫の居所が悪い」という。怒りが消えないのは「腹の虫がおさまらない」からである。男が突然婚外情事に誘惑されるのは、「浮気の虫」のせいだとされる。子供が癇癪をおこした場合、母親のなかにはその子を神社につれていき、「癇の虫」を治めてもらう人もいる。日本人は、昔から、直情的行動に個人で責任をとりたくないので、外から身体に入ってくる「虫」のせいにするのである。虫は、「封じ込める」ことができ、「犠牲者」はあまり罪の意識も持たずに社会に帰ってこられるのである。

"crushed" (*kao o tsubusareru*), he is disgraced. When face is saved, one's *kao* is "made to stand" (*kao o tateru*). *Kao* is almost synonymous with *memboku*. *Memboku* may also be "sullied," "ruined," or "smeared with ash." What is signified by these words is the individual's social self or the self as properly presented to the public. To maintain a good reputation and to avoid shame to one's name have long been cardinal principles of personal conduct in Japan.

mushi

(literally, "worm" or "bug"). The word *mushi* is used in a number of idioms to describe emotions or feelings. When a person is depressed, he is said to be "possessed by the worm of depression" (*fusagi no mushi*). When a person is in a bad temper, "the worm is in the wrong place" (*mushi no idokoro ga warui*). When a person persists in anger, it is because "the worm in his abdomen has not calmed down" (*hara no mushi ga osamaranai*). When a man is suddenly tempted to have an extramarital affair, it may be explained as the result of "the worm of fickleness" (*uwaki no mushi*). If a child has violent temper tantrums, the mother may take the child to a shrine to have "the worm of tantrums (*kan no mushi*) sealed off." It might be that the Japanese, in their traditional reluctance to hold an individual responsible for impulsive behavior, attribute such behavior to an external agent, the "worm," which has made its way into his body. The *mushi* can always be "sealed off," and the "victim" can then return to the community without too much guilt.

気

伝統的大衆心理学と人間関係の重要な概念。
「気」は、およそ、「意志」「精神」「心」など
を表し、さまざまな心の状態を表す四十以上
もの成句に使われている。これを大きく分け
ると、次の四つになる。(1) 意識、自覚、正
気。正気でなくなると「気が狂う」、卒倒す
ると「気が遠くなる」、注意がそれると「気
が散る」という。(2) 興味、意向、意欲。個
人が積極的なときは、「気が進む」当初の興
味を失うことを、「気が変わる」という。(3)
気分、感覚、感情。気落ちしているときは、
「気が沈む/ふさぐ」、神経質になっていると
きは、「気がくしゃくしゃする」という。(4)
気質、心、精神。すぐ興奮する人は「気が短
い」、性格のいい人は「気がいい」、辛抱強い
人を「気が長い」という。しかし、ほとんど
の成句の主語は人間ではなく、「気」である。
人が辛抱強いとき、長いのは人ではなく、
「気」である。人が気落ちしたとき沈むのは、
人ではなく「気」である。

ki

An important concept in Japanese popular psychology and in interpersonal relationships. The word *ki,* which means loosely "mind," "spirit," or "heart," is used in over forty idiomatic expressions to describe various states of mind. They may be classified roughly into the following categories. (1) Consciousness, awareness, or sanity: when a person becomes insane, it is said that his "*ki* is out of kilter" (*ki ga kuruu*); when he faints, his "*ki* becomes distant" (*ki ga tōku naru*); when he is distracted, his "*ki* becomes scattered" (*ki ga chiru*). (2) Interest, intention, or volition: when an individual is willing, his "*ki* proceeds" (*ki ga susumu*); when he loses his initial interest, his "*ki* changes" (*ki ga kawaru*). (3) Mood, feelings, or emotions: when a person feels depressed, his "*ki* sinks or becomes closed" (*ki ga shizumu/fusagu*); when he is nervous, his "*ki* becomes ruffled" (*ki ga kusha kusha suru*). (4) Temperament, heart, or mind: of a quick-tempered person it is said that his "*ki* is short" (*ki ga mijikai*); of a good-natured person that his "*ki* is good" (*ki ga ii*); of a patient person that his "*ki* is long" (*ki ga nagai*). However, in most expressions it is *ki,* not the individual, that is the subject of the statement. When a person is patient, it is not *he* but the *ki* (in him) that is long. When an individual feels depressed, it is not *he* but *ki* that sinks.

気質
<small>かたぎ</small>

伝統的大衆心理学の大切な概念。この語の語源は、紙や布にプリントするための形木（版木）である。後に、習性や習慣を表すようになり、やがてそれぞれの職業、年代、身分に共通する精神、特色、思考態度を意味するようになった。いろいろな社会的階層（愛人、商人、農民など）を描く物語が、江戸時代に気質物という大衆文学になった。たとえば、職人気質は、利益を無視してまで仕事にうるさく、製品に誇りを持つことを特徴とした。これは、職人は機転がきかず、複雑な人間関係に無関心で、正直で素朴であることを表していた。

素直

「素直な」という形容詞の形で用いられ、「まっすぐで従順な」という意味を表す。日本では、子供にとってもっとも望ましい人格特性の一つであると考えられ、「ひねくれた」の反意語である。精神医学者土居健郎は、「甘え」が満たされないとき、人は激しい欲求不満を感じ、「すねる」とか「ひがむ」という動詞の表す不機嫌な心境に陥る。これが長年月にわたり人格の一部になってしまうと、その人は「ひねくれた」人といわれる。対して、

katagi

(character, turn of mind, spirit). An important concept in Japanese popular psychology. The word originally meant a wooden board with carved designs used to print designs on paper and cloth. It later came to mean customs and habits and, eventually, the spirit, traits, or mind-set common to members of an occupational, age, or status group. Stories describing the *katagi* of members of various social categories (such as mistress, merchant, student, and farmer) constituted a genre (*katagi-mono*) of popular literature in the Edo period. *Katagi* among artisans (*shokunin katagi*), for example, was characterized by a fastidious devotion to work and pride in their product, to the point of ignoring profit. It also implied the artisan's lack of social tact, his indifference to complicated interpersonal relations, and his honesty and *naïveté*.

sunao

Used in the adjectival form *sunao na,* meaning "upright and compliant." Considered one of the most desirable personality traits in Japanese boys and girls, *sunao na* is the opposite of *hinekureta* (warped, twisted). According to the psychologist Doi Takeo, when a Japanese person's *amae* (dependency need) is not satisfied, he or she feels acute frustration and resorts to the kind of sulking described by the verb *suneru* (to pretend indifference to one's *amae*) or the verb *higamu* (to pretend not to need to depend, while envying others who are apparently

子供時代から「甘え」が十分に満たされた「素直な」人は、権威を基本的に信用して受け入れ、何かあった時には面倒を見てもらえるという仮定のもとに行動するのである。

頑張る

対人関係で重要な言葉。たぶん「我を張る」から出た言葉で、集団の決定や規範に反対するという、否定的意味を含んでいた。しかし、1930年代から後、「頑張る」は肯定的な言葉にかわり、主として集団の目的を達成するための意気込みと努力を説く意味に用いられた。たとえば、村の青年は、都会での新しい仕事に出かけるときに、友人や両親や、先生に、「頑張ります」と約束した。その意味するところは、その人たちをがっかりさせない、ということであった。また、この語は、集団の中で、お互いを励ますときに、しばしば「頑張れ」という命令形で用いられる。

生き甲斐

個人の人生目標を語るときや、世論調査の項目としてもよく使われる。日本の母親は、子供だけが「生き甲斐」だとよく言うし、男性

favored). When this becomes a chronic attitude and is seen as an integral part of the personality, the person is described as a *hinekureta* person (distrustful, embittered, begrudging, and resentful). In contrast, a *sunao na* person, whose *amae* has been sufficiently gratified since childhood, has a basic trust in and acceptance of authority and acts on the assumption that he or she will always be taken care of.

gambaru

(to persist, to hang on, to do one's best). An important word in Japanese interpersonal relationships. Probably derived from *ga o haru* (to be self-willed), the word originally had the negative connotation of asserting oneself against group decisions and norms. Since the 1930s, however, *gambaru* has become a positive word, commonly used to exhort enthusiasm and hard work, usually toward a group objective. For example, when a village youth leaves for a new job in the city, he promises his friends, parents, and teachers that he will *gambaru*. The implication is that he will try not to disappoint them. The word is also used among members of a group to encourage each other in cooperative activities, often in the imperative form *gambare*.

ikigai

(that for which life is worth living; from *iki*, "living," and *kai*, "value, effectiveness, meaning"). A popular phrase often used in discussions of individual life goals

には仕事に「生き甲斐」を見つける人もいる。「生き甲斐」がなくなった人は、自殺するかもしれない。

1960年代以来、この言葉は、社会的関心の中心となった。第二次世界大戦での敗戦により、多くの古い価値や考え方が失われた。日本人は、伝統的に倹約や勤勉や集団への無私の奉仕への反発から、物質的満足と幸せな家庭生活に「生き甲斐」を捜し始めた。「生き甲斐」に関する世論調査のいくつかは、この傾向を肯定しているように見える。この傾向を肯定しているように、女性は、幸福な家庭と子供に、人生最大の価値をおいている。男性にとっては、四十代までは仕事が一番で、そこから仕事派と家庭派に分かれていく。

分

社会の一員として与えられた地位と任務。英語で最も近いのは、status または role である。分は独立した名詞として、「分をわきまえる」のように使われたり、複合名詞の一部として、「身分」のように使われる。「分」の概念は、日本社会では重要であるが、すべての人が封建的階級制の中で明確に定義された身分を割り当てられた江戸時代以降は、とくに重要視された。徳川幕府は、身分制度を固定し、身分間の移動はほとんど不可能にした。日本社会が、家柄や身分を重視するのは、こ

and a frequent subject of public opinion surveys in Japan. A Japanese mother will often say that her children are her only *ikigai,* or a man will find his *ikigai* in his job. Individuals may commit suicide when they no longer have an *ikigai.*

Since the early 1960s this word has become a focal point for public concern. With Japan's defeat in World War II, many old values and beliefs were lost. The Japanese began to look for *ikigai* in material comforts and a happy family life, no doubt in reaction to the traditional stress upon frugality, hard work, and selfless dedication to collective causes. A number of opinion surveys on *ikigai* seem to confirm this new attitude. Women consistently rank a happy home and children as their highest value in life. For men, work ranks highest until their forties, when they split into work-oriented and family-oriented groups.

bun

A position and set of duties assigned to each member of society in relation to other members. The closest English equivalent is "status" or "role." The term is used either as an independent noun, as in *bun o wakimaeru* ("know your place"), or as part of a compound noun like *mibun* ("social standing"). The concept of *bun* has been important in Japanese society since the Edo period especially, when each person was assigned to a well-defined position in the feudal hierarchy. The Tokugawa rulers froze the social hierarchy, and movement between social classes became virtually impossible. This

の徳川時代の慣習によるのであろう。社会的移動があたりまえになり、ほとんどの日本人が同質的中産階級に所属すると考えている現在でさえ、個人の地位は、最終的には、家系、教育、職業、年齢、性などによって決定される。

集団

日本の社会では、集団意識は、若いときから、最も身近で大切な「集団」、家庭の中で学習される。家庭は、社会生活に順応する環境を用意し、学校、地域、学校内外のクラブ、職場の集団など、より広い「集団」で応用できる、相互影響の行動様式も養う。日本人は上下関係に敏感で、「集団」では構成員の地位がかなりはっきりしている。個人はすべて直属の上司につながっている。「集団」のトップは一人で、それ以外の人はすべて、従属的な関係でトップにつながっている。

先輩が後輩にほどこすのは、すべて好意であり、場合によっては恩とよばれる。恩であろうとなかろうと、その好意には、尊敬、奉仕、忠誠という形で報いなければならない。恩に報いる義務は義理とよばれる。「集団」の仲間の関係は、「機能的に広汎で」、特定の

Tokugawa practice seems to have been responsible for making the Japanese highly status-conscious concerning family background and occupation. Even today, when social mobility is common and most Japanese consider themselves part of a homogeneous middle class, a person's status will in the end be determined by such factors as his family background, education, occupation, age, and sex.

groups

(*shūdan*). In Japanese society, group consciousness is learned from an early age in the family, which is the most important primary group for the individual. The family provides the context in which socialization takes place, as well as patterns of interaction that are applied in other, secondary groups such as school and neighborhood cliques, clubs in and out of school, and groups in the workplace. The Japanese are highly rank-conscious, and Japanese groups have fairly clear-cut ranking among members. Each person is linked to a particular individual above him. At the top of the group is one individual to whom all others are related through subordinate linkages.

Whatever is imparted or provided by a senior to his subordinate is considered a favor and is in some contexts called *on*, an especially profound debt. Whether *on* or not, the favor must be repaid in the form of respect, service, and loyalty to one's superior. The obligation to repay one's debt is often called *giri*. The relationship

役割に限定されず、生活のあらゆる面にかかわってくる。

普通、温かく親しい関係が保たれるのは「集団」の構成員の間だけで、「集団」は外部の人に門戸を閉ざすのである。外部に同一目標を目指す競合「集団」を認めたとき、「集団」内の結束は強まる。たとえば、銀行の支店は、預金高を増やそうと互いに競い合う。政党の派閥は、総裁選や大臣ポストなどの政治目的ではりあう。

閥

現代の日本には、昔ながらの徒党や派閥がいまなお存在する。いろいろな派閥主義が何百年もの間存在しているが、「閥」という言葉が使われるようになったのは、明治時代である。

「閥」は、機関や地域や家族、あるいは共通の知人などの縁で結びつき、企業、政府、政党、出身学校などで排他的小集団を作る。「閥」は基本的には階級的父子主義で、雇用、昇進、政治や取引での便宜などを支配する。「閥」の構成員はお互いを助け合う義理があり、目上のもの、とくに、「閥」の長の恩に報いなければならない。「閥」の長は、家父長的仁愛をほどこすだけでなく、下位の者に忠誠を求める。この疑似家族、あるいは親分子分関係は、先輩後輩関係に基づく階級関係をもそなえている。

among group members is "functionally diffuse," that is, it is not circumscribed in terms of specific roles, but tends to encompass almost all aspects of one's life.

As a rule, warm, intimate relationships are maintained only among group members, and the group closes its doors to outsiders. A group's internal cohesion is often heightened by recognizing a rival group with which it competes in obtaining certain resources. Branches of a bank, for instance, may be pitted against one another for increasing deposits. Factions *habatsu* of a political party compete for such political resources as the presidency of the party or ministerial posts.

batsu

A traditional type of clique or faction that is still found in modern Japan. Although varieties of factionalism have existed in Japanese society for centuries, the word *batsu* became common in the Meiji period.

A *batsu* is a group with common ties based on institution, geographic region, family, or connection to the same person. Its members form an in-group, as, for example, in industry, a political party, or an educational institution. A *batsu* is basically hierarchical and paternalistic and frequently controls hiring, promoting, and the granting of political and business favors. Members of a *batsu* carry an obligation (*giri*) to help each other and to repay their debt (*on*) to their superiors, particularly to the group leader, who not only exercises paternalistic benevolence but also claims loyalty from subordinates. This pseudo-familial or *oyabun-kobun* ("parent-child") rela-

　「閥」の種類は、学閥、戦前なら、軍閥などのように、接頭語によって区別できる。「閥」は、教育、医学、経営、公務、政治など、訓練を要する職業に多い。「閥」の中でも古いのは婚姻を通じて形成される閨閥で、政治的、経済的力もそなえている。明治維新（1868年）の後、薩摩、長州、土佐、肥前出身者が、藩閥をなして、政府と軍の中枢を占めた。財閥は、金融、ビジネス、産業の複合企業体（コングロマリット）である。学閥は出身大学に基づく「閥」である。最近の「閥」に関係したこととしては、政党や労働組合の派閥による主導権争いがある。

派閥

大きな集団の中で、主導権争いの結果できるグループ。この語は「閥」の同義語ではあるが、「閥」が大きな組織内の小グループ一般に使われるのに対し、「派閥」は、政党、企業、労働組合内の小グループに対して用いられる。たとえば、自由民主党にはいくつかの「派閥」があり、各「派閥」には、総理大臣候補の名前がつけられている。「派閥」は、

tionship is accompanied by a hierarchical structure of authority deriving from length of service (*sempai-kōhai*).

Particular types of *batsu* may be distinguished by different prefixes, as in *gakubatsu* (school or university clique) or, in pre–World War II days, *gumbatsu* (military clique). *Batsu* are usually found in professions requiring training, such as teaching, medicine, business management, civil service, and politics.

One of the oldest kinds of *batsu* is *keibatsu*, a clique formed through marriage alliances and having some political or economic power. After the Meiji Restoration (1868), men from the former domains (*han*) of Satsuma, Chōshu, Tosa, and Hizen came to dominate the government and military through domain-based cliques called *hambatsu*. *Zaibatsu* (financial cliques) are financial-business-industrial conglomerates. *Gakubatsu* are cliques based on the college or university from which one has graduated. A particularly modern incidence of *batsu* is found in political parties and trade unions in which factions (*habatsu*) vie for leadership.

habatsu

(factional clique). A group or faction resulting from a struggle for leadership within a larger group. Although this term is essentially a synonym for the word *batsu*, which refers to the cliques found in many large organizations, *habatsu* is most often used to refer to factions within political parties, business corporations, and trade unions. For example, there are several factions within the Liberal Democratic Party (LDP), each named for a

組織内の主導権争いの内部抗争を引き起こす。その抗争は、しばしば金で解決される。

親分・子分

架空の親（親分）と子（子分）の間に作られた関係で、相互の経済的利益や社会的扶助を目的としている。

「親分・子分」関係は、小規模な共同組織のかなめであったが、現在でも、近代化されていない組織には残っている。この関係の基本は、親分の経済的、政治的、社会的権力が大きいことである。「親分」は、「子分」の厚生、行動、指導に責任を負う。親分の支配を受けいれた子分は、その恩に報いるために、従順と忠誠と奉仕をささげる。「親分・子分」の関係は19世紀に急激に衰えたが、親分と子分という言葉は、伝統的な形の人間関係のあるところでは、よく使われる。古い形の「親分・子分」関係は、やくざの世界に見られる。いろいろの分野で、実力者は、冗談めかして、親分と呼ばれる。

「親分・子分」関係は、芝居や映画の人気のテーマであった。その物語の中では、親や恋人への愛といった個人的な感情と、親分と組への忠誠の対立が悲劇を生むのである。

person who could potentially become prime minister. *Habatsu* generate internal power struggles for the leading position within the organization. Often the struggle hinges on money.

oyabun–kobun

(literally, "parent role–child role"). A relationship posited between a fictive parent (*oyabun*) and child (*kobun*), established for mutual economic benefit or social support.

Oyabun-kobun ties have traditionally been the backbone of small-scale cooperative organizations and are still common in the less modernized sectors of Japanese society. The basis of the relationship is the greater economic, political, or social power of the *oyabun*. He assumes responsibility for the welfare, behavior, and guidance of the *kobun*. The *kobun* accepts the authority of the *oyabun* and is thus obligated to obedience, loyalty, and certain services as repayment for the benefits he receives. The incidence of *oyabun-kobun* relations has declined radically during the last century, but the terms *oyabun* and *kobun* themselves are still heard quite frequently today in reference to relationships that resemble the traditional pattern. A classic example of *oyabun-kobun* patterns can be seen in gangster groups. Powerful individuals in any sphere may be jokingly referred to as *oyabun*.

The *oyabun-kobun* relationship has been a popular theme in Japanese dramas and movies. The conflict between personal feelings, such as affection for a parent or lover, and loyalty to an *oyabun* and his group often provides the tragedy for these stories.

学閥

同じ学校の卒業生が作る相互扶助の組織。

　どの大学にも、卒業生が自動的に所属する同窓会がある。同窓会は、大企業や官庁のなかに「学閥」を作る力となる。採用や昇進のときは、同じ「学閥」の構成員は好意的扱いを受ける。「学閥」内の調和と協力関係を強化するため、全員の認める基準、たとえば卒業年次が、先輩・後輩、恩師と教え子、同級生を区別するのに適用される。「学閥」には、義理人情の要素もある。

　明治時代には、日本政府は近代化の機関として、学校制度を重視した。東京大学を中心とする高等教育機関が、高級官僚と学者を生み、産業、教育、軍の指導者を育てることを目的に設立された。これら高等教育機関の卒業生の多くが、政府や大企業に職を得た。

　「学閥」の横行が、日本の社会を、人間の価値が学位や出身大学によって決められる学歴社会にしてしまった、と論ずる人もいる。今日は、経歴よりも能力のほうが重視されるようになってきたと指摘する人もいるが、

gakubatsu

(academic cliques or alumni cliques). Mutual support groups formed by graduates of the same school.

Most universities and colleges have alumni associations (*dōsōkai*) to which all graduates automatically belong. These associations facilitate the formation of *gakubatsu* within large corporations and government bureaus. When employment openings occur or opportunities for advancement arise, members of the same alumni group will receive preferential treatment. In order to strengthen harmony and cooperation within the graduate group, standards recognized by all members, such as the year of graduation, are applied in making the important distinctions of *sempai-kōhai* (senior-junior), teacher and student, and classmate. The *gakubatsu* also contains elements of *giri* and *ninjō* relations.

During the Meiji period, the Japanese government placed great importance on the school system as a modernizing institution. Tōkyō University and a network of higher educational facilities were established to produce high-level bureaucrats and scholars and to develop business, educational, and military leaders. Great numbers of graduates from these institutions took posts in government or large enterprises.

Some have contended that the prevalence of *gakubatsu* has transformed Japanese society into a "credential society" (*gakureki shakai*) where a person's worth is measured by academic degree and school. There are some indications that ability is beginning to take prece-

「学閥」はまだ大きな影響力を持っている。

先輩・後輩

日本の組織、学校、協会などに見られる非公式の人間関係で、年上で経験の豊富な人が、経験の浅い人たちに友情や援助や助力を与え、与えられるほうは感謝、尊敬、それに、ときには個人的忠誠を捧げる。

「先輩・後輩」の関係は、組織への加入の日付によって決定される。同じ学校の卒業生や職場の先任者である先輩は、友人ないしは保護者として、新参者を訓練し、適切な行動を教え込む。「先輩・後輩」関係は日本の社会に行き渡っている。「派閥」や「閥」などの人間関係が「先輩・後輩」関係にもある程度はたらき、「先輩・後輩」関係は、問題を早く満足がいくように解決することに役立っている。昇進はこのような長年にわたる人間関係で果たされることが多いが、先輩が後輩を利用するなど、否定的側面もある。

村八分

村からの追放。一つの家族に、村の社会経済生活への全面参加を禁じること。追放された家も村八分と呼ばれる。

dence over background in Japanese society, but the *gakubatsu* still exert a powerful influence.

sempai-kōhai

(senior-junior). An informal relationship ubiquitous in Japanese organizations, schools, and associations, in which older, experienced members offer friendship, assistance, and advice to inexperienced members, who reciprocate with gratitude, respect, and, often, personal loyalty.

The *sempai-kōhai* tie is determined by the date of entrance into a particular organization. The *sempai,* perhaps a graduate of the same school or a senior in the work group, acts as a friend and patron, disciplining and teaching the neophyte appropriate conduct. *Sempai-kōhai* ties permeate Japanese society. *Habatsu, batsu,* and other personal networks function to some extent in *sempai-kōhai* terms, and *sempai-kōhai* alliances often smooth the way toward a quick, satisfactory resolution of a problem. Successful careers have often been promoted by these long-term relationships, though they can also have negative aspects, as when the *sempai* exploits his *kōhai.*

murahachibu

Loosely, village (*mura*) ostracism. The practice of barring a household from full participation in the social and economic life of the rural community. The ostracized household is itself also called *murahachibu.*

最近まで、日本の村落は、共同組織の役割を担っていた。各「家」は共同の宗教儀式を定期的に行い、相互援助や労働の手助けをしてきた。とくに米の生産と灌漑でそれが著しかった。入会林で許可なしに薪を切ることや、違法行為や恥ずべき行為を警察や村外の人に漏らすようなことをすれば、村の寄り合いで、その「家」は告発された。告発が全員一致で支持されれば、その「家」に正式に「村八分」の通告がされた。しかし、農業に代わって都会での雇用が増えると、村落の力はなくなり、「村八分」は急激に減少した。

縄張り

藩、領土、勢力範囲を意味する比喩的単語。縄を境界線に張って神の神聖な地を線引きする民俗習慣からきたもの。

鎌倉時代以後、軍陣の設営地や城の敷地などを意味した。「縄張り」という言葉は、島、庭場などの語とともに、江戸時代からは、やくざや博徒が自分たちの勢力範囲を表すために使うようになった。「縄張り」の概念は、企業や官庁でも重要である。

Until recently, the Japanese hamlet acted as a corporate entity. Its member households regularly performed communal religious rites and exchanged mutual aid and labor, particularly for the purpose of rice production and irrigation. Conduct such as cutting firewood in the communal forests without permission or revealing illegal or shameful village actions to the police or outsiders was cause for a charge of wrongdoing to be brought against a household at a hamlet council meeting. If it was unanimously agreed that the charges were valid, an official notification of ostracism was delivered to the household. As urban employment replaces farming, however, the power of the hamlet and incidences of ostracism have steadily diminished.

nawabari

(literally, "rope stretching"). A figurative term meaning domain, territory, or sphere of influence. It is derived from the folk custom of land demarcation by stretching a straw rope along boundaries to delineate an area that was supposed to be sacred to the gods.

From the Kamakura period onward, *nawabari* signified the location of a military camp or the area in which a castle was to be built. *Nawabari*—along with terms such as *shima* (island) and *niwaba* (garden)—has been used since the Edo period by *yakuza* and gamblers to refer to their territory. The concept of *nawabari* is also important in business and bureaucratic organizations.

根回し

意思決定するとき、争いを避けて意見の一致をみるための日本的方法。文字通りの意味は、移植する前に木の根のまわりを掘り、木を移動しやすくすること。しかし、とくに、政治やビジネスで、意見の一致や特定の目的を達成するために、見えないところで繰り広げる作戦、という比喩的な意味で使われることが多い。各種利害が入り乱れているときは、まともな正面突破では、合意に達したり政治的目的を達成することはきわめて困難である。日本の政治やビジネスでは、前もって利害関係のある人々と解決方法を討議し、できる限りその人たちの見解を最終提案に組み込むのが、ならわしである。最終決定の行われる会議の前に、決定への地均しがほとんど終わっているので、もし「根回し」が成功すれば、討論での抗争は回避できるのである。意思決定のために「根回し」をすると時間がかかるが、最終決定とその実施は、まともにぶつかりあって決定したり上から押しつけられるよりも、円滑にいくのである。

nemawashi

(prior consultation). A technique used in Japan to avoid conflict and obtain a consensus in decision making. The literal meaning of *nemawashi* is to dig around the roots of a tree prior to transplanting, thus making the uprooting and movement much easier. But the term is used much more widely in a figurative sense to describe maneuvering behind the scenes to reach a consensus and obtain certain objectives, especially in politics and business. When various interests are potentially in conflict, reaching a consensus and attaining political objectives are very difficult through direct, public confrontation. Instead, in Japanese politics and business the practice is to discuss decisions in advance with various interested parties and to incorporate their views, wherever possible, into any final proposals. Much of the groundwork for decisions is therefore laid well in advance of the meetings where final decisions are made, and, if the *nemawashi* is successful, conflict can be avoided during public discussion. As with decision making in general in Japan, the process involved in *nemawashi* is time-consuming, but final decisions and their implementation generally go much more smoothly than when decisions are made through confrontation or are imposed from above.

談合

本来の意味は、話し合うこと、相談であるが、事業の入札に先立つなれ合いの意味あいがきわめて強い。建設業のように、「互いに邪魔せずにやっていく」体質の強い業界では、大きな建設計画の入札の前に、業者が相談を行うのが習慣である。従って、入札の前に、いちばん低い値段で落とす業者を、継続的に行われる相談やそれまでの関係を考慮して決めるのである。「談合」は、公共または半公共事業でもっとも頻繁に行われていると考えられる。民間の計画では、入札はもっと厳しい基準で行われる。

dangō

Literally translated, *dangō* means "consultation" or "conference," but it has strong overtones of collusion prior to submitting bids for projects. Especially in industries such as construction, where there is a strong "live and let live" mentality, the practice is often for industry participants to consult among themselves before making bids for large construction projects. Thus, prior to the submitting of bids, construction companies will essentially decide which among them should be the low bidder on a particular contract based upon an ongoing series of negotiations and established relationships. *Dangō* is believed to be most common in bidding for public or semipublic projects. For private-sector projects there is usually a more stringent set of bidding criteria.

宗教観
Religious Concepts

宗教と自然

中国と日本の世界観を、西方の一神教（ユダヤ教、キリスト教）と比べると、人間と神の間の距離は近く、自然の地位はきわめて高い。中国と日本の文化の大きな特徴は、自然を神聖視し人間にふさわしい場所は、自然の中にあると考えたことである。

　日本人は、有史以前から、自然の中の神聖な力と考えられる神を崇拝してきた。『古事記』と『日本書紀』では、神は日本列島創造にかけがえのない役割を演じている。宗教儀式は、季節の経過、とくに米作りの各行程に深くかかわっている。神道がより高度な組織的宗教になってくると、正月や田植えから刈り入れまでの米作の各行程に応じた宗教儀式や、漁業などの自然経済に関係する祭りなどが行なわれるようになった。社会的行事に関して言えば、天皇の即位式は、米の収穫にあわせて行われた。このように、古代日本の宗教活動は、特定の「自然宗教」は台頭していないものの、すでに自然の力とその移り変わりと密接に関係していた。

　自然観においては、神道と仏教は多少異なり、時代によっても違いはあるものの、その伝統と歴史を通じて、一定の通則が見受けら

nature in Japanese religion

(*shūkyō to shizen*). In both the Chinese and Japanese worldviews, there is less distance between man and the divine than in the Western (Judeo-Christian) monotheistic tradition, and nature is elevated to a very lofty position. A major thrust of Chinese and Japanese culture has been to locate man's proper place within the lap of nature, which is seen in terms of the divine or sacred.

From prehistoric times, the Japanese people seem to have venerated *kami* or gods which most often were seen as the sacred powers within nature. In the *Kojiki* and *Nihon shoki,* the *kami* are portrayed as taking an integral part in the creation of the Japanese islands. Rituals were closely related to the passing of the seasons, especially to the cycle of rice agriculture. As Shintō developed into a more highly organized religion, there emerged more formal festivals for honoring the New Year and the various stages of rice agriculture from transplanting to harvesting, as well as festivals related to other aspects of the natural economy, such as fishing. Regarding worldly matters, enthronement ceremonies for a new emperor were timed to coincide with the natural cycle of the rice harvest. Thus religion in early Japan was already closely attuned to the powers and patterns of nature, even though a specific "nature religion" did not emerge.

Although views of nature differ somewhat between Shintō and Buddhism, and from age to age, some general patterns cut across traditions and periods. First,

れる。まず、自然は、神々の創造という二次的な重要性の故に崇拝されるのでなく、自然そのものに備わる神聖と美の故に崇拝される。第二に、自然は、抽象的存在としてではなく、特定の地域の特定の山、木、川のように、具体的にとらえられる。第三に、人間も神も自然の中に住んでいると考えられる。第四に、自然には、不幸や災難などの暗い側面があるものの、それは人間の動機づけのあいまい性や、悪神にも見られる二面性の一面に過ぎないのである。

祈り

人間と神の間の対話として、祈りは日本のすべての宗教で重要な役割を果たしている。神道でも仏教でも、国や地域の繁栄と国家の安泰や自然災害防止などを願う祈りは、しきりに行われた。個人の行いが未来の果報を生じるという仏教の思想が入ってくると、人は自分のために祈るようになった。個人の祈りは、「百度参り」とか、呪いをかけるために朝の二時から四時ごろ神社に参る「丑の刻参り」などの形をとることもあった。古来の土着の祈りには、魔術的要素が強く、密教によってさらに神秘的になった。祈りの言葉の意味内容に重点が置かれるようになっても、まじないの場合は、魔力は言葉そのものの中に存在すると考えられた。密教の加持祈禱に使われる真言（呪文）はその見本である。

nature is revered for its sacredness and for beauty in its own right, not through any secondary importance as a creation of divinities. Second, nature is revered not so much as an abstract entity but more concretely in terms of specific mountains, trees, and streams in particular locales. Third, both humans and *kami* are understood to dwell within nature. Fourth, although nature has its dark side, with calamities and disasters, this is just one aspect of a duality also reflected in the ambiguous character of human motivation and even in malevolent deities.

prayer

(*inori*). As the dialogue between humans and the divine, prayer has played an important part in all Japanese religions. In both Shintō and Buddhism there were many prayers for the welfare of the community and the nation, seeking national security, the prevention of natural disasters, and so on. With the introduction of the Buddhist idea that one's actions will result in future rewards, individuals began to recite prayers for their own benefit. Personal prayer sometimes took the form of one hundred visits to a shrine for worship (*hyakudo mairi*) or visiting a shrine from 2:00 to 4:00 in the morning to place a curse on someone (*ushi no toki mōde*). The magical element was strong in indigenous forms of prayer from primitive days, and was further developed by esoteric Buddhism. Importance was placed on the meaning and content expressed by the words of ordinary prayers, but, in the case of incantations, a magical

天

『古事記』（712年）の神話では、天あるいは
高天原は、神のすみかとされていた。太陽神、
天照大神は、神道の神々では最高の地位を与
えられ、神話の中では皇室の先祖とされてい
る。大乗仏教では、天は徳の高い人の未来の
すみかとされる。これは、一般民衆の心には、
仏の救済の力によって浄土や極楽に行くこと
であった。天は、道徳と肉体の宇宙の究極原
理であるという中国の思想は、儒学者には受
け入れられたが、日本では広い支持を得られ
なかった。キリスト教でいう heaven は、天
または天国と翻訳されている。

神

神道の「神」で、自然、生き物、ある種の人
間の中に住み、創造と破壊の神秘的な力と解
釈されている。恐れと感謝という相反する気
持ちを起こさせ、神道儀式の中心である。天
の「神」が高天原に住んで、神社にまつられ
るのに対し、地の「神」は、自然現象の中に
住んで、自発的にあるいは神官の呼び出しで

power was thought to reside in the words themselves. The *shingon* (mantra) employed in the prayer for grace (*kaji kitō*) in esoteric Buddhism is an example of this.

heaven

(*ten*). In Japanese mythology, as recorded in the *Kojiki* (712), heaven, or the High Celestial Plain (Takamagahara), is depicted as the abode of the deities. The sun goddess, Amaterasu Ōmikami, was given the highest place in the Shintō pantheon and is described in the mythology as the progenitor of the imperial line. In Mahāyāna Buddhism, heaven is conceived of as the future dwelling place of the virtuous. In the popular mind it was understood to mean the Pure Land (Jōdo) or Paradise (Gokuraku) to which one went through the saving power of the Buddha. The Chinese concept of heaven as the ultimate principle of the moral and physical universe was accepted by Confucians but never gained wide acceptance in Japan. The Christian notion of heaven is translated as *ten* or *tengoku*.

kami

Term used to refer to the divine in Shintō religion, traditionally interpreted as a superior and mysterious force of either creative or destructive character, which resides in natural elements, animals, and certain human beings; it causes ambivalent feelings of fear and gratitude and is the focus of ritual behavior. Whereas heavenly divinities tend to reside in the High Celestial Plain (Takama-

現れる。「神」の数ははっきりしないが、伝統的に「八百万の神」といわれる。一般に、「神」は正しく礼拝すれば情け深い。しかし、自然災害は、無実の罪にとわれて自殺したり、追放のうちに死んだ人の霊のなせるわざであるから、その御霊は鎮め、情け深い力に転換する必要があった。「神」にはそれぞれ「魂」と呼ばれる特別の力、あるいは意志があり、それには「荒御魂」と「和御魂」の二種があって、儀式でそれぞれ相応に礼拝される。神道が、仏教、儒教、道教の影響を受けると、「神」の概念は、哲学的、倫理学的に発展をとげた。10世紀に始まった神道と仏教を融合した本地垂迹説では、特定の「神」は特定の仏と結び、重要な変化を遂げたとされる。神々の頂点に立ちすべてを包み込む「神」をうちたてようとする試みは成功せず、多くの「神」は、地方性と時代性を残している。

魂

御魂ともいわれる。神道における形而上の存在をさす。物質的存在と切り離せない精神的存在である。「もの」や「み」と異なり、「魂」は物質的存在を通じて機能するが、物質的存在そのものからは独立している。病気や不幸

gahara) and to be worshiped at shrines, earthly divinities tend to reside in natural phenomena and to manifest themselves either spontaneously or through summoning by priests. The number of these divinities varies—tradition refers to "The Eight Hundred Myriads" (*yaoyorozu no kami*). On the whole, *kami* appear to be benevolent if properly worshiped. However, natural calamities were attributed to the spirits of humans wrongly accused who had therefore committed suicide or died in exile, leaving a "vengeful spirit" (*goryō*) needing to be pacified and transformed into a benevolent force. Each *kami* is endowed with a particular force, or will, called *tama*, which may have a "coarse" aspect (*aramitama*) "gentle" aspect (*nigimitama*), and is worshiped accordingly. As Shintō interacted with Buddhism, Confucianism, and Taoism, the notion of *kami* developed philosophically and ethically. Within the Shintō-Buddhist syncretic systems (*honji suijaku*), beginning around the tenth century, particular Shintō *kami* were associated with particular Buddhist divinities and thus transformed in important ways. Attempts to establish an all-encompassing *kami* at the very top of the pantheon failed, and many *kami* retain their local and historical character.

tama

Also called *mitama*. Name applied in the Shintō tradition to a metaphysical substance of being. Different from *mono* and *mi*—spiritual entities inseparable from material being—*tama* functions through the medium of material substance but is independent from that sub-

は、「魂」の力が衰えたとき起こり、死は霊魂が肉体から離れたとき来る。歴史的に見ると、「魂」には四つの異なる働きがある。調和の和御魂、行動的で雄々しい荒御魂、慈悲にあふれ幸いを与える幸魂、驚異と不可思議をもたらす奇御魂である。神道の神々は、「魂」の格式と働きに応じてその数を増やした。太陽神天照大神の荒御魂は、伊勢神宮の別宮である荒祭宮にまつられ、大国主命の幸魂と奇御魂は大神神社にまつられている。悪魂は怨霊または御霊とされ、鎮撫の祭りを通じて鎮めなければならなかった。

地獄

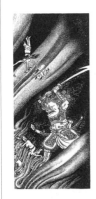

古代の日本神話には、死者の住む世界、黄泉の国があったが、悪人を罰するための地獄という思想は、仏教とともに入ってきた。仏教の地獄は、もともとはヒンズー教から来ている。ヒンズー教の聖典には、いろいろの地獄が出てくるが、その中には、阿鼻地獄または無間地獄や叫喚地獄がある。地獄の支配者は閻魔として知られ、死者の生前の行状を取り調べた後、それぞれの地獄に送り込む恐ろしい裁判官である。地獄の思想は、平安時代末に、浄土教が地獄の罰に対する浄土での救済を説くようになると、しだいに広まった。こ

stance. Disease or misfortune occurs when the power of the *tama* declines, and death when this *tama*-spirit escapes from the body. Historically, four separate aspects or functions of *tama* have been recognized: the harmonious and harmonizing *nigimitama,* the active and valiant *aramitama,* the gracious and beneficent *sakimitama,* and the wondrous and wonder-working *kushimitama*. Shintō deities have proliferated in accordance with the degree and function of *tama*. Thus there is separate enshrinement and worship of the *aramitama* of the sun goddess and imperial ancestress, Amaterasu Ōmikami, at the Aramatsuri no Miya, a subshrine of the Ise Shrine, and the *sakimitama* and *kushimitama* of the god Ōkuninushi no Mikoto at the Ōmiwa Shrine. Evil *tama* are regarded as vengeful spirits (*onryō* or *goryō*) that must be placated through rites of pacification.

hell

(*jigoku*). Although ancient Japanese myths mention Yomi no Kuni, an underworld of the dead, the concept of hell (*jigoku*) as a place of punishment for the damned was introduced with Buddhism. The Buddhist hell itself was of Hindu origin. Hindu sacred texts usually refer to many distinct hells, which include Abi Jigoku or Muken Jigoku (Interminable Hell) and Kyōkan Jigoku (the Hell of Sorrowful Crying). The ruler of hell is known as Emma, a fearful judge who reviews a person's past deeds before, consigning him to the appropriate hell. The concept of hell became increasingly widespread from the late Heian period, as Pure Land Buddhism

の時代に、地獄の責め苦を描く地獄草紙が多く制作された。

空 <ruby>空<rt>くう</rt></ruby>

概念化と言語表現に基づく存在を実体ある実在と認識しないことを表す仏教用語。この境地を達成することは、存在を全否定することではなく、虚無主義を肯定することでもない。インドの大乗仏教僧、ナーガールジュナ（200年前後）によると、すべての事象には縁起があり、単独では存在し得ない、すなわちすべての事象には物質的現実はなく、「空」である。概念化と言語表現による認知は、あらゆる事物を固定した存在ととらえ、それに具体的実在性を与える。あらゆる事象は、このような通常の認知によって存在すると考えられるから、人間の愛情、感情、苦悩、幻想なども存在するのである。これを排除して悟りに到達するには、「すべては空」であることに気づかなければならない。この境地に立ったとき、あらゆる事象の原形が見えてくる。この「空」の境地は、平常の認識に必ず伴う否定と肯定、存在と非存在の区別を超越する。

　日本における「空」は、インド仏教のように、仏教の理論には力点を置かず、直感的、感情的側面、すなわち無常観を強調した。

preached salvation in the Pure Land in contrast to punishment in hell. Many *Jigoku-zōshi* (Scrolls of Hells)
produced in this period depict the torments of hell.

emptiness

(Japanese: *kū*; Sanskrit: *sūnyatā*). Buddhist term that
indicates the elimination of cognition, based on conceptualization and verbal expression, of objects as substantial reality. The achievement of this state is neither a
total negation of existence nor an affirmation of
nihilism. Nāgārjuna (fl ca. 200), an Indian Buddhist of
the *Mahāyāna* tradition, stated that all things are dependent on causes and conditions for their existence (*engi*)
and do not exist by themselves; they are devoid of substantial reality and are empty. Perception based upon
conceptualization and verbal expression grasps all things
as fixed entities and attributes substantial reality to
them. It is because all things are assumed to exist
through such ordinary perception that human attach-
ments, passions, suffering, and illusions come into
being. To eliminate them and reach enlightenment, it is
necessary to realize that "all is empty." When this
occurs, the original form of all things is grasped. This
standpoint of emptiness transcends distinctions of affirmation and negation, existence and nonexistence,
which necessarily accompany ordinary cognition.

The emphasis in Japan has been not on Buddhist
theory, as was the case in Indian Buddhism, but on its
intuitive and emotional aspect, chiefly the awareness of
impermanence (*mujōkan*).

無

中国の道教の基本理念。絶対的非存在を表す
語で、あらゆる存在はここから生じ、人間は
最終的にここに帰る。倫理と政治を超越した
「無」の思想は、倫理と政治問題にどっぷり
つかっている儒者を批判する道士たちによっ
て発展した。この「無」の哲学は、中国と日
本の仏教、とりわけ禅宗において、インドの
「空」の哲学と結合した。しかし、仏教が説
明しているように、「無」は、非存在の状態
ではなく、存在と非存在の対立を超越した絶
対的なもの、あるいは悟りに等しい理想的、
絶対的な人間の状態と考えられるのである。

悟り

悟りの概念は、仏教信仰の中心に位置し、と
りわけ禅宗で顕著である。あらゆる人間はす
でに仏であり、「悟り」は絶対的でなければ
ならないことから、急進的禅宗では、「漸進
的でない瞬間の悟り」を主張した。演繹的な
悟りの認識だけで、人は生得の仏性に目覚め
ることができるのである。この経験は「風呂
の底が一瞬にして抜ける」ことにたとえられ
た。悟りは本人が認識するものであるが、伝
統的には師の印可が必要とされる。

nothingness

(*mu*). Fundamental Chinese Taoist concept; the term for absolute nonexistence, from which all existence arises and to which mankind ultimately returns. The idea of nothingness transcending ethics and politics was developed by Taoists critical of the Confucian preoccupation with ethical and political problems. This philosophy of nothingness merged with the Indian Buddhist philosophy of emptiness (*kū*) in Chinese and Japanese Buddhism, especially Zen Buddhism. As defined by Buddhism, however, nothingness is seen not as a state of nonexistence as opposed to existance but as an absolute, transcending the opposition of existence and nonexistence, or as an ideal and absolute human state identical to religious enlightenment (*satori*).

satori

(awakening; enlightenment). At the heart of the Buddhist faith, the concept of *satori* achieved prominence particularly in the Zen tradition. Because all people are considered to be already Buddhas and because enlightenment must be total, the radical Zen tradition has insisted on "sudden, not gradual, enlightenment." By mere recognition of one's a priori enlightenment, an individual can awaken immediately to innate Buddhahood. The experience has been compared to that of a "sudden falling out of the bottom of a wooden bathtub." Although self-validating, the *satori* experience

涅槃
（ね はん）

サンスクリットの「吹き消す」を意味する、
ニルヴァーナの音訳。生死を超越し、知恵を
獲得し煩悩を滅却して、悟りを完成した状態
をいう。これは、生死の彼方の存在、存在と
非存在、と逆説的に称される。

　日本の仏教の源流といわれる大乗仏教で
は、涅槃と輪廻を内包する無の概念を発展さ
せることによって、涅槃と輪廻が最終的には
同一であるという、逆説的概念を定めた。こ
の概念には、すべての存在に仏性がそなわる
という信仰、あらゆるものが悟りを得る可能
性を拡げること、悟りをえたにもかかわらず、
人を救うために輪廻に止まることを選んだ菩
薩を重視することなどが付加された。大衆的
信仰のレベルでは、涅槃は仏の浄土に生まれ
変わることであり、ある点では西洋の宗教的
伝統である天国の概念に似通っている。

禊
（みそぎ）

神道の沐浴の儀式。肉体的、精神的汚れを水
で洗い清める儀式。神道は清浄と清潔を強調
するので、身体を洗い清めることはきわめて
大切なことで、あらゆる儀式の前に必ず行わ

traditionally requires the seal of approval from one's master.

nehan

A transliteration of the Sanskrit term *nirvāna,* which literally means the extinction of a flame. It refers to the state of enlightenment that is achieved, either in life or in death, when one attains wisdom and eliminates the flames of craving. It is paradoxically described as being beyond life and death, being and nonbeing.

Mahāyāna Buddhism, to which Japanese Buddhism belongs, posited the paradoxical notion of the final identity of *nirvāna* and *samsāra* (*rinne*) through the development of notions such as emptiness, which embrace the two. This was accompanied by a belief in the Buddha nature within all beings, an extension of the possibility of attaining enlightenment to all, and an emphasis on the bodhisattva (*bosatsu*) who has achieved enlightenment but chooses to stay in *samsāra* to help others. At the popular, devotional level, *nirvāna* is often understood as a rebirth in a Buddha's Pure Land, which is similar in some respects to the notion of heaven in Western religious traditions.

misogi

The Shintō rite of ablution. The word *misogi* refers to the ritual cleansing of the body with water to remove both physical and spiritual defilements. Since Shintō lays great stress on purity and cleanliness, the act of

なければならない。『古事記』（712年）によると、「禊」の儀式は伊弉諾尊に始まったとされる。伊弉諾は黄泉の国に下り、死んだ妻を捜した。この世に帰ってきた伊弉諾は、川で滅亡と死にまつわる不浄を洗い流したという。

水を使う清めは色々あるが、もっともよく見られるのは、神社に参拝するとき手を洗い口をすすぐ儀式である。神宮はあらゆる儀式の前に、潔斎といって、沐浴しなければならない。水垢離というのは、裸で滝に打れたり、おけで冷水を浴びることである。水垢離は、ほかの「禊」とちがって、特定の期間に行う苦行である。現在でも、祭りには「禊」が行われる。

祓

清め、贖罪、ざんげなど、広い範囲にわたる神道の儀式の総称。「祓」の儀式は神道のあらゆる場面で見られ、神道が清めを何よりも大切にしていることを反映している。「祓」の基本的役割は、神道儀式の参加者が、神道のしきたりにのっとって神の訪れと神との交わりを準備するための、清めの儀式であった。清めの基本には、(1)「禊」(2) 神官が清める対象の頭上で祓串を振る (3) 聖なる力で清め

cleansing the body assumes enormous importance and must be performed before any ceremony begins. According to the *Kojiki* (712), the rite of *misogi* originated with Izanagi no Mikoto. Izanagi descended to the nether-world (Yomi no Kuni) to search for his deceased wife. When he returned to this world he went to a river and washed away the impurities associated with decay and death.

Various types of purification rituals using water are still performed. The one most frequently observed is the rinsing of the hands and mouth before worshiping at a shrine. Before all festivals the priest is required to bathe thoroughly, in the practice known as *kessai*. *Mizugori* (literally, "removing impurities by water") entails standing virtually nude under a waterfall or dousing oneself with buckets of cold water. Unlike other *misogi*, it is basically an ascetic practice undertaken for a specified period. In many parts of Japan the ritual of *misogi* still survives in festivals.

harae

General term for a wide range of Shintō rites of purifi-cation, atonement, and penitence. *Harae* rites permeate Shintō and reflect its preoccupation with the process of purification. A basic functions has been ceremonial purification to prepare participants in Shintō obser-vances for visitations from and union with gods. Some of the basic methods of purification are: (1) ritual ablu-tion or *misogi*, (2) the waving of *harae-gushi* by priests over those to be purified, (3) the recitation of *harae*

てくれるという祓詞（はらえごと）をとなえる (4) 神に供物
をささげること、などがある。

「祓」には、聖なるもの、政治、社会秩序
にそむいたことへのあがないと罰が含まれ
る。その例は、日本神話の天照大神に乱暴を
はたらいた素戔嗚尊の祓の話である。「祓」
はまた、神道の最終目的でもある。大祓は、
六月と十二月の晦日（つごもり）、および、天皇の即位の
後に祝われる大嘗祭の前に行われるのが伝統
で、国全体を清め改新する大式典であった。

穢（けが）れ

清浄と「穢れ」、純粋と不純という観念は、
古今を通じて日本の社会、文化で重要な意味
を持っている。古代の「穢れ」の一大特徴は、
それが罪の概念と密接な関係を持っていたこ
とである。善は純粋で清浄と考えられ、悪は
善を汚したり堕落させるよごれたものと考え
られた。したがって、この二つの概念は、一
つになって罪穢れという言葉になり、神が忌
を嫌ういっさいを含むところとなった。罪穢
れのもう一つの特徴は、接触によって人から
人に直接伝わることである。そのため、罪穢
れに染まった人は、「禊」をするか、一定の
期間日常生活から遠ざかる必要があった。
『延喜式』（927年）の祝詞には、いくつかの

kotoba, believed to purify by their sacred power, and (4) the presentation of offerings to the gods.

Harae include acts of atonement and punishment for transgression of the sacred, political, and social orders, as illustrated in Japanese mythology by accounts of the penance (*harae*) extracted from Susanoo no Mikoto following his offenses against Amaterasu Ōmikami. In addition, *harae* might also be viewed as forming the final goal of Shintō practice. *Ōharae,* for instance, is a grand rite of purification and renewal of the entire country traditionally performed on the last day of the sixth and twelfth months and before the imperial rite of thanksgiving (Daijōsai) celebrated after a new emperor's formal enthronement.

kegare

(ritual impurity or defilement). The concepts of clean and unclean, pure and impure, have been of cultural and social significance in Japan from ancient times up to the present day. A special characteristic of the concept of *kegare* in ancient times was its close connection to the concept of *tsumi* (sin or crime). Thus, good was understood as pure and clean, while evil implied something dirty that defiled or contaminated the good. Consequently, the two concepts were fused in the term *tsumi-kegare,* inclusive of all that was abhorred by the Shintō deities (*kami*). Another characteristic of sinful and unclean things is that they can be passed from one person to another through direct contact. Hence, persons thought to have been contaminated were required to

「穢れ」が列挙されている。第一は衛生的に汚れたもの、第二は人間の血、第三は人間のみならず動物を含めた死にかかわるすべて、第四は自然災害への屈服、第五は人間社会を害するすべての行動である。

性行動では、近親相姦と獣姦が「穢れ」とされた。血にまつわる「穢れ」は、女性に関係することが多かった。出産や月経は死と並んで神がもっとも忌む汚れとされた。

縁起

あらゆる物は、「因」と「縁」の調和ある相互作用を通じて存在するという仏教の基本命題。南方仏教では、人間存在を説明するのに十二因縁を明らかにし、対法蔵論は、あらゆる存在を説明するのに、六因四縁を確立し、中観派経論は因縁を空であるとした。日常語では、(1) 事物の源泉、(2) 前兆、(3) 寺社縁起（創建の言い伝え）を意味する。

undergo purification (*misogi*) or to separate themselves from everyday life for a period of time. Such early Shintō writings as the collection of *norito* contained in the Engi Shiki (927) enumerate several categories of *kegare*. The first includes things unclean from a sanitary viewpoint; the second involves human blood; the third involves everything related to death, including not only human death but also the death of animals: the fourth takes in subjection to all sorts of natural disasters; and the fifth are all actions that serve to disturb human society.

In the area of sexual acts, incest and bestiality were treated as *kegare*. The *kegare* involving blood was largely associated with women. Such events as childbirth and menstruation ranked along with death as forms of *kegare* that were particularly abhorred by the Shintō deities.

engi

(Sanskrit: *pratītya-samutpāda*; "interdependent origination"). Key Buddhist thesis that holds that all things exist through the harmonious interaction of causes (*in*) and conditions (*en*). The Pāli Theravāda texts set forth the twelve fold chain of interdependent origination to explain human existence, the scholastic *Abhidharmakosabhāsya* established the theory of six causes and four conditions to explain all existence, and the *Mādhyamikasāstra* defined interdependent origination as emptiness. In common Japanese usage, *engi* has come to mean: (1) the origin of some event or thing, (2) omens or portents, and (3) legends surrounding the founding of a shrine or temple (*jisha engi*).

因果

仏教の重要な概念。「因」とは内的、直接的原因をさすが、「縁」は、外的、間接的原因を意味する。この二つが一体となって果を生む。仏教の因果応報では、善因には善果、悪因には悪果がかならずあるという。人間は自分の善あるいは悪行によって楽か苦の報復を受ける。因果の世界は、生死の永久の繰り返しを伴って、輪廻と呼ばれる。敬虔な仏教徒は、苦しみの原因である因果応報からの解放を願い、涅槃に入ることを願う。

輪廻

生死の繰り返しを表す仏教用語。仏教思想では、あらゆる生あるものは死後の再生を経験する。苦楽どちらの世界に生まれ変わるかは、前世での行いのカルマによるという。仏教の転生は、六つの世界のうちどれか一つである。下位から列挙すると、地獄、餓鬼、畜生、修羅、人間、天上である。生まれ変わりごとに、生前

inga

(Sanskrit: *hetu* and *phala*; cause and effect). An important concept of Buddhism. The term *in* refers to an inner and direct cause, while another term, *en*, refers to an external and indirect cause. The two combine to produce effect (*ka* or *ga*). In the Buddhist conception of karmic retribution (*inga ōhō*), a good karmic cause will invariably produce a good karmic effect, and a bad karmic cause will produce a bad karmic effect. Depending on one's good or bad actions, one will obtain pleasurable or painful karmic retribution. The karmic realm of cause and effect, with its perpetual cycle of death and rebirth, is called *rinne*. The devout Buddhist hopes to achieve deliverance from karmic retribution, the cause of suffering, and enter *nirvāna*.

rinne

(Sanskrit: *samsāra*; "wandering through [the cycle of birth and death]"). A Buddhist term denoting the process of transmigration and rebirth. According to Buddhist belief, all sentient beings undergo rebirth after death. Whether they are reborn in a pleasant environment or one of torment depends upon the moral nature (karma) of the acts they committed during their lifetime. Buddhism holds that rebirth takes place in one of six realms, which, in ascending order, are the undesirable realms of hell, hungry spirits (*gaki*), and animals, and the favorable realms of bellicose spirits (*ashura*),

の業によって、上の世界から下の世界に落ち
る可能性があるので、仏教徒は、最終的には
輪廻から逃れたいと願う。その道は、悟りを
開くか阿弥陀のように浄土に入るしかない。

他力

仏教では、衆生を救う仏・菩薩の力とともに、
その力を通して悟りへの道に導く過程を表
す。浄土宗では、阿弥陀仏の名を唱える衆生
を救う阿弥陀仏の願力を表す。この願力を信
ずる者は極楽に入り、悟りを開き、仏になれ
る。浄土真宗は、阿弥陀の力に頼る者は極楽
に生まれ変わり、念仏はそれに対する感謝の
表現であるという。この反意語、自力は仏の
力を借りず、自分の知と努力で悟りを開くこ
とである。

即身成仏

真言宗の中心的教義で、真の悟りは現世で得
られるものであり、それは精神だけでなく肉

man, and the heavens. Since there is always the possibility, depending on one's actions, of falling from a higher to a lower realm whenever rebirth occurs, the Buddhist seeks ultimately to escape from this cycle of transmigration, which can be accomplished only by attaining Buddhahood or entering the Pure Land of a Buddha such as Amida.

tariki

(literally, "another's power"). In Buddhism, *tariki* refers to the power of the Buddhas and bodhisattvas to save others as well as to the process of approaching enlightenment through the power of Buddhas and bodhisattvas. In the Jōdo sect, *tariki* refers to the vow made by the Buddha Amida to save all who invoke his name. People who place their trust in the power of this vow are born into paradise (*gokuraku*), achieve *satori* (enlightenment), and become Buddhas. The Jōdo Shin sect teaches that any person who relies on the power of Amida is assured rebirth in paradise, and the practice of *nembutsu* (reciting the name of the Buddha) is interpreted as an expression of thanks. The opposing term *jiriki* (literally, "one's own power"), refers to enlightenment through one's own resources and efforts, but not without Buddha's assistance.

sokushin jōbutsu

("Buddhahood in this very body"). A central tenet of the Shingon sect of Buddhism, which holds that perfect

体の変化でもある。この教義は、空海が、
『即身成仏義』で明らかにしている。即身成
仏の概念は、仏性はあらゆる生き物にひそん
でいるので、特別に引き出す必要はないとい
う、極度に内在論的な思想から出ている。こ
の概念は、進化的な「始覚」に対して、内在
的な「本覚」と関連している。

　広く解釈すると、即身成仏は、生成発展す
る多神教的宇宙観を示唆している。これは日
本の仏教にとって、明示的教義であるばかり
でなく、解釈の方法論としても重要である。

念仏

人々は、阿弥陀の浄土に生まれ変わることを
念じて、南無阿弥陀仏、と念仏を唱えた。念
仏は、阿弥陀以外の仏に対し、浄土に生まれ
変わること以外の願い、たとえば悪いカルマ
を打ち払うとか、一刻も早く悟りを開くこと
を念ずることもあった。

　法然は、今日の念仏の概念をうちたて、一
般化した。また、浄土宗の独立を主張し、仏
の名をくりかえし唱えることが唯一の救済へ
の道であると説いた。法然は浄土宗を、親鸞
は浄土真宗を開き、念仏を修行の第一とし
た。

enlightenment can be attained in one's present lifetime and is as much a bodily as a spiritual process. The doctrine was explicated by Kūkai, in his *Sokushin jōbutsu gi* (*Attaining Enlightenment in this Very Existence,* 1972). The concept of *sokushin jōbutsu* derives from the radically immanentalist view that the potential for Buddhahood exists latently in all creatures and needs not so much to be developed as simply evoked. This is related to the immanentalist *hongaku* (primordial enlightenment) ideal, in contrast to the developmental *shigaku* (incipient enlightenment) viewpoint.

Broadly construed, *sokushin jōbutsu* suggests an organic, pantheistic view of the universe. It is important for Japanese Buddhism not only as an explicit doctrine but also as an interpretive tendency.

nembutsu

The invocation Namu Amida Butsu (I take my refuge in the Buddha Amida), uttered in the hope of rebirth into Amida's Pure Land. *Nembutsu* were sometimes directed to Buddhas other than Amida and for goals other than Pure Land rebirth, such as the cancellation of bad karma or the immediate realization of enlightenment.

Hōnen formulated and popularized the modern notion of *nembutsu*. He asserted the independence of the Pure Land movement and taught that the simple utterance of the Buddha's name was the only path to salvation. The Jōdo sect founded by Hōnen and the Jōdo Shin sect founded by Shinran took *nembutsu* as their primary religious exercise.

Chapter

5

民間信仰
Folk Religion

民間信仰

既成宗教の外で、民衆によって支持され、実行され、伝承される信仰や慣行や儀式。民間信仰は、神道や仏教と明確に区別できるものではなく、これら既成宗教からさまざまな慣行を吸収している。

　日本には、単一の正統な民間信仰というものは存在しない。民間信仰には、地域や職業によってかなりの変化がみられる。慣行は、「新年の賀」とか「田植え祭」のような具体的な名称で知られる。慣行には二つの大きな流れがあり、一つは、季節毎の行事であり、もう一つは、一生の節目の儀式（通過儀礼）である。日本人のほとんどすべてが、このうちのいくつかに参加する。

　季節の行事でもっとも重要なのは正月である。正月の慣習でもっとも広く行われているのは、神社や寺への初詣であるが、多くは家庭内で行われる。正月にはいろいろな行事にその年の事始めとして、特別の意味が与えられる。初夢や書き初めがそれである。これと並んで大切なのが、夏も終わり近くに、死者のために行われる儀式、盂蘭盆である。

　日本は明治時代初期から西洋暦を採用しているが、現在でも複雑な中国暦を、とくに結婚式や葬式の日取りをきめるときに使っている。中国の影響で五節句の祝いも行なう。五

folk religion

(*minkan shinkō*). Beliefs, customs, and rituals that are held, practiced, and transmitted by the people or "folk" outside organized religion. Folk religion cannot always be separated easily from Shintō and Buddhism for it has assimilated and preserved many practices of these established religions.

There is no single "orthodox" folk religion for the Japanese people. In fact, folk religion has varied considerably among different regions and occupations. Practices are known by their concrete names, such as "greeting the New Year" or "holding the rice-transplanting ceremony." Two of the most important patterns are the round of seasonal customs and rituals related to the life cycle. Nearly all Japanese people have participated in some of these customs.

The most important seasonal celebration is the New Year. While one of the most conspicuous of New Year's customs is the practice of visiting Shintō shrines and Buddhist temples, many important customs are observed in the home. On New Year's Day, special ritual significance is attached to the first occurrence of an activity for that year, such as the first dream or first calligraphy. Also important is the observance in late summer for the spirits of the dead, the Bon Festival.

Although Japan formally adopted the Western calendar in the Meiji period, people retain observances of the complex Chinese calendar, especially when choosing a propitious day (and avoiding an unlucky one) for

節句とは、一月七日（人日の節句：七草の節句）、三月三日（上巳の節句）：雛祭、五月五日（端午の節句）：子供の日、七月七日（七夕）、九月九日（重陽の節句）である。

　民間信仰のもう一つの流れは、一人の人間のゆりかごから墓場までの一生を貫くさまざまな儀式である。妊娠した女性、誕生、幼児期、結婚、死などには、特別の宗教的儀式が行われる。

　季節の行事と通過儀礼は、日本人の伝統的な時の経過の指針となってきた。家族も村も、季節の行事を繰り返すことで世の中とのつながりを維持し、個人は次々に起こる通過儀式によって自分の進歩をしるしたのである。

祖先崇拝 (仏教)

日本人は「家」の死者の霊のために、位牌を納め、ろうそくと線香、それに花と食物を供えた仏壇にお経をあげ、定期的に供養を行う。

　7世紀以来、死者を慰め、その御利益を願い、恨みを防ぎ、極楽浄土への道を守るために、いろいろな儀式を行ってきた。1665年に、大名は幕府から、人別帳の作成を命じら

a wedding or funeral. The five central Chinese-inspired festivals celebrated in Japan are known as Gosekku and are as follows: 7 January (Jinjitsu no Sekku), commonly referred to as Nanakusa no Sekku (Seven Herb Festival); 3 March (Jōshi no Sekku; Doll Festival); 5 May (Tango no Sekku; Children's Day); 7 July (Tanabata Festival); and 9 September (Chōyō no Sekku).

Another major pattern of Japanese folk religion is the traditional round of rituals that follow the individual from the cradle to the grave. There are special religious observances for the pregnant woman, birth, early childhood, marriage, and death.

Patterns of seasonal and life-cycle rituals helped orient the traditional Japanese in their passage through time. Families and villages maintained their sense of belonging in the world by marking the recurring seasonal rituals, and the individual marked his or her progress in life by observing the successive life-cycle rites.

ancestor worship

(*sosen sūhai*). The Japanese regularly conduct rites on behalf of the souls of the dead of their households. Sutras are recited before Buddhist family altars (*butsudan*) that contain memorial tablets (*ihai*) for the individual dead and on which candles and incense are burned and flowers and food are offered.

Since the seventh century, ceremonies have been conducted to comfort the dead, to solicit their beneficence and prevent vengeful acts by them, and to secure their safe passage into paradise. Since the mid-seven-

れ、家庭での先祖をまつる儀式は、寺院や僧侶と分かちがたく結びつけられた。これはキリスト教の根絶を確かめる意味もあったが、各戸を寺院の檀家として登録することにより、年毎の正確な信徒数を確認できた。寺院のさまざまな責務の中には、檀家の先祖供要の法養があるが、そのお布施が今日でも寺院のおもな収入になっている。

人が死亡すると、僧侶は戒名を贈る。死から数えて四十九日目に、仏壇に新しい位牌を納める。

死者のための儀式は何回も行われる。正月の三が日、春秋の彼岸、盂蘭盆には、先祖を礼拝する。

法事の大きな目的は、新しく亡くなった人の魂を、穢れと地上に呪縛されている状態から解放して、「家」と村の先祖のいる、清められた国へ送り込むことである。三十三回忌または五十回忌（まれには百回忌）には、個人の魂の概念は消滅する。地方によっては、位牌から戒名と本名を削り、火で焼いたり、海に投ずるか、寺か墓に納める。その法事は、

teenth century, domestic ancestral rites have been inextricably linked to the fortunes of the Buddhist temple and its clergy. By 1665, the domainal lords (*daimyō*) were required by the central government to establish a household registry system. Partly in order to ascertain that Christianity had been completely eradicated, every household was required to register as a *danka* (parishioner-household) of a Buddhist temple, whose priests would then certify the accuracy of the annual enumeration of its members. Among the many responsibilities of the temple was the overseeing of the performance of ancestral rites by its parishioners, and the contributions received in return for this remains the chief source of revenue for temples today.

When a person dies, the Buddhist priest is asked to devise an appropriate posthumous name. On the forty-ninth day after death the tablet is placed with others in the altar.

Ceremonies are held and offerings are made to the dead of the household on a number of occasions. The ancestors are venerated as a group at the New Year, 1–3 January; at the vernal and autumnal equinoxes (*higan*); and at the Festival of the Dead (Bon Festival).

One of the major purposes of the ancestral rites is to move the soul of the newly dead from its ritually polluting, still-earthbound state, into the purified collectivity of the long-dead ancestors of the house and community. At the thirty-third or fiftieth (far more rarely at the one-hundredth) anniversary of death, a transition is marked that obliterates the concept of the individual soul altogether. In some parts of Japan, the posthumous

弔上げまたは弔切りと呼ばれ、個人は村と村
人を守る神々に加わり、以後その個人だけの
儀式はなくなる。

山岳信仰

山岳信仰は、山や火山や山脈を対象にする自
然崇拝の一つの形として始まった。山には霊
と神が住むという信仰が発達した。猟師は山
の神をあがめ、農民は春の初めには山に登っ
て、神を村に迎え、豊作を祈願した。日本人
は、山を祖先の霊の住む場所と考えた。神は
山で冬をすごし、春の初めに田圃に下りてき
て田の神となり、農作業を守り、収穫が済む
とまた山に帰っていった。村には、この神の
ために神社を作り、春と秋には祭りを奉納し
た。

　平安時代の仏僧、最澄と空海は、山での宗
教活動を唱道した。平安時代には、また、修
験道という一種の宗教が発達したが、その目
指すところは、山岳での苦行を通じて神通力
を獲得することであった。現代でも、山岳信

and real-life names are shaved from the tablet and it is then burned, cast into the sea, or left in a temple or at the grave by the head of the household. From that anniversary of his death—known as *tomurai* age or *toikiri* (the final rites)—the individual has merged with the collectivity of deities that protect the community and its residents, and no further rites are directed to him alone.

worship of mountains

(*sangaku shinkō*; literally, "mountain beliefs"). *Sangaku shinkō* began as a form of nature worship centered upon mountains, volcanoes, or mountain ranges. The belief that spirits and gods (*kami*) lived in mountains developed gradually. Hunters in the mountains revered mountain *kami* (*yama no kami*), and farmers climbed mountains in early spring to welcome the *kami* to the village and pray for a good harvest. Japanese also thought of mountains as the dwelling place of ancestral spirits. Folk belief held that the *kami* spent the winter in the mountains, came down to become a *kami* of the rice paddies (*ta no kami*) in early spring to protect farming endeavors, and returned to the mountains after the harvest. Shrines to these *kami* were built in villages, and the spring and autumn festivals were dedicated to them.

During the Heian period, the Buddhist monks Saichō and Kūkai advocated a religious life in the mountains. At the same time, a form of religion called Shugendō developed, the goal of which was to attain supernatural powers through mountain asceticism. In

仰は、霊山の神社や寺院で、修験道とともに行われている。

あの世

死後の世界とか黄泉（よみ）の国ともいわれる。死後についての日本人の伝統的基本的信仰では、死霊は時とともに個を失い、三十三回忌を終えると祖霊に同化するとされた。祖霊は生者を見守り、正月には血族を訪れ、夏のお盆には稲を守りにやってくる。非業の死をとげた者は御霊（ごりょう）となるので、鎮める必要があった。

　仏教は、輪廻（りんね）や来世の概念を世に広めて、日本人の伝統的考え方を変えていった。とくに鎌倉時代以降は、極楽浄土信仰と並んで地獄信仰が盛んになった。人間は死後四十九日間は人間と霊の中間の存在で、山を越え、三途の川を渡って、閻魔（えんま）大王または十王（じゅうおう）の裁きをうけ、来世に入っていくと考えられた。

modern times, the worship of mountains has continued to be practiced along with Shugendō in certain shrines and temples on sacred peaks.

afterlife

(*ano yo*; literally, "that world"). Also referred to as *shigo no sekai*, "the world after death," and Yomi no Kuni, "the Land of Darkness." The traditional, fundamental Japanese belief about life after death has been that the spirits of the dead gradually lose individuality and finally, after the thirty-third anniversary of death, merge with the spirits of the ancestors. The spirits then keep watch over the living, visit kinsmen over the New Year holidays, and, at the summer Bon Festival, come to protect the rice crop. An exceptional individual, especially if he has died a tragic or violent death, is believed to become a vengeful god (*onryō* or *goryō*) who needs to be placated.

Buddhism modified this traditional view, introducing such notions as reincarnation and different realms of being into which the dead might be reborn. Especially from the Kamakura period on, belief in various hells as well as in the paradise of the Buddha Amida's Pure Land became popular. It was believed that during the forty-nine days after death—the period of intermediate existence—the dead passed through mountains and crossed a river (Sanzu no Kawa) before being judged by the lord Emma or the Ten Lords (Jūō) and assigned to a realm for the next life.

喪

日本における喪の習慣は、死にふれることは、死者の親族の禁忌をまねく穢れであるという信仰に結びついていた。喪の期間は、死者との血縁の距離によって異なる。親や子の場合が百日、兄弟姉妹が四十九日、いとこが七日と決めている地方もある。喪には家にこもる、魚・肉をたつ、仕事を休む、神道の神に触れないなどが含まれる。最も重い喪が忌で、死から七日間、次が服で死から四十九日間とされた。親や兄弟姉妹が亡くなった次の年の年賀状を出さない習慣は、今でも行われている。

御霊 (ごりょう)

怨霊 (おんりょう) ともいう。地位や影響力のある人で、不自然な、あるいは非業の死を遂げた人の、恨みのこもった魂。死者の魂は生者に影響を与えると信じられ、とくに、尋常でない人生を生きたり、不自然な死を遂げた人は、たたりをおこさぬよう、畏怖し、鎮められなければならないと考えられた。仏僧や修道者は、そのような御霊を鎮める宗教儀式を行ったが、

mourning

(*mo*). The observance of mourning in Japan was originally connected to the belief that exposure to death
constituted a form of ritual impurity (*kegare*) that called
for taboos surrounding relatives of the deceased. The
period of mourning thus varied according to the close-
ness of one's relation to the deceased: in some regions
there were set periods of mourning of one hundred
days for a parent or child, forty-nine days for a sibling,
and seven days for a cousin. Mourning consisted of
remaining at home in seclusion, abstaining from fish
and meat and the performance of one's usual occupation, and, above all, avoiding contact with Shintō
deities. Heavy mourning (*ki*) was observed during the
first seven days following a death, light mourning (*fuku*)
until forty-nine days after. The practice of not
exchanging New Year's greetings in the year following
the death of a parent or sibling is still observed.

goryō

Also called *onryō*. Malevolent spirits of persons of rank
or influence who died unnaturally or in a state of anger
or resentment. It was believed that the spirits of the
dead influenced the living and that in particular, the
spirits of those who lived extraordinary lives or died
unusual deaths were to be feared and placated lest they
cause harm. Buddhist monks and ascetics were solicited
to perform religious services on behalf of such vengeful

御霊は、その復讐を防ぐために神に祀り上げられることさえあった。奈良時代後期に盛んになった御霊信仰は、平安時代の朝廷内の陰謀で大きな役割を果たした。中世の武士もまた、殺した敵の魂を鎮めようとした。御霊祭は夏に行われ（祇園）、伝統的な氏神祭は春と秋に行われる。

生き神

神とあがめられる生きた人。天皇は現つ神（あきがみ）または現人神（あらひとがみ）と呼ばれたが、1946年、それまで国家神道によって支持されてきたその地位を、天皇自らが放棄した。江戸時代までは、並外れたカリスマを持った人は、死後神格化されたり、生きているうちに神格化されることもあった。現代のカリスマ的宗教家、天理教の開祖中山みきや天照皇大神宮教の開祖北村サヨなどは生き神を自称した。これに相当する仏教用語は、生き仏である。

巫女

古代の女性のシャーマンで、初期の神道儀式では、祭りで神が地上に降りてきたとき、神意をうかがって神託を告げるという大切な役割を果たした。現代の巫女には二つの意味がある。(1) 恍惚状態の中で、超自然的存在の

spirits, who were sometimes deified to avoid their wrath. The *goryō* cult, prominent in the late Nara period, played a significant role in the court intrigues of the Heian period. Feudal warriors also tried to appease the spirits of slain enemies. The festivals of such deified spirits usually take place in summer (Gion Festival), while those of traditional deities (*kami*) are observed in spring and autumn.

ikigami

(living human deity). Living individual revered as a deity (*kami*). Emperors were called *akitsukami* or *arahitogami* (living deity) until 1946, when the status, which had been supported by the State Shintō (Kokka Shintō) system, was renounced by the emperor. Individuals with extraordinary charisma were generally deified after their death until the Edo period, when the concept was also applied to the living. Some recent charismatic religious leaders, such as Nakayama Miki, founder of Tenrikyō and Kitamura Sayo, founder of the Tenshō Kōtai Jingū Kyū, were declared *ikigami*. The Buddhist counterpart of this concept is *ikibotoke*.

miko

In ancient times a female shaman who played a prominent part in the early Shintō cult by acting as a medium for the *kami* during his descent to Earth at the time of a ritual (*matsuri*). The term now has two meanings: (1) a woman capable of transmitting the utterance of a super-

言葉を伝達する女性、(2) 神社の女性祭式執行者で、通常若く、必ずしも心霊的あるいはシャーマン的能力を持っていない。

昔は、巫女は霊的存在で神によって選ばれてその地位についたとされる。その超能力は、夢や神懸かりを通じて授けられたという。7世紀中頃の大化改新により、巫女は朝廷の儀式から追放され、都の外で行われる儀式に加わった。仏教の伝来は、さらにその地位を下げ、神を招くのは仏僧や山伏の役目になった。

古代巫女の現代版は、いくつかの新興宗教の開祖に見られる。天理教の中山みきや大本教の出口ナオなどである。神や仏の口寄せをする女性は、地方、とくに東北地方には、今でも見られる。青森県の盲目のイタコは、シャーマン的霊媒の伝統を残すものとして、高く評価されている。

陰陽道

中国古代の陰陽五行説に基づく信仰と、日本に伝わってから発達した占いなどの習慣。陰陽道は、元来は世界観と『易経』に出てくる卦を説明するものであった。『易経』には、陰と陽は、宇宙の根元である太極から生じたとある。陰と陽が、この世のあらゆる変転をもたらすのである。漢（紀元前206～紀元

natural being while in a trance; (2) a female officiant at a Shintō shrine, often a young girl, who does not necessarily have psychic or shamanistic power.

In the early cult, the *miko* is thought to have come to her office through election by a spiritual being, usually a *kami*. The gift was bestowed either through a dream or through sudden, involuntary possession (*kamigakari*). With the Taika Reform of the mid-seventh century, the *miko* was banished from the ceremonies of the court and relegated to cults practiced outside the capital. The advent of Buddhism further reduced her status. The role of active summoner came instead to be carried out by a Buddhist priest or *yamabushi*.

Modern counterparts of the ancient *miko* may be found among the founders of certain *shinkō shūkyō*, such as Nakayama Miki, founder of Tenrikyō and Deguchi Nao, founder of Ōmoto. Women acting as mouthpieces for gods or *hotoke* may also still be found in many rural districts, particularly the Tōhoku area. The blind *itako* of Aomori Prefecture are rightly regarded as the remnant of a true shamanic medium tradition.

ommyōdō

(literally, "The Way of Yin and Yang"). A system of belief based on the ancient Chinese theories of *yin* and *yang* and the five elements (Ch: *wuxing*), and the magical practices that developed after their importation into Japan. Ommyōdō originally referred to the world view and practices found in the ancient Chinese Yi Jing or Book of Changes. In this work the two essences of *yin*

220年）の時代に、あらゆるものを五つの原素（木、火、土、金、水）に分ける思想が変転の理論と結びついた。方位と位置、五つの色、四霊（聖獣）もまたこの五元素の思想と結びついた。7世紀に朝廷には陰陽寮がおかれ、暦を作ったり将来を占うために天文を研究した。今日も行われている特定の日の縁起、方角の善悪、数の吉凶など多くの俗信は、陰陽道からでたものである。

瞽女
ごぜ

唄を歌い、三味線を弾いて旅をした盲目の女性。瞽女は、16世紀に始まり、江戸時代には全国に広まったが、明治以後その数は減り、現在はほとんど残っていない。

　瞽女は、大名の保護のもと、城下町に建てられた共同屋敷を基盤に固い結束を保って生活していた。地方に娯楽の少なかった時代には、瞽女は温かく迎えられた。瞽女は、民謡の普及や発展にも重要な役割を果たした。その演目は、民謡や俗謡ばかりでなく、神道や仏教に基づく、形式の整った、何時間にもわたる語りと組み合わせた連続ものの唄も含まれていた。旅をする身体障害者にして遊芸者

and *yang* are said to stem from *taikyoku,* the source of the universe. The ebb and flow of *yin* and *yang* bring about the changes observed in the world. In the Han dynasty (206 B.C.–A.D. 220), this theory of change was combined with the theory dividing all things into five elements (wood, fire, earth, gold, and water). Direction and position, the five colors, and the guardian animals were also related to this five-element theory. In seventh-century Japan, the central government established the Ommyōryō, or Bureau of Yin and Yang, to study the stars in order to make a calendar and foretell the future. Many popular beliefs today, such as the auspiciousness of certain days, lucky and unlucky directions, and numerology, stem from Ommyōdō.

goze

Blind women who traveled about Japan singing and playing the *shamisen.* After first appearing in the sixteenth century, the *goze* spread throughout Japan during the Edo period. Their numbers have gradually dwindled, and few now remain.

Goze lived in tightly organized groups, each based in a communal house, usually established in a castle town under the protection of the local *daimyō.* At a time when entertainment was scarce in the countryside, they were welcomed warmly. *Goze* also played an important part in the spread and development of Japanese folk song. Their repertoire included not only folk and popular ballads but also sequences of song mixed with formalized recitation several hours long, based on Shintō

である巫女の多くは霊力を持っているとされ、いやす人であり、農業の豊作祈願者でもあった。

山伏

平安時代に、山中で禁欲生活をすることによって魔力を獲得しようとした修行者で、普通は男。この呼称は、後世になると、修験道修行者にあてはめられた。

　山伏の伝統的服装には、十六の品目があり、山での修行で実際に使用されるとともに、修行者を世俗から聖(ひじり)に変身させる象徴的意味をもっている。その主なものは、頭巾(ときん)、篠懸(すずかけ)の衣、六色の飾りふさのついた結袈裟(ゆいげさ)、念珠(ねんじゅ)、法螺貝(ほらがい)、錫杖(しゃくじょう)、後ろ腰に下げる皮敷(ひしき)などがある。山伏のおもな仕事は加持(かじ)と厄払いであるが、火渡りや刃渡りなどの荒行でも知られる。

座頭

1. 室町時代の芸人や商人の座の頭。

2. 室町時代初期に定められた盲人四官（検校(けんぎょう)、別当(べっとう)、勾当(こうとう)、座頭(ざとう)）の最下位で、

or Buddhist teachings. Wanderers, the handicapped, and performing artists were often thought to have supernatural powers, and many *goze* served as healers and casters of agricultural fertility spells.

yamabushi

(literally, "one who lies in the mountains"). The name given during the Heian period to ascetics, usually men, who practiced austerities in the mountains in order to attain holy or magical powers. It was later applied to the members of the Shugendō order.

The traditional costume of the *yamabushi* comprises sixteen items that *are* of practical use during an ascetic sojourn in the mountains and that symbolically transform the disciple from a profane to a sacred state. The items *include* a small black cap (*tokin*), a tunic with baggy trousers (*suzukake*), a collar with six colored tufts (*yuigesa*), a Buddhist rosary (*nenju*), a conch-shell trumpet (*horagai*), a staff with rings (*shakujō*), and a fur rug hanging down from the back of the waist (*hishiki*). Although the principal tasks of the *yamabushi are* healing and exorcism, they *are* also celebrated for such spectacular feats as fire-walking and climbing up ladders of swords.

zatō

1. Heads of guilds (*za*) of entertainers or merchants in the Muromachi period.
2. Lowest of four ranks (*kengyō, bettō, kōtō,* and *zatō*) given to members of a guild of blind male entertain-

男の盲人の芸人の座（当道座）に属していた。座頭は、後に、盲人（普通、当道座にはいる）の一般名称となり、一様に頭を剃って仏僧の衣を着るようになった。生活の糧は、琵琶をひいたり、唄を歌ったり、物語を語ったり、鍼や按摩から得た。江戸時代には、幕府から仕事に対して支払いを要求し、その金（座頭金）を高利で貸すことを許された。この制度は1871年まで続いた。

地蔵

日本仏教でもっとも大衆的な菩薩。その姿は、片手に宝珠、片手に錫杖を持った僧である。苦しむ人々を助け、その役に立つという地蔵は、平安時代から大衆に敬われてきた。地蔵は、土着の神と習合されることが多い。特に子供と地獄の魂を救うとされている。

道祖神

道路と村境の守り神で、道ばたに石の彫像として立っている。またの名を障の神（塞の神）といい、これは障（悪霊）を追い出す役割を表していた。道祖神は猿田彦と結びつけられることがよくあるが、猿田彦は、天皇の先祖といわれる瓊々杵尊が地上に降ったとき先導

ers (*tōdōza*) formed early in the Muromachi period. *Zatō* later became a general term for blind men (usually members of the *tōdōza*) who shaved their heads and wore the vestments of a Buddhist priest. They earned their living as musicians, singers, and storytellers, or as practitioners of acupuncture or massage (*amma*). During the Edo period, members were permitted by the shogunate to demand payment for their services and to use their earnings (*zatōgane*) to make high-interest loans, a practice that was discontinued in 1871.

jizō

("womb of the earth"). One of the most popular bodhisattvas in Japanese Buddhism. Jizō is usually represented as a monk with a jewel in one hand and a staff in the other. Jizō's vow to aid and benefit all suffering beings has made him an object of popular veneration since the Heian period. Jizō is often syncretized with native deities. He is particularly regarded as the savior of children and souls in hell.

dōsojin

Guardian deity of roads and village boundaries, worshiped in the form of stone images along the roadside. Also known as *sae no kami* (or *sai no kami*), an ancient designation that suggests the function of "obstructing" or "keeping out" *sae* (evil spirits). The *dōsojin* is often identified with the god Sarudahiko, who guided Ninigi

したといわれる。崇拝の対象としては、いろいろの形をとる。今日では、道祖神は、結婚、誕生を司る神もかねている。道祖神は、正月の注連飾（しめかざり）を一月十四、十五日に焼く「どんど」のとき、日本全国で拝まれる。この日、子供たちが各戸を訪問して、道祖神に供える餅などをもらい、どんど小屋あるいはとり小屋という特別に作った小屋で、それを食べて唄を歌う地方もある。

山の神

山の神と呼ばれる神はいろいろあるが、それぞれが特定の職業とかかわりを持っている。

　農民はそれを田の神として拝む。春の初めに山の神が山から下りてきて田の神となり、取り入れが済むと山のすみかに帰る。この山の神は先祖の霊をも表す。猟師や木こりや炭焼きなどの山の民は、男神または女性神として拝み、木地屋（きじや）は山の神を夫婦神として信じる。神道の山の神は、大山祇神（おおやまつみのかみ）または女性神の木花開耶姫（このはなさくやひめ）のことである。一般的に、山の神は恐ろしいものとされる。

　山の神の祭りは、ふつう、二、十、十一月

no Mikoto, the supposed ancestor of the imperial line, on his descent to earth. The object of worship takes various physical forms. Today, *dōsojin* function also as gods of marriage, birth, and other rituals. They are widely feted throughout Japan during the burning of the New Year's ornaments (*dondo*) on 14 and 15 January. Children in some regions go door-to-door to solicit *mochi* (rice cakes) or other offerings "for the *dōsojin*"; in a specially constructed hut called a *dondo-goya* or *tori-goya,* they eat the *mochi* and sing songs.

yama no kami

(god of the mountain). There are various types of deities called *yama no kami,* each of them associated with a different occupational group.

Farming folk venerate a mountain deity that is identical with the *ta no kami* (god of the paddies): the *yama no kami* descends from the mountains in early spring to become the *ta no kami* and after the harvest returns to his abode in the mountains. This particular type of *yama no kami* also embodies the spirits of the people's ancestors. Mountain folk such as hunters, woodcutters, and charcoal makers venerate either a male or a female *yama no kami,* whereas lathe workers (*kijiya*) believe the *yama no kami* to be a married couple. When these deities are worshiped in Shintō, *yama no kami* are identified with the god Ōyamatsumi no Kami or the goddess Kono-hana no Sakuyahime. In general these *yama no kami* are fearsome and terrifying.

Festivals honoring *yama no kami* are generally held

の七、九、十二、十七日に行われる。その日に山に入ることは禁じられるが、それは山の神が自分たちの木の棚卸しをするので、森に入られることに神経質になるからだという。

田の神

稲を守り、米の豊作をもたらす神道の神。田の神の祭りは、米の生育の各段階と結びつけて行われることが多い。春の稲作に先立って田の神を迎える種まきの前の神迎え、苗床に籾を蒔く日の水口祭、田植えを始める日のさおりの祝い、田植えが済んだ祝いの祭りのさなぶり。それに数々の収穫の祭りなどがある。田の神は、人間界に住んでおらず、祭りのときに下りてくる去来神であると信じられている。古代の言い伝えでは、山の神が春に下りてきて、田の神として米の生長を守り、秋の収穫ののちに、山に帰り再び山の神になる。

歳神

若歳神ともいう。年の変わり目に各家庭で礼拝されたり歓迎される神。古くは「とし」に

on the seventh, nineth, twelfth, or seventeenth day of February, October, or November. It is forbidden to go into the mountains on such days, since that is when the deity is believed to take an inventory of his or her trees, and an aroused *yama no kami* would be sensitive to any intrusion into the forest.

ta no kami

(god of the paddies). Shintō god who protects rice plants and brings about abundant rice crops. Festivals to this god are often observed in conjunction with the various stages of rice cultivation. These include the major festivals "welcoming of the god of the fields" (*kamimukae*), just prior to spring planting; "the festival of the water gates" (*minakuchi matsuri*), held on the day when seed rice is sown in the rice plant nurseries; the festival of the first rice planting (*saori*); the festival held on the final day of planting seedlings in the paddies (*sanaburi*); and many harvest festivals. It is believed that the god of the paddies does not dwell in the human world but descends for festivals (*kyoraishin*). Old legends tell that the god of the mountain (*yama no kami*) comes down to the villages in the spring in the form of the god of the paddies to protect the growth of the rice and returns to his mountain abode after the fall harvest.

toshigami

("god of the New Year;" also *wakatoshisama*, "lord of the New Year"). A type of deity invoked and wel-

は「年」のほかに「米」の意味があり、歳神を迎えることは農耕儀礼の一部であった。

　歳神は、正月に家庭に幸福をもたらし、農家には豊かな収穫を、商家には商売繁盛を、漁師には大漁を約束した。各家庭は、大晦日には伝統の料理を作り、正月に酒と餅とともに歳神に供えた。歳神は、老夫婦から女神までいろいろあるが、老人と見るところが多く、先祖の集合的な霊を表している。

荒神

崇拝しない人に呪いをかける神で、神道の和魂（にぎみたま）と並び称される荒御魂（あらみたま）の一種である。荒神は以下の三つに大別できる。(1) 竈神（かまどがみ）。汚れをきらう。東北地方では、新生児のおでこに竈の煤（すす）をぬると健康になるといわれる。また、火事を防ぐといわれ、仏教では頭が三つ、腕が六本あり、信者を守る三宝荒神（さんぼうこうじん）として信仰されている。(2) 南西日本では、地荒神（じこうじん）として知られ、屋敷神、同族神、部落神とされる。(3) 馬や牛の守り神。

comed in each household at the turn of the year. In archaic Japanese, *toshi* means "rice" as well as "calendar year," and this observance was part of an annual cycle of agricultural rites.

On New Year's Day, the *toshigami* pays his annual visit to bring blessings to each family, promising such benefits as a good crop to farmers, good business to merchants, and a big catch to fishermen. Traditional dishes are prepared on New Year's Eve and offered to the visiting deity on New Year's Day with *sake* and *mochi*. Images of the *toshigami* vary from those of an aged man and wife to that of a goddess, but most depict aged men and may represent the collective ancestral spirit of each family.

kōjin

Kōjin are said to cast evil spells on people unless properly revered; they fall into the category of malevolent deities (*aramitama*) that are juxtaposed in the Shintō tradition with beneficent deities (*nigimitama*). *Kōjin* include: (1) A god of the kitchen fire who dislikes uncleanliness. In northeastern Japan this god is thought to bring vigor to newborn babies on whose foreheads soot from the kitchen fire has been rubbed. Also believed to prevent fires, it has been adopted into Buddhism as the three-headed, six-armed god *sampō kōjin*, who protects the faithful. (2) Gods worshiped in southwestern Japan, known as *jikōjin* (earth *kōjin*), that are treated as protectors of houses, family gods, or community gods. (3) A god widely worshiped as a guardian deity of horses and cattle.

産土神

生まれた土地の守り神。氏神と混同される。
氏神は同族の神であり、産土神は地理的領域
の神である。一つの村の家族がすべて血縁関
係にある場合、この区別は無意味であったが、
血族外の家族が村に入ってくると、住民全体
を守る神が必要になった。地域を守る神は、
通常、産土神あるいは鎮守の神と呼ばれ、氏
神よりも広い地域を守る必要があった。同じ
産土神を拝む人たちは、産子と呼ばれ、氏神
を拝む人たちは氏子と呼ばれた。

氏神

本来は氏（一族）の守護神。古代の日本社会
は多数の氏で構成されていて、氏の構成員は、
氏全体の利益を守ってくれる共通の先祖の子
孫であると信じていた。この神格化された先
祖、氏神は、氏の特権的支配によって神社に
祀られた。氏神は氏の直接の先祖ではなく、
氏と密接な関係がある神であることもあっ
た。たとえば、源氏は、武勇と関連のある八
幡を氏神に選んだ。

　氏子だけが氏神を参拝する資格を持ってい
た。氏の神社での神事は、氏の代表によって

ubusunagami

The protective deity of one's birthplace. The category of *ubusunagami* has become confused with that of *ujigami,* the local tutelary god. The *ujigami* is the god of a consanguineous family or people, while the *ubusunagami* is the deity of a geographic region. When all families of a village were related by blood, this distinction was irrelevant, but as unrelated families came to occupy the same village, a need was felt for a deity who could protect all the inhabitants. The newly adopted territorial deity was usually called an *ubusunagami* or *chinju no kami* and was responsible for a larger territory than the *ujigami.* Worshipers of a single *ubusunagami* came to be called its *ubuko*; the *ujigami*'s worshipers were termed *ujiko.*

ujigami

Originally, the tutelary deity of an *uji* (clan). Early Japanese society was composed of many *uji,* the members of which believed themselves to be descended from a common ancestor who looked after their interests. This deified ancestor, *ujigami,* was worshiped at a shrine under the exclusive control of the *uji.* Occasionally the *ujigami* was not the direct ancestor of an *uji,* but rather a deity closely connected with it. The Minamoto, for example, adopted as its *ujigami* the deity Hachiman, who is associated with military prowess.

Only members of the *uji* were entitled to worship the *ujigami.* Services at the *uji* shrine were led by the nomi-

執り行われた。この特権は注意深く守られて
いた。

氏子制度は、13世紀から16世紀にかけて
急激に衰え、氏神という名称は、地域住民全
体を守る神を意味するようになった。氏子の
代表の役割は、職業的神主、あるいは年ごと
に選出される宮座（みやざ）に取って代わられた。

同一の氏神を祀る地域の信者は氏子と呼ば
れる。地方によっては、氏神は各自の屋敷裏
の小さな祠にまつられた屋敷神をさすことも
ある。

鎮守の神

特定の地域の守護神。鎮守の神は、神社を維
持している領主あるいは地主が公認したその
地域の神であった。この名称は、守護する神
という意味で、寺や城や私邸の敷地を守る神
にも適用された。

神棚

神道の神を礼拝するために家庭内に置かれた
祭壇。客を迎える部屋の鴨居の上に作った棚
に置かれるのが普通である。ここには、通例、
伊勢神宮や鎮守の神のお札をあげる。神棚の
位置は、神によって変わることがある。七福
神の恵比須と大黒天は、通常台所の楣（まぐさ）（入り
口の横木）に貼り、火と台所の神荒神は竈（かまど）の

nal head of the *uji*. This privilege was carefully guarded.

The *uji* system declined steadily from the thirteenth to the sixteenth centuries, and the term *ujigami* came to refer to the local deity who protects all the inhabitants of a region. The priesthood shifted to professional priests (*kannushi*) or to a household head chosen yearly (*miyaza*).

Supporters in the region of an *ujigami* are called *ujiko*. In some areas of rural Japan today, the term *ujigami* refers to a specific *yashikigami* (household deity) enshrined at a small outdoor shrine (*hokora*) in the family plot.

chinju no kami

(literally, "pacifying guardian god"). The tutelary deity of a given locale. A *chinju no kami* was often officially recognized as a regional deity by local lords and land-holders, who contributed to the upkeep of its shrine. The term *chinju no kami* has also been applied, in its specific sense of "guardian deity," to the gods who protect the grounds of a temple, a castle, or a private residence.

Shintō family altars

(*kamidana*; literally, "god shelf"). Altar placed in the home for traditional worship of Shintō deities (*kami*). Typically, it is placed on a shelf built above a door lintel of the room where visitors are received. It is customary to place talismans of gods such as those of the Ise Shrine or the local tutelary deity (*chinju no kami*) on the altar. The location of the altar may differ, however, accord-

そばに祭壇をおく。正月に来る歳神を迎える
ときや、お盆に先祖の霊を迎えるときは、臨
時の祭壇を作る。神棚には酒や食物やろうそ
くをあげる。最近神棚を持つ家は少なくなっ
た。

仏壇

仏像と先祖の位牌を納めた小さな厨子または
壁龕。仏壇は、多くの家庭で、神棚とともに
神聖な場所である。この語のもとの意味は、
仏像の置かれた本堂の高くなった壇のことで
あった。小さな厨子の仏壇は、徳川幕府が、
各「家」を仏教の寺院に登録させたころから
一般的になった。仏壇には、仏像か図像が納
められ特別の部屋に置かれる。定期的に、食
物、花、線香などを供え、お経をあげる。

貧乏神

貧乏をもたらすといわれる神。福の神や疫病
神と並んで、家の中に住む善悪さまざまな神
の一つである。貧乏神は、神送りという儀式

ing to the god or gods being worshipped: Ebisu and Daikokuten, two of the Seven Deities of Good Fortune, are usually lodged above a kitchen lintel; the fire and kitchen god *kōjin* has his own altar next to the oven. A temporary altar may be built to receive the *toshigami*, gods who visit at New Year, or the returning ancestral spirits during the Bon Festival. Offerings placed on the *kamidana* include *sake*, food, and candles. The number of households that have *kamidana* is declining.

butsudan

Small cabinet or niche containing an image of the Buddha flanked by the family ancestral mortuary tablets (*ihai*). Along with the *kamidana* (Shintō family altar), the *butsudan* is a sacred place in many households. Originally, the term meant a platform in a Buddhist hall where images were placed. The small cabinet-form *butsudan* became common when the Tokugawa shogunate required each household to register with a Buddhist temple. The image placed inside the *butsudan* may be a statue or a picture of the Buddha, and the cabinet may be placed in a special room. Offerings of food, flowers, and incense are regularly placed before the *butsudan*, and Buddhist scriptures are read in front of it.

bimbōgami

Type of deity said to bring poverty. Along with deities like the *fukunokami* (deity of good luck) and the *yakubyōgami* (deity of illness), it is one of the many bearers of

で追い払われる。江戸時代の小説に初めて書かれた貧乏神信仰は、都会生活の一現象であった。貧乏神は、破れた団扇を持ち、やせて青白い姿をしている。比喩的には、いつも貧乏で不運な人のことをさす。

水神

水に住む神で、川神、滝神、井戸神などとして知られる。竜と蛇が水神の化身とされるが、いたずらな河童もその化身とされる。稲作には水が不可欠なことから、田植え歌の多くは、田の神あるいは米の収穫の神を、太陽と女性である水神の子としている。農村では、水神が正しく拝まれるように、水神講が作られた。家庭によっては、井戸のそばに水神の石像を置いた。水神の祭りは六月と十二月に行われ、川の氾濫や病気を防ぐために、川に餅を投げ入れた。

船霊

船、船乗り、漁師に安全と豊漁を保証する守護神。船大工の手によって、船霊の神体が、

good or bad fortune traditionally believed to reside in the home. *Bimbōgami* are exorcised in a rite called *kamiokuri* ("sending off the gods"). Belief in the *bimbō-gami,* first mentioned in the literature of the Edo period, is a phenomenon of city life. The *bimbōgami* is commonly portrayed as a thin, pale figure with a tattered fan. Figuratively, the term refers to a person who is constantly indigent and unlucky.

suijin

Type of god who lives in water; known variously as the god of the river, of the waterfall, of the well, and so forth. Dragons and serpents are commonly regarded as incarnations of the water god, while the mischievous *kappa* may also be a degenerate form. Since water is absolutely essential for rice cultivation, many rice-planting songs refer to the gods of the fields (*ta no kami*) or of rice harvests as the offspring of the sun and a female water deity. In farming communities, special fraternities (*suijinkō*) are established to see that the deity is properly honored. In some households a stone statue of a *suijin* is placed near the well. Festivals honoring water gods are held in June and December; in some areas, rice cakes are tossed into rivers to ward off floods and other disasters.

funadama

(literally, "spirit of the ship"). Tutelary deity of ships, seamen, and fishermen; ensures safety and a plentiful

秘儀のもと、帆柱の下の穴に納められる。この神体は、女性の毛髪、二つのさいころ、男女一対の人形、一枚か二枚の硬貨、穀物、化粧品、あるいは鼠のふんでさえあることもある。神体を納める儀式は、必ず左舷から始めるが、これは、習慣として、おぼれた人の身体を右舷から引き上げるからである。船霊は女神であるという信仰や、女が一人で船に乗り込むのを忌む迷信があるので、神体をまつらない船もある。船霊は音を鳴らして、危険や嵐の接近を知らせるといわれる。また、不漁が続くと、船霊を新しいのにかえることもある。

七福神

富と長寿をもたらすと言われる七人の神。15世紀から17世紀にかけて広く信仰された。普通は、恵比須、大黒天、毘沙門天、弁財天、福禄寿、寿老人、布袋である。恵比須、大黒天、毘沙門天は富の神であり、恵比須は漁の神でもある。大黒天は民間信仰では、神話の神である大国主命と習合した。弁財天は水と音楽の神であり、福禄寿と寿老人は長寿の神である。布袋は風変わりな禅僧で、弥勒菩薩の化身とも言われる。今日では、正月に、七福神ゆかりの神社やお寺を巡り歩くことがよくある。元日の夜、七福神が宝船に乗った絵

catch. In a secret ceremony, the *shintai* (physical representation), of the *funadama* is placed in a hole at the base of the mast by the ship's carpenter. The god may be represented by a lock of women's hair, a pair of dice, a pair of male and female dolls, one or two coins, grain, cosmetics, or even mouse droppings. The ceremony for installing the *shintai* is always performed from the port side because by custom the bodies of drowned people are hauled aboard from the starboard side. Because the belief that the *funadama* is a female deity sometimes provokes the superstition against having a lone woman aboard ship, some vessels refrain from enshrining the god's *shintai*. The *funadama* is said to warn of approaching danger or storms by making a chiming sound. If there is a succession of poor catches, the existing *funadama* may be replaced by a new one.

Seven Deities of Good Fortune

(*Shichifukujin*). The seven gods who are said to bring wealth and long life. Widely worshiped from the fifteenth to seventeenth century, the group usually consists of Ebisu, Daikokuten, Bishamonten, Benzaiten, Fukurokuju, Jurōjin, and Hotei. The grouping includes gods and sages of Indian, Chinese, and Japanese origin. Specifically, Ebisu, Daikokuten, Bishamonten, and Kichijōten are gods of fortune; Ebisu is also venerated as the fishing deity; and Daikokuten is identified in folk religion with the mythic figure Ōkuninushi no Mikoto. Benzaiten is the deity of water and music, and Fukurokuju and Jurōjin the deity of long life. Hotei is thought to

を枕の下に入れる習慣があるが、こうするとすばらしい初夢が見られるという。

恵比須

七福神の一人で、生業（なりわい）の守護神として広く信仰されている。地方によって、漁業、農業、商業の神や家庭の守護神とされる。恵比須という名前は、もとは「外国人」、「異人」という意味で、異郷人（まれびと）の信仰を反映していた。恵比須は、また、大国主命の子の事代主神（ことしろぬしかみ）ともされる。

　恵比須の祭りは、地域にもよるが、一月か十月に行われる。農村では、恵比須は、大黒天と並んで台所にまつられる。漁村の初漁の獲物は、恵比須への供え物として、海に投げ入れる。恵比須は耳が聞こえないという俗信から、神社にお参りする人は、祈る前に、足をどんどん踏みならす。恵比須は、着物と袴をつけ、風折烏帽子（かざおりえぼし）をかぶり、右手に釣り竿を持ち、左脇の下に幸運の象徴の鯛を抱えている。

have been an eccentric Zen priest who was believed to be an incarnation of the bodhisattva Maitreya. Today it is quite common to make a New Year's pilgrimage to a series of shrines and temples associated with these deities. Particularly popular is the custom of placing a picture of the seven gods aboard a treasure ship under one's pillow on the night of 1 January, to guarantee that the first dream of the year will be a lucky one.

Ebisu

One of the seven deities of good fortune (Shichifuku-jin); venerated throughout Japan as the tutelary deity of one's occupation. In some communities, Ebisu is regarded specifically as the god of fishing, farming, and commerce and as the tutelary deity of the house. The name Ebisu means "foreigner" or "barbarian" and reflects the belief in deities who have come from afar (*marebito*). He is also identified as Kotoshironushi no Kami, the son of the god Ōkuninushi no Mikoto.

The feast of Ebisu is celebrated in either January or October, depending on the area. In farming communities, Ebisu is worshiped in the kitchen along with Daikokuten. The first catch of the season is tossed into the sea as an offering to Ebisu. In accordance with a folk belief that Ebisu is hard of hearing, devotees thump on his shrine before reciting their prayers. Ebisu is usually represented as wearing a *kimono,* a divided skirt (*hakama*), and a tall cap folded in the middle (*kazaori eboshi*), holding a fishing rod in his right hand and carrying a sea bream (a symbol of good luck) under his left arm.

大黒天

福の神。大黒とも摩訶迦羅（マハーカーラ）ともいう。インドのマハーカーラは、悪の軍勢と戦う神であった。特に三宝（仏・法・僧）に献身したという。最澄が日本に紹介し、京都郊外の比叡山に祀（まつ）られた。大黒天と大国主命の韻が似ているので、二者は混同されるようになった。大黒天は、恵比須と並んで、七福神で最も重要な神とされた。この二つの神は、台所の守護神とされる。大黒天は、黒い頭巾をかぶり、右手には打ち出の小槌、左の肩には大きな袋をしょっている。

庚申（こうしん）

十干十二支による年や日につけられた名称。庚申は十干第七の庚（かのえ）と十二支第九の申（さる）にあたり、六十周期の五十七番目にあたるすべての年と日を表す。

　道教の言い伝えによれば、庚申の日の夜に、

Daikokuten

The god of wealth. Also known as Daikoku or as Mahakara, from the Sanskrit Mahākāla. In India, Mahākāla was a god who fought the forces of evil. He was believed to be especially devoted to the Three Treasures (Sambō; Buddha, the Law, and the Priesthood). He is said to have been introduced to Japan by the priest Saichō, who subsequently dedicated a shrine to him at Mount Hiei outside Kyōto. Since Daikokuten's name sounds identical to an alternate reading of the ideograms for Ōkuninushi no Mikoto, the two have become confused. Daikokuten came to be regarded, along with Ebisu, as one of the most important of the so-called seven deities of good fortune (Shichifukujin). Together with ith Ebisu, he is venerated as the tutelary deity of the kitchen. Daikokuten is usually represented as wearing a black hat with a round crown, holding a wish-granting mallet in his right hand, and carrying a big bag slung over his left shoulder.

kōshin

Year or day designation in the sexagenary cycle (*jikkan jūnishi*). *Kōshin* designates any year or day that falls on the combination of *kō*, the seventh of the "ten stems," and *shin*, the ninth of the "twelve branches" or zodiacal symbols, a combination representing the fifty-seventh year or day of a complete cycle of sixty.

According to Taoist tradition, on the night of a *kōshin*

人間の身体に住むといわれる三匹の虫（三尸）が、人の睡眠中に抜け出してその人の罪を天の神に告げて、命を縮めるという。平安時代には、一晩中眠らずに虫が体内から逃げ出すのを防ぐ道教の習慣が、宮廷の貴族の間で盛んだった。貴族たちは、眠気を追い出すために、双六や碁をしたり、音楽を演奏したりした。この習慣は庚申待ちといい、江戸時代には一般にも広がった。徹夜の庚申待ちは過去のものとなったが、省略した形で残っている地方もある。

講

仏典を講義する会として出発し、後に神道信者に広がった宗教および親睦のための団体。最勝講、仁王講、法華講などの仏典講義の会は、奈良時代や平安時代の貴族の間で盛んに行われ、鎌倉時代に急速に広まった。大師講や阿弥陀講といった、当時作られた講が、今日も残っている。神道では、伊勢講や熊野講などが古く、規模も大きい。明治時代に独立した出雲大社教や御岳教などの神道分派も、講の基礎がなければ不可能だった。多くの講は地域の組織で、中でも修験道と関係あるものが目立っている。山岳信仰と結びついている講に、富士講がある。講はまた、相互扶助の役割もはたし、金融扶助を行う頼母子講や無尽講の発生にもあずかった。

day the "three worms" (*sanshi*) believed to dwell in the human body escape during sleep and report a person's sins to the Celestial God, resulting in a possible shortening of that person's life. During the Heian period, the Taoist custom of staying awake all night to prevent the worms' escape was practiced among Japanese court nobility, who fought off sleep with games of *sugoroku* and *go* and the playing of music. This custom, known as *kōshin machi*, became widespread among the general populace during the Edo period. All-night *kōshin machi* are a thing of the past, but the custom survives in some areas in an abbreviated form.

kō

Religious or fraternal associations that developed from lecture meetings on Buddhist sutras and later spread among the Shintō faithful. *Kō* such as the Saishōkō, Ninnōkō, and Hokkekō, all lecture meetings on Buddhist sutras, were popular among the aristocracy during the Nara and Heian periods. The institution spread rapidly during the Kamakura period. Several Buddhist *kō* formed at this time, such as the Daishikō and the Amidakō, survive to this day. Within Shintō, the Isekō and the Kumanokō are among the oldest and largest. Many Shintō sects that became independent in the Meiji period, such as the Izumo Ōyashirokyō and the Ontakekyō, could not have done so without the structural base provided by their *kō*. Many *kō* are regional organizations, with those related to Shugendō (mountain worship) being particularly prominent. Also associ-

願掛け

願立てともいう。神や仏に特定の願いを叶えてもらうように祈ること。願掛けには普通、何らかのささげ物や行動や苦行の成就を申し出る。共同で行う場合と個人の場合とがある。共同の場合、村全体や集団全員が、豊作のための雨乞い、日照り祈願、戦禍や伝染病からの厄除け、あるいは村の重病人のために祈る。健康や結婚の幸せなど、個人の願掛けの場合、家族全員がかかわることもある。現代では、霊験あらたかな有名な寺や神社に行って願掛けをするのが普通である。

　神社や寺巡りも願掛けの一種と考えられる。神への供え物は食物や品物（餅、酒、布）などである。薬師如来に、身体の病む部分を描いた絵馬を奉納するならわしもある。入学試験合格祈願を書いた絵馬が、現代の日本ではもっとも多い願掛けである。願掛けは、祈願した人の願いが叶ったときに、社寺にお礼参りをして完結する。

ated with mountain worship are the Fujikō. The *kō* also came to function as mutual assistance associations, leading to the development of the *tanomoshi* and the *mujin,* both *kō* providing financial assistance.

gankake

Also termed *gandate*; prayers or petitions to a Shintō or Buddhist deity to obtain a specific request. *Gankake* are accompanied by offerings or promises to fulfill certain acts or penances and may be made either by groups or individuals. In the former case, *gankake* often involve an entire village or community in prayers for the rain or sun necessary for a good harvest, for protection from the ravages of war or epidemic, or for a villager who is gravely ill. Individual *gankake*, generally for personal health or marital happiness, may involve the entire family; they are the more common form in modern times, being made at temples or shrines noted for their miraculous powers.

Pilgrimages to shrines and temples are considered a form of *gankake*. Offerings made to the deity may include food or goods (such as *mochi, sake,* or cloth). One popular practice is to offer a votive tablet (*ema*) inscribed with a picture of an afflicted organ to Yakushi Nyorai. *Ema* inscribed with prayers for success in school and university entrance examinations are probably the most common form of *gankake* in contemporary Japan. The process of *gankake* is concluded by a visit of thanks to the shrine or temple in question upon fulfillment of the petitioner's request.

雨乞い

日本は水稲栽培に依存してきたので、昔はいろいろな雨乞い儀式や祈りがあった。そのなかには、村人が神社に籠っての祈願、鉦と太鼓（雷のまね）を打ちならす雨乞い踊り、神社や特定の場所に水をもらいに行く儀式的な旅、池の中に汚物を投げ込むなどして水の神を怒らせて雨を降らせる、などがあった。雨乞い踊りは、民俗芸能として今でも残っている。

護符

お守りとかお札と呼ばれる魔除けで、神社やお寺で配ったり売ったりする。健康、家内安全、商売繁盛などの御利益があるという。これらの長方形の紙の札（時には木のものもある）は、神棚にあげたり、門口に貼りつけたり、身につけたりする。お札には、普通、神の名前が書いてあり、お寺でつくるものには仏像が描かれている。埼玉県の三峰神社が出す護符には、神の御眷属のやまいぬ（狼）の絵が描いてある。このお札を玄関に貼ると泥棒よけになり、蚕を飼っている部屋に貼ると、ネズミの害を防ぐという。群馬県の榛名神社のお札は、鳥や虫の害を防ぐため、竹竿につけて畑に立てる。

rituals for rain

(*amagoi*). Since Japan is dependent upon wet-rice agriculture, there were in the past many rites and prayers for rain. These included formal prayers offered by villagers while in seclusion at a shrine; a group rain dance, usually accompanied by gongs and drums (in imitation of thunder); the ceremonial journey to receive water from shrines or certain specified places; and the throwing of dirty objects into a body of water or other acts in an attempt to provoke the water god into making rain. Rain dances (*amagoi odori*) survive as one of the folk performing arts.

gofu

Protective amulet commonly termed *omamori* or *ofuda,* distributed or sold at Shintō shrines and Buddhist temples and believed to bring good health, household safety, financial success, and so forth. These rectangular slips of paper (or occasionally wood) can be placed in the *kamidana*, affixed to a doorway, or carried on one's person. They usually bear the name of a deity; those issued by Buddhist temples may also display a Buddhist image. The *gofu* issued by the Mitsumine Shrine (Saitama Prefecture), for example, carries the image of a wolf which is the familiar of the god. It is said to prevent burglary when affixed to doorways and to prevent rat damage if displayed in rooms where silkworms are tended. Amulets from the Haruna Shrine (Gumma Prefecture)

断ち物

重要な祭礼や願掛けのために、個人的に一定期間禁忌する食物のこと。多くは、好物や日常的にとっているお茶、塩、米、酒などである。これは基本的には個人の慣習であるが、特別の場合、村中が断ち物をすることもある。

直会
<small>なおらい</small>

神と人が交わる神道の儀式で、前もって神に供え、神によって清められた酒、米、魚、野菜などを、神と参加者が分けあう。古代には、直会は神道の中心的儀式だった。参加者は、信徒、神職ともども、断ち物をして身を清め、忌みごとを守らなければならなかった。供える料理は、浄められた火で調理し、神と共通の食事として、参加者は神棚の前で食べた。しかし、現代では、断ち物はせず、直会の食事は供え物を神棚から降ろして別の部屋でとることが多い。このように、直会は神事の中心ではなく、神事の最後に、日常生活に復帰するために行われる。

are often displayed in the fields, attached to a bamboo pole, in order to prevent damage by birds and insects.

tachimono

(literally, "that which is cut off"). Certain types of food that an individual voluntarily abstains from as an ascetic practice in preparation for an important festival or to fulfill a personal or religious vow (*gankake*). In many cases it involves abstinence from a favorite or basic food such as tea, salt, rice, or *sake*. Usually this is an individual practice, but there are examples of whole villages avoiding *tachimono* on special occasions.

naorai

(communion). Shintō ceremony of communion between a god (*kami*) and human worshipers in which the participants share *sake,* rice, fish, and vegetables previously offered to and sanctified by the god. In the ancient past, *naorai* formed a central part of a Shintō rite. All participants—parishioners and priests alike—were required to purify themselves through abstinence and to observe various taboos prior to the rite. Food offerings were prepared over a purified fire and subsequently eaten by participants in front of the altar as a common meal with the god. In modern practice, however, the rules of abstinence are not generally observed, and the *naorai* feast is held, often in another room, after the food offerings have been removed from the altar area. *Naorai* thus now forms not the central but the last stage of the rite

巡礼

日本での巡礼は、大きく二つに分類される。一つは、「西国三十三箇所巡礼」や「四国八十八箇所巡礼」で、時には相当離れている寺や聖所を決められた順に巡り歩くものである。巡礼の順序も重要なポイントである。もう一つは、熊野三社や伊勢神宮、あるいは特定の霊山など単独の特別な場所への旅である。一般的には、第一のタイプを意味する。

　巡礼が始まったのは奈良時代と考えられるが、一般的になるのは平安時代になってからである。和歌山県南部の熊野は、修験道信者の中心地となった。長谷寺、四天王寺、高野山、金峰山寺なども代表的な巡礼地であった。江戸時代には、四国、琴平神社、善光寺、伊勢神宮、木曽御岳、富士山など、西方への巡礼が急速に広まった。明治時代以降の旅行は、基本的に、江戸時代の巡礼の継続といえよう。

before the return to daily life in the community.

pilgrimages

(*junrei*). In Japan, pilgrimages can be divided into two general types. The first is the type exemplified by the "Pilgrimage to the Thirty-three Holy Places of Kannon in the Western Provinces" and the "Pilgrimage to the Eighty-eight Temples of Shikoku," in which one makes a circuit of temples or holy places, sometimes separated by great distances, in a set order. The order of visitation is an important feature of this type of pilgrimage. The second type is a journey to one particular holy place. Pilgrimages to the Kumano Sanzan shrines and Ise Shrine, as well as to certain holy mountains, belong to this type. In common usage the term *junrei* usually refers to the first type only.

It is thought that pilgrimages were first undertaken in the Nara period, although the custom did not become popular until the Heian period. Kumano, in southern Wakayama Prefecture, became a large center for adherents of the Shugendō sect. Hasedera, Shitennōji, Kōyasan, and Kimpusenji were also popular pilgrimage sites. In the Edo period the number of pilgrims who made journeys to the western provinces, Shikoku, Kotohira Shrine, Zenkōji, Ise, Kiso Ontake, and Mount Fuji increased rapidly. Travel since the Meiji period has basically retained the Edo-period pattern of pilgrimage.

女人禁制

霊場や宗教儀式に、穢れ（けがれ）を理由に、女性が立ち入ることを禁ずること。古代日本の宗教では、女性は高い地位を与えられていたが、生理や出産の出血に対するタブーがあった。そのタブーを仏教が強化したと考えられている。神仏の聖所、比叡山、高野山、大峰山、御岳山などは、厳しい女人禁制で知られていた。漁師も、船霊が女性をひどく嫌うので、女性の乗船を拒んだ。今日では、女人禁制は事実上消滅している。

法螺貝

法螺貝に簡単なマウスピースをつけたラッパ。インド原産で、奈良時代に朝鮮経由で日本に入ってきた。法螺貝は仏教の儀式で用いられ、禁欲的な修験道修行者の宗教的装具の一つになった。また、中世には、戦場の合図に使用された。

nyonin kinzei

("no women allowed"). The exclusion of women from sacred places or events, because of their supposed impurity. Although women had high status in ancient Japanese religion, it is thought that Buddhism reinforced certain indigenous taboos against the blood associated with menstruation and childbirth. The mountains Hieizan, Kōyasan, Ōminesan, and Ontakesan, all sacred to Shinto or Buddhism, were known for their strict prohibition of women. Fishermen also banned women from their boats, because of the supposed aversion of the boat spirit (*funadama*). Today, such practices have virtually disappeared.

horagai

A horn formed by attaching a simple mouthpiece to the end of a conch shell. Of Indian origin, the instrument entered Japan via Korea in the Nara period. It was employed in Buddhist ceremonies and as one of the religious accoutrements of the ascetic Shugendō practitioners. The *horagai* was also used to sound commands in premodern warfare.

俗信
Folk Beliefs

占い

占いという言葉には、超自然的存在と交信したり、普通の人間の能力では解くことのできない疑問に解答を得るために、宇宙の力を解釈するさまざまな方法を含んでいる。日本でも、古代からいろいろな方法が採用されたが、以下の五つがもっとも重要なものである。

1. 太占（ふとまに）：鹿の肩甲骨を熱してできた亀裂を解釈する。アジア大陸から渡来したと考えられている。

2. 亀占（きぼく）：亀の甲羅を切り取って熱することによりできた亀裂を解釈する。紀元200年ごろ中国から持ち込まれたといわれる。7世紀半ばから1868年まで神祇官（じんぎかん）でとりおこなわれた。

3. 占いを目的として、夢で神々と霊的交感をすることは、平安時代から室町時代にかけて、神社や寺院で行われた。巡礼者は聖地におもむいて、夢の中の神や菩薩に悩みに対する答えを求めた。神託は和歌の形をとることが多かった。

4. 巫女を通じて占いをするならわしが、かつて託宣祭（たくせんまつり）という村の祭りで広く行われた。今日では、この祭りはなくなったが、儀式は特定の講で行われることがあり、行者や山伏が神を霊媒の体内に呼び込む。

divination

(*uranai*). The term *divination* comprises the various methods used to communicate with a supernatural being or interpret cosmic forces in order to obtain answers to questions insoluble by ordinary human faculties. In Japan a number of such methods have been employed since early times, of which the following five are the most important:

1. *Futomani*, or divination by interpreting patterns of cracks made on a deer's shoulder blade when heated, is thought to have been brought to Japan from the Asian continent.

2. *Kiboku*, or divination by interpreting cracks on a turtle shell that has been incised and heated, is believed to have been imported from China around A.D. 200. From the mid-seventh century until 1868, *kiboku* was used in the Jingikan (Office of Shintō Worship).

3. Communion with the gods through dreams for divinatory purposes was practiced in shrines and temples from the Heian through the Muromachi periods. The pilgrim journeyed to a holy spot to solicit the answer to a problem from the presiding god or bodhisattva in a dream. The oracular answers were often delivered in the form of *waka* poetry.

4. Divination by means of a shamanistic medium was once in widespread use in village rituals termed *takusen matsuri*. Now virtually extinct, these rites are still practiced by certain *kō* and involve an ascetic (*gyōja*) or *yamabushi* (mountain priest) who sum-

5. 易経_{えききょう}：中国伝統の筮竹_{ぜいちく}を使って行う。職業的占い師によって、今日も神社やお寺で行われている。

忌_{いみ}

不吉または神聖であると思われる物、人、場所、時、行為、言葉などを避けること。「忌」は穢れ_{けが}の概念と密接な関係にあった。不純なものは、神聖なものを損なったり穢さないように、避けなければならない。同時に、神聖なるものも、ときには、その神聖さを損なわないよう避けなければならない。前者は、例をあげれば、出産、月経、死などをとりまく伝統的な「忌」である。縁起の悪い事と同音異義の忌詞_{いみことば}や忌数_{いみかず}も「忌」である。したがって、死と同じ発音の四は避ける。平安時代には、神の住む方角を避けるために「方違え_{かたたが}」という習慣があった。

忌詞_{いみことば}

縁起の悪い言葉や表現、および、それに代わる婉曲な言いまわしや、代わりの表現のことをいう。たとえば、神道の儀式では、死や血

mons the *kami* (deity) into the medium's body for questioning.

5. Divination by the *Yi jing* (Ekikyō), employing the traditional Chinese method with yarrow stalks, is still widely practiced in both shrines and temples by professional diviners.

taboo

(*imi*). Ritual avoidance of things, persons, places, times, actions, or words believed to be inauspicious or, equally, sacred. The concept of taboo is closely allied to the notion of ritual impurity (*kegare*): anything impure must be avoided so as not to offend or defile the sacred; at the same time, the sacred itself must occasionally be avoided to insure that no offense to its sanctity occurs. Examples of the former category are the traditional taboos surrounding birth, menstruation, and death. Inauspicious words (*imikotoba*) or numbers (*imikazu*) that are homonyms of proscribed phenomena may also be taboo: hence the avoidance of the number four (*shi*), which is a homonym of the word for death (*shi*). In the Heian period, directional taboos (*katatagae*) were observed so as to avoid the directions in which certain deities were believed to reside.

taboo expressions

(*imikotoba*). Words or expressions associated with or considered to bring bad luck; also, the euphemisms and alternative expressions used in their place. For example,

という言葉とともに、仏や僧などの仏教用語は避けられる。仏教は葬式と関係があるからである。夜になると避ける表現もある。死と通ずる「塩」のかわりに「波の花」という。結婚式の祝辞では、「帰る」とか「戻る」という言葉は注意深く避ける。忌詞のなかには、外部の人を排除して結束を強めるため、職人、芸人、やくざなど特定のグループ内だけで使う、隠語の一部になったものもある。

隠語
いんご

部外者を排除したり、仲間意識を強めるために、特定の集団だけで使う言葉や表現。隠語は特定の職業グループ、飲食業あるいは芸能関係者、さらには、泥棒、賭博師、浮浪者などの社会の周辺部の人々によって、とくによく使われる。隠語の多くは、「おやじ」を「やじ」とする省略語、「やど」を「どや」とする倒置語、「茶」を「宇治」とする関連語、「盗む」を「もらう」とする意味の拡張などの形をとる。「酒」のことを「さんずい」とする文字からくるものもある。

　犯罪の世界で使われる隠語には、「警察」をさす「さつ」、「場所」をさす「しょば」などがある。同時に、警察にも隠語はある。

in Shintō ceremonies, Buddhist terms such as *hotoke* (Buddha) and *sō* (Buddhist monk) are generally avoided (Buddhism being associated with funerals), as are words like *shi* (death) and *chi* (blood). There are expressions to be avoided after nightfall; instead of saying *shio* for salt (a near-homophone of *shi*), one says *nami no hana* (flowers of the waves). In speeches at wedding parties, words like *kaeru* and *modoru* (to go back home) are carefully avoided. Some *imikotoba* have become part of the secular argot used exclusively by particular groups (such as craftspeople, entertainers, and gangsters) to reinforce in-group solidarity and exclusivity.

ingo

(secret language; argot). A general term for the specialized vocabulary and idioms employed by a particular group in order to exclude outsiders or to reinforce in-group feeling. *Ingo* appears particularly among certain professional groups, in the restaurant and entertainment business, and among thieves, gamblers, vagrants, and others on the fringes of society. Many *ingo* words result from abbreviation, as in *yaji* from *oyaji* (father); inversion, as in *doya* from *yado* (lodgings); association, as in *uji* (from Uji, a city famous for its tea) for *cha* (tea); or extension of meaning, as in *morau* (receive, take) for *nusumu* (steal). Some are references to the way a word is written, as in *sanzui* for *sake*.

Ingo words from the criminal subculture include *satsu* for police and *shoba* for place or territory (from *basho,* place). Conversely, the police have their own

「容疑者」をさす「ほし」、「強盗」をさす「たたき」などである。

　飲食業や芸能界の隠語で、一般人に使われるようになったものもある。「醤油」をさす「むらさき」、「お茶」をさす「あがり」、「勘定」をさす「おあいそ」などがそれである。そのほかによく使われるのは、「賄賂」をさす「鼻薬（はなぐすり）」、「顔はいいが下手な役者」をさす「大根」などである。

厄年

民間信仰による、人生でいちばん不幸や災難のおこりやすい年齢のことである。地方や時代によっても差はあるが、陰陽道によると、男は二十五歳と四十二歳、女は十九歳と三十三歳が厄年である。なかでも、男の四十二歳と女の三十三歳が大厄といって、とくに危険だという。厄年には、寺院や神社に詣でる習わしになっている。六十一歳と七十歳も、男女共通の厄年と言われるが、これには長寿のお祝いの意味も含まれる。

家相

土占いに基づく建築物の位置、方位、構造をいう。土占いの思想は、中国の殷時代（紀元前16〜11世紀）にさかのぼり、占星術等の占いとともに、黄河の氾濫予想、宮殿や都市

vocabulary: *hoshi* (star) for suspect, *tataki* (beating) for armed robbery, and so on.

Much of the *ingo* of the restaurant and entertainment business has found its way into the common vocabulary: *murasaki* (purple) for soy sauce, *agari* (to finish; the last item) for tea, and *oaiso* (pleasant treatment) for the bill. Also frequently heard are *hanagusuri* (snuff) for bribe money and *daikon* (a large white radish) for a good-looking but untalented actor.

yakudoshi

(critical or unlucky years). According to Japanese folk belief, those ages when an individual is most likely to experience calamities or misfortunes. Although there are local and historical variations, according to the Ommyō-dō school of divination the ages 25 and 42 for men and 19 and 33 for women are deemed critical years. Of these, the ages 42 for men and 33 for women are considered especially critical. It is customary in these unlucky years to visit temples and shrines. The sixty-first and seventieth years of life are also deemed *yaku-doshi* for both men and women, but their observance is accompanied by celebrations of longevity as well.

kasō

Physical aspect i.e., (location, direction, or construction) of buildings according to the art of geomancy. The basic concepts of geomancy originated in China during the Shang dynasty (sixteenth to eleventh cen-

の計画、方違えや忌日の決定など、日常生活にも適用された。日本では、家相は、藤原京と平城京建設の時に用いられているので、その少し前に大陸から紹介されたと思われる。家相の中核になるのは、鬼門、すなわち不吉な方角であり、普通東北とされる。今日でも、玄関や風呂、便所などは、この方角を避ける。

方違え
<small>かたたがえ</small>

陰陽道に基づく方角の禁忌。平安時代には、外出先が自宅から見て天一神の居る方角なら、前の晩よその家に宿泊して方角を変えた。天一神は、良くも悪くも、人の運命を左右すると信じられていた。特定の日に天から降り、定められた順序で四十四日間かけて各方角を順次にまわり、十六日間天に帰る。このサイクルは終わることなく続くが、方違えとは、天一神を避けることなのである。神が天にいる十六日間なら、どの方角に行っても安全であるとされた。

turies B.C.) and were practiced, along with astrology and other forms of divination, in predicting the flooding of the Yellow River, in laying out palaces and cities, and in carrying on daily activities such as determining directional taboos (*katatagae*) and taboo days. In Japan, *kasō* was used in the planning of two early capitals, Fujiwarakyō and Heijōkyō, and so was probably introduced to Japan from the continent shortly before their construction. A concept central to this form of geomancy is *kimon,* or inauspicious direction, generally regarded as being the northeast. Even today, houses are located and constructed so that entrances and rooms such as the bathroom and toilet avoid this direction.

katatagae

Taboos about directions, based on Ommyōdō. During the Heian period, if travel from one's home was in the direction presided over by the god Nakagami, it was customary to stay elsewhere overnight. Nakagami was believed to govern people's fortunes, both good and bad. He descended from heaven on a certain day, traveled from one direction to another in a prescribed order for a total of forty-four days, and returned to his celestial abode for sixteen days. The cycle was repeated endlessly, and it was in order to avoid Nakagami that *katatagae* was observed. It was considered safe to travel in any direction while the god was in heaven.

形代 (かたしろ)

神道の儀式で、穢れ(けが)を祓(はら)うために身代わりとしたもの。災厄を形代に負わせて水に流すか焼いた。

　形代は、普通人形や人の形を模したので、「人形(ひとがた)」ともいわれ、災厄を祓うために、それで人の身体を撫でることから「撫物(なでもの)」ともいわれた。三月三日の雛祭には、夕方、人形で身体をなで、それを川に流す「流し雛（巳の日の悪魔払い）」が行われた。

　夏越(なごし)には、日本各地で形代を使う行事が行われた。村の鎮守様では、氏子に形代を配り、氏子はそれに家族の名前や年齢を書いて神社に納め、お祓をした。

丙午 (ひのえうま)

十干十二支の四十三番目で、火の馬と結びつけられている。この年には火災や自然災害が多いといわれる。また、この年に生まれた女性は、気性が荒く、夫を食い殺すという迷信があり、嫁のもらい手がなかった。今日では少なくなったが、まだ、「丙午」の年に妊娠

katashiro

Object employed as a scapegoat in the exorcism of ritual impurities or evil influences through Shintō rites. The malignant influences are drawn into the *katashiro,* which is then floated away or burned.

Katashiro are also termed *hitogata* (literally, "dolls"), from their common occurrence in the form of dolls or human effigies, or *nademono* ("things for rubbing"), from the practice of rubbing the scapegoat against the worshiper's body to absorb evil influences. The observance of the Doll Festival on the third day of the third month used to include a "Snake Day Exorcism" in which a doll was rubbed against the body and then set adrift on a river.

Rites employing *katashiro* occur throughout Japan during the *nagoshi* observance. Local tutelary shrines distribute paper *katashiro* among their parishioners; the names and ages of family members are written upon the *katashiro,* which are then returned to the shrine for purification.

hinoe uma

The forty-third year in the traditional sixty-year cycle (*jikkan jūnishi*), identified with the fire horse. It was traditionally believed that many fires and other natural disasters occur during this year of the cycle. There was also a superstition that women born during this year had a wild disposition and ate their husbands, and such women

したり子供を産むことを避ける傾向がある。最近の例は1966年で、この年には出生率が大幅に下がった。

六曜

六輝(ろっき)ともいう。日本の暦につけられた名称と運勢。吉凶を表す。暦に先勝(せんしょう)、友引、先負(せんぷ)、仏滅、大安、赤口(しゃっこう)の六つの異なった運勢を、六日周期で割り当てたもの。この習慣は、14世紀に中国から伝わり、江戸時代中期から実際に使われている。六曜は現在でも日本のカレンダーの多くに記載されていて、日常生活で使われることもある。たとえば、結婚式の日取りを決めるとき、仏滅は避け、大安がいちばん望ましいとされる。葬儀は伝統的に友引の日を避ける。六曜の内容は以下の通りである。

1. 先勝。朝は吉、午後は凶。このような日には、すべてを効率的に行わなければならない。急ぎの仕事と訴訟に適している。
2. 友引。昼間をのぞいて吉。しかし葬式や仏事は凶。この日葬式を行うと、友を引く（死を招く）という。

were shunned as brides. Such beliefs became wide-spread during the Edo period. Today, there is still a tendency for pregnancy and childbirth to be avoided during *hinoe uma*; the most recent occurrence of that year, 1966, saw a marked drop in the birth rate.

rokuyo

("six days"). Also called *rokki*. Designations or fortunes added to Japanese calendars indicating whether or not a given date is auspicious. In the old Japanese solar calendar, six different fortunes—*senshō, tomobiki, sempu, butsumetsu, taian,* and *shakku*—were applied in continuous six-day cycles. This custom was imported from China in the fourteenth century and was practiced in Japan from the mid-Edo period onward. These fortunes still appear on many Japanese calendars and are observed to some extent in everyday life. For example, when selecting a wedding date, the *butsumetsu* designation is avoided and *taian* is regarded as most desirable. Funerals are customarily not scheduled on dates with the *tomobiki* designation. The following is a glossary of the six designations.

1. *Senshō.* The morning is auspicious, but the afternoon will bring bad luck. On this type of day, everything should be done efficiently. It is a good day for urgent business and litigation.

2. *Tomobiki.* Except for noontime, the day is auspicious. But it is bad luck to hold funerals and other Buddhist services on this day. To hold a funeral on this day is said to be inviting another death.

3. 先負。急用と論争は避ける。平静を守って吉。午後は吉。

4. 仏滅。万事に凶。慶事の計画や創業は凶。

5. 大安。万事吉。結婚式、宮参り、慶事の計画によし。

6. 赤口。万事に凶。正午のみ吉。

賀の祝

長寿を祈って、一定の年齢で祝われる通過儀礼。「年祝い（としいわい）」あるいは「算賀（さんが）」ともいう。中国からもたらされ、はじめは数え年四十歳から十年ごとに祝われた。「賀の祝」は、常に数え年で数える。

　数え年では、人間は生まれた年に1歳で、正月に1歳ずつ年をとる。この計算方法だと、西洋式よりも一歳から二歳上になる。室町時代後期になると、「賀の祝」は六十一歳（還暦（かんれき））に始まり、七十歳（古希（こき））、七十七歳（喜寿（きじゅ））、八十歳（傘寿（さんじゅ））、八十八歳（米寿（べいじゅ））、九十歳（卒寿（そつじゅ））、九十九歳（白寿（はくじゅ））に祝われるようになった。お祝いは親戚や友達といっしょに、誕生日または九月十五日の敬老の日

3. *Sempu*. Urgent business and controversy should be avoided on this day. It is a good day for going about all activities in a serene manner. The afternoon is auspicious.

4. *Butsumetsu*. This day is bad luck in all respects. It is best to avoid scheduling auspicious events and opening a business.

5. *Taian*. This day is auspicious in all respects—a good day for scheduling celebrations, such as weddings and shrine visits (*miyamairi*).

6. *Shakku*. This day is bad luck in all respects; the only auspicious time is noon.

ga no iwai

A Japanese rite of passage celebrated at various ages that involves praying for long life; also called *toshiiwai* or *sanga*. Imported to Japan from China, *ga no iwai* was originally celebrated once every ten years often a person turned 40, according to the traditional Japanese method of calculating age (*kazoedoshi*). *Ga no iwai* dates are always decided on the basis of *kazoedoshi*.

In *kazoedoshi,* a person is considered to be one year old in the year of his birth and becomes one year older at the beginning of each subsequent New Year. This calculation results in an age that ranges from one to two years greater than that calculated by the usual Western method. Toward the latter part of the Muromachi period, *ga no iwai* came to be celebrated from the age of 61 (*kanreki*) and subsequently at ages 70 (*koki*), 77 (*kiju*), 80 (*sanju*), 88 (*beiju*), 90 (*sotsuju*), and 99 (*hakuju*). The rit-

に行われる。「賀の祝」をおこなう年齢は、地方によって異なる。この年齢は、厄年と深い関係があり、ある地方での厄年が、別の地方の「賀の祝」のことがある。

還暦

六十歳（数え年六十一歳）の祝い。六十歳に意味があるのは、伝統的な暦は、十干十二支の六十年周期でできているからであり、六十歳の誕生日に、自分の生まれ年の干支に戻り、新しい周期が始まるからである。還暦の祝いは中世に始まり、江戸時代に一般に広まった。六十歳の祝いには、親戚や友達が招かれる。地方によっては、赤い衣服を着るが、赤は伝統的に赤ん坊の着物の色で、生まれなおすという意味がある。最近まで、六十歳になった人は、配偶者といっしょに、隠居するものとされていた。

達磨

インドの菩提達磨の人形。菩提達磨は、中国に渡り禅宗の始祖となった。洞窟で九年間座

ual is usually celebrated with relatives and friends on the person's birthday or on Respect-for-the-Aged Day (15 September). The ages at which *ga no iwai* is celebrated can differ from region to region. These ages are closely related to *yakudoshi* (the ages determined to be critical or unlucky according to Japanese folk belief), and what is considered a *yakudoshi* in one region can be a year for *ga no iwai* in another.

kanreki

Celebration of a person's sixtieth birthday (sixty-first as reckoned by *kazoedoshi*). The significance of the age 60 is that the traditional calendar was organized on sixty-year cycles (*jikkan jūnishi*), and on the sixtieth birthday one begins a new cycle, returning to the calendar sign under which one was born (*honke-gaeri*). The celebration of *kanreki* began in the medieval period and became popular during the Edo period. On the day of a person's sixtieth birthday, relatives and friends are invited to a celebratory feast. In some areas it is customary for the person to wear something red, this traditionally being the color for infants' clothing and hence symbolic of the beginning of a new cycle. Until recently, a man of 60 was expected to become, with his spouse, an *inkyo* (retired person).

daruma

Dolls representing the Indian priest Bodhidharma (Bodai Daruma or Daruma), the founder of Zen Bud-

禅を組み、腕と脚が使えなくなってしまったといわれる。達磨は、豊作や選挙での当選等特定の願いを達成するためのお守りとされる。片方の目をいれて神棚にあげ、願いが叶うと、もう片方の目をいれる。

　たおしても起きあがるので「起き上がり小法子」と呼ばれる達磨の原型は、16世紀に普及した。達磨が今日のような形になったのは江戸時代で、天然痘の魔除けとされた。年末から年始にかけて、東日本の達磨市で売られることが多い。

魔除け

悪霊や鬼、およびそれが引き起こす人の不幸や自然災害を追い払うためのお守りや儀式。門や庇に護符を貼って家に悪霊が入ってくるのを防いだり、死者の枕元に刀剣を置いたりするのが、魔除けの例である。子供を守る魔除けは特別の形を取る。子供の魔除けとしては、着物の背に色鮮やかな印を縫いつけたり、おでこに灰で×印や悪霊の敵とされる「犬」の字を書いたりする。お寺や神社が配布するお札や護符は、神社で正月に売られる破魔矢や破魔弓と同様、悪霊を追い払うとされている。

dhism in China, who is said to have lost the use of his arms and legs after spending nine years meditating in a cave. They are used as charms for the fulfillment of some special wish, such as a plentiful harvest or successful election to public office; the custom is for the purchaser to paint in one eye, place the *daruma* in the family shrine, and paint in the other eye when the wish is fulfilled.

Prototypes of these dolls, called *okiagari koboshi* ("the little priest who stands up") because they return to an upright position when tipped over, were popular during the sixteenth century. The present form of the doll dates from the Edo period, when it was regarded as a talisman for protection against smallpox. *Daruma* are often sold in special *darumaichi* (*daruma* fairs), generally held in eastern Japan between the end of the year and early spring.

mayoke

Talismans or rituals believed to dispel evil spirits and demons and the personal misfortunes and natural disasters presumably caused by them. Hanging charms from gates and eaves to prevent evil spirits from entering the home, or placing a sword at the pillow of a corpse, are examples of *mayoke*. There are special forms of *mayoke* for the protection of children. These include embroidering brightly colored protective insignia on the back of a child's *kimono* or tracing an *X* or the Chinese character for "*dog*" (the natural enemy of malevolent spirits) on a child's forehead with ash. The charms and amulets (*gofu*) issued at temples and shrines are also believed to

虫封じ

病気の子供のために、まじない、祈禱、護符などで行う魔除け。病気は、子供の身体にすむ虫のせいにされることがあった。虫を封じるには、民間薬を与えたり、神社やお寺で、特別な祈禱をしてもらうほかに、子供の手のひらに神様の名前を書いたり、かかとに「端午」の漢字を書いた。護符を、玄関や神棚に貼りつけることもあった。

丑の刻参り

丑の刻（午前二時〜四時）に神社に参詣して、怨みのある人が死ぬよう呪いをかける行為。呪う相手に擬した藁人形を、鳥居や境内の木に釘で打ちつけて、祈願した。この儀式は、七日連続して行い、それが終わると、呪われた人は、藁人形の釘を打ち込まれた部位に痛みを感じて死ぬと信じられた。

ward off evil spirits, as are other special appurtenances, such as the *hamaya* and *hamayumi* (lucky bow and arrow) sold at shrines at the New Year.

mushifūji

(literally, "sealing up of a worm or insect"). Kind of exorcism formerly used on sick children, commonly employing spells, prayers, and talismans. Disorders were sometimes attributed to a *mushi*, or worm, that was believed to inhabit the child's body. To exorcise the *mushi,* one could give the child a folk medicine or take the child to a shrine or temple, have special prayers recited, and have the name of a Shintō deity written on the palms of his or her hands, or the characters for the fifth day of the fifth month (Children's Day) written on the soles of the feet. Another method was to affix a paper talisman to the front doorway or to the Shintō family altar.

ushi no koku mairi

The act of going to a shrine at approximately 2:00 A.M. to place the curse of death on an enemy. To place this curse, the petitioner nails a straw doll resembling the object of his or her enmity to a shrine gate (*torii*) or a tree on the shrine grounds, and then offers a prayer. The rite is repeated for seven consecutive days, after which it is believed that the accursed person will die after experiencing pain in the same part of the body where the straw doll was nailed.

物の怪

死霊・生霊は、人に祟り死や病気を招くといわれ、特に平安時代に広く信じられた。人間の魂は、死んでからは永久に、興奮のきわみでは一時的に、肉体から離れると信じられた。そのような魂が、怒りや嫉妬や復讐のために他人にとりつくと、物の怪といわれた。

化け物

怪物、幽霊、鬼など、さまざまな超自然的存在。化け物はお化けともいうが、普通、人間の形をしている幽霊と区別して、妖怪と呼ぶのが一般的である。妖怪は、音、火、風などを含めてさまざまな人間以外の形態をとり、特定の場所の暗がりの中に出現する。とくに多いのは、山、道ばた、水辺、部屋などである。化け物には、天狗、山姥、一つ目小僧、河童などがあるが、総数五百を上回るという。

鬼

角があり、凶暴で、赤い顔をしている。民話や諺や俗な言葉では、悪魔や怪物と同じものとされる。その性格は複雑で両面性を持ち、

mononoke

Vagrant spirits of the living or the dead believed to possess a person and to cause death or illness. *Mononoke* are associated mainly with the Heian period. The human spirit was believed to detach itself from the body permanently at death, or temporarily during times of emotional stress. Such a spirit was termed *mononoke* when it possessed another person either from anger, jealousy, or vengeance.

bakemono

Any of various monsters, apparitions, or goblins; preternatural beings in general. *Bakemono* (sometimes called *obake*) are generically termed *yōkai,* as distinguished from ghosts or *yūrei,* which typically appear in their original human form. *Yōkai,* by contrast, may appear in various nonhuman forms, including sounds, fire, or wind, and usually manifest themselves at dusk in a specific place (typically a mountain, roadside, body of water, or room). *Tengu, yamamba, hitotsume kozō,* and *kappa* are just a few of the types of *bakemono,* which number more than five hundred.

oni

Horned, ferocious, scarlet-faced figure usually equated in folktales, proverbs, and common parlance with a demon or ogre. His true nature, however, is more com-

悪魔の顔と同時に、情け深い守護者の顔も持
っている。鬼の悪魔的側面は、オニの語にあ
てられた漢字の「鬼」に込められた意味や、
仏教のさまざまな地獄の拷問者としての鬼の
連想で強調された。昔の鬼の優しい役割は、
祭りや儀式で、悪い勢力を追い払いながら行
列の先頭を歩くことに残っている。

天狗

日本の民話に出てくる奇怪な両義性を持つ妖
怪。長いくちばしと羽を持ち、目は光り、人
間の胴体と腕と脚を持っている。位の高い天
狗は、長くつきだした鼻、白髪、赤い顔をし
て、羽団扇を持っている。天狗は、第一に、
大木を好む山の守護者である山の神の化身と
考えられている。中世の文学では、天狗は仏
教の悪賢い敵であり、僧を誘拐して、木のて
っぺんにつるしたり、強欲やうぬぼれを吹き
込んだり、糞をおいしい料理と思わせて食べ
させる。また、子供の誘拐者、幻覚を引き起
こす力と神通力の持ち主としても恐れられ
る。逆に、超自然的技の保護者であり、伝達
者とすることもよくある。天狗は山伏と似た
服装で描かれることが多く、山伏と近い関係
にあると考えられている。

plex and ambivalent, in that he has a benevolent, tutelary face as well as a demonic one. The demonic side of the *oni* was strengthened by the connotations of the Chinese character with which the word is written and by the *oni*'s association with the demon torturers of various Buddhist hells. Evidence of the *oni*'s ancient benevolent role, however, may still be seen in a number of festivals or rituals, in which he marches at the head of the procession, sweeping away evil influences.

tengu

Uncanny and ambivalent creature in Japanese folklore, with a long beak and wings, glittering eyes, and a man's body, arms, and legs. A variant form, sometimes credited with higher rank, has a long nose, white hair, and red face and carries a feather fan. The *tengu* is seen principally as a *keshin* or transformation of a *yama no kami*, the guardians of certain mountains with a particular affinity for huge trees. References in medieval literature reveal him as a subtle enemy of Buddhism, kidnapping Buddhist priests and tying them to the tops of trees, implanting thoughts of greed and pride in their minds, or feasting them on dung magically disguised as delicious food. He is also feared as an abductor of children and for his powers of illusion and demoniacal possession. Conversely the *tengu* is often represented as a benign protector and transmitter of supernatural skills. He is closely associated with the *yamabushi*, being often depicted as wearing items of the *yamabushi*'s distinctive costume.

山姥

山に住むと信じられている女の妖怪。もとは
山の神ないしは山の神の巫女であったとされ
る。人間を食うといわれるが、愛嬌のある、
間の抜けた鬼婆として、伝説や民話に登場す
ることもある。

神隠し

突然、わけもなく人がいなくなることで、天
狗や狐や悪霊のしわざだと考えられた。誰か
が神隠しにあうと、村全体が、村中や近くの
山を鉦（かね）・太鼓をたたきながら探した。被害者
は、病気の子供であることが多く、霊界に連
れ去られ、一日か二日、時には何年もしてか
ら帰ってきたという。

河童

日本の水界に住むといわれる水陸両生の超自
然的存在で、水神が姿を変えたものという。
その姿と呼び名は地方によって異なる。大き
さは、十二〜十三歳の子供ぐらいで、顔は虎
に似て鼻はとがり、髪はオカッパをしており、

yamamba

Female demon believed to live in the mountains. The *yamamba* is thought to have been originally a mountain deity (*yama no kami*) or a mountain deity's female servant. Commonly described as a female demon who devours humans, the *yamamba* sometimes appears in legends and folklore as a humorous, stupid old hag.

kamikakushi

(literally, "hiding by the spirits"). The sudden and unexplained disappearance of a person from home that was traditionally believed to be the work of the supernatural beings called *tengu*, of foxes, and of other malevolent spirits. When someone fell victim to *kamikakushi*, it was customary for the entire community to conduct a search of the village and neighboring mountains with ringing of bells and beating of drums. It was believed that the victim—usually a sickly child—had been carried off to the world of spirits (*reikai*) and that he would return after a day or two, or even after several years.

kappa

An amphibious supernatural creature said to inhabit Japan and thought to be a transformation of a water deity. The description and name of the *kappa* vary from region to region. Generally, the *kappa* is believed to be about the size and shape of a twelve- or thirteen-year-

頭には皿のようなへこみがあり、水をためている。その水がなくなると、陸上での超能力は弱まるという。つるつるした身体は青緑色の鱗でおおわれ、魚のようなにおいがし、手と足には水掻きがある。腕と脚の関節を自由にぐるぐるまわせるので、すぐわかるという。くちばしと羽があるものや、亀かカワウソのような形の河童もいるという。地方によっては、田植えや灌漑の手伝いをする河童もいるが、たいていは人間や動物を餌食にしている。河童は、餌食をつかまえて、尻の穴から肝臓を引っぱり出すのを好むという。また、キュウリが好きで、相撲を好む。芥川龍之介の小説『河童』は有名。

海坊主

海入道または海小僧とも呼ばれる。日本の民話では、海坊主は丸い大きな頭をした海の妖怪だという。伝説によると、海坊主に話しかけた人の船は一瞬のうちに転覆させられるという。大きな魚、大波、あるいは入道雲を海坊主と間違えたとするのが通説だが、無縁仏、あるいは不慮の死をとげた人の魂が、海に避難するという迷信からきた信仰とみなされる。

old child, with a face much like a tiger and with a snout; its hair is bobbed, and a saucer-like depression on top of the head contains water. When the supply of water diminishes, the *kappa*'s supernatural power on land is impaired. The *kappa*'s slippery body is covered with blue-green scales and emits a fishy odor. It has webbed feet and hands. Human beings can recognize the *kappa* by its ability to rotate its arm and leg joints freely. In other variations, *kappa* have beaks and wings or resemble turtles or otters. Although in some areas *kappa* help with rice-planting or irrigation, usually they prey on humans and animals. In particular the *kappa* delights in grabbing its victim and tearing out the liver through the anus. The *kappa* is also said to be fond of cucumbers and partial to *sumō* wrestling. Akutagawa Ryūnosuke wrote a popular novel entitled *Kappa*.

umibōzu

Also called *uminyūdō* or *umikozō*. In Japanese folklore, the *umibōzu* is a ghost of the sea said to have a large round head. According to legend, if anyone speaks to this ghost, it will immediately capsize that person's boat. It is thought that people have mistaken large fish, large waves, and thunderheads for this ghost, but the origin of the belief is probably the superstition that the souls of people who have no one to look after their graves or have suffered an untimely death take refuge at sea.

座敷童

東北地方、とくに岩手県の旧家の座敷に住む
とされる守護神。男の子の姿をして、長髪で
顔が赤く、富をもたらすという。また、いた
ずらなところもあり、夜中に寝ている人の胸
にのしかかるという。

一つ目小僧

民話に出てくるおでこに目が一つついた空想
上の妖怪。小僧の格好をしているが、山の神
や田の神とも関係があるという。関東地方や
東北地方では、旧暦二月八日と十二月八日の
忌日、事八日(ことようか)に訪ねてくるとい
われ、家の前に立てた棒に、目籠をさかさま
にして掲げ、これを追い払う。目籠の多くの
「目」が、一つ目小僧をはずかしめ、脅かす
のだという。

雪女

雪女郎ともいう。雪の夜に白い着物を着て現
れる女の幽霊。雪のように蒼白で冷たく、神
秘的な出来事は雪女のせいにされることが多

zashiki warashi

Household tutelary god traditionally believed to live in the homes of old and well-to-do families in northern Honshū, particularly in Iwate Prefecture. Said to appear in the form of a young boy with long hair and a red face and to bring riches to the family, it can also be mischievous, bearing down on the chests of sleeping people during the night.

hitotsume kozō

Goblin with a single eye in the middle of its forehead; one of the fantastic and grotesque creatures that appear in Japanese folktales. It generally takes the form of a young boy (*kozō*) but is sometimes associated with the Shintō gods of mountain or field (*yama no kami; ta no kami*). In the Kantō and Tōhoku regions it was believed to appear on the night of *kotoyōka,* a taboo day falling on the eighth day of the second and twelfth lunar months, and was warded off by attaching an open mesh basket upside down to a pole set up before a house. The many mesh "eyes" of the basket were believed to shame and intimidate the goblin.

yuki onna

(snow woman). Also called *yuki jorō*. Apparition of a woman dressed in white, believed to appear on snowy nights. Pale and cold like the snow, she is often blamed

い。赤ん坊を抱いて現れることが多いので、子供と関係づけられ、出産の時死んだ女とされることもある。また、一つ目、片足のこともある。雪女は、年末か年始に人を訪れる歳神と考えられている。

幽霊

幽霊は、死んだ人の魂で、その人にそっくりの姿で現れる。この世に戻ってくる特別の理由を持っていて、親族や親しい知人など、特定の人にしか姿を見せない。激しい死に方や不自然な死に方をした人は、死の世界への最後の関門をくぐれないので、親族や知人の前に現れて、この世から去り難いことを訴えると考えられている。江戸時代中期以降の『東海道四谷怪談』や『牡丹灯籠』などの幽霊物

語では、幽霊は
髪をふりみだし、
長い腕をだらり
とさせて、脚が
ない。

人魂

人が死んだときか、すぐ後に肉体から離れる霊魂で、尾のある青白い火の玉の形をしているとされる。人魂を見ることは、自分の死の

for mysterious happenings. Frequently appearing with a baby in her arms, she is associated with children and is sometimes thought to be a woman who died in childbirth. At other times the spirit is described as a woman with one eye and one leg. The *yuki onna* is thought to be a form of New Year's deity (*toshigami*) who visits people at the end or beginning of each year.

ghosts

(*yūrei*). A *yūrei* is a departed human soul, that appears as a shadowy likeness of the deceased. A *yūrei* is said to have a specific purpose for returning to the world of the living and to reveal itself only to certain persons, most often surviving relatives but occasionally other intimate acquaintances. The spirits of those who died violently or unnaturally are believed to be unable to make their final passage into the world of the dead; they appear before their relatives and acquaintances and express their reluctance to depart this world. Since the mid-Edo period, *yūrei* in such ghost stories as *Tōkaidō Yotsuya kaidan* (The Ghost Story of Tokaido Yotsuya) and *Botan-dōrō* (Peony Lantern) have been depicted as having disheveled hair, elongated and dangling arms, and no legs.

hitodama

Spirit that is supposed to depart from the human body at the time of death or shortly afterward; commonly believed to take the form of a bluish white ball of fire

前兆であると考えられたが、中世の文学には、それを追い払ういろいろな方法が書かれている。今日でも、夜、屋根の上や墓地をただよう人魂を見たという人がいる。流れ星や、燐光など、自然現象が人魂だと思われることもある。

憑物

人間にとりついて、肉体的、精神的苦痛を与える。この言葉は、もともと、姿を消して身体にある穴の一つから体内に入り込む動物をさした。この動物には、大別すると、狐とされる四つ足の動物と、とうびょうとして知られる蛇の二つのタイプがある。つけられた名前に似ず、狐は小さなイタチに似ていて、蛇は魚のように短くて太っているといわれる。

憑物は二種類に分類される。自らの意志で人間を悩ますものと、狐使いに命令されるものである。狐使いは、餌を与えて憑物を誘い出し、私的恨みを晴らすために、憑物を召使いや使者として使う。憑物による苦しみは、肉体の苦痛から、被害者の口を借りて狐がしゃべる、明らかに魔がついた状態になるものまで広範囲にわたる。憑物を落とすには僧侶か修験者の力を借りなければならない。憑物には、この他に怠慢な子孫にとりついた先祖の霊や、神社を穢されて激怒する神もいる。

with a tail. Seeing *hitodama* was traditionally regarded as a premonition of one's own death, although various ways of exorcising them are mentioned in medieval literature. Even today, one hears of people who claim to have seen *hitodama* hovering over rooftops or in graveyards at night. Shooting stars, phosphorescence, and other natural phenomena are sometimes taken for *hitodama*.

tsukimono

Entities believed to "possess" a human being, causing a variety of bodily and mental torments. The term applies primarily to certain animals supposedly capable of becoming invisible and entering the human body through one of its orifices. Such animals are of two broad types: a four-legged creature usually described as a fox and a snake known as a *tōbyō*. Instead of resembling their namesakes, the "fox" is described as resembling a small weasel, and the snake as short and fat like a fish.

Tsukimono can be divided into two categories: those that molest human beings by their own volition and those that are directed by another person, known as a *kitsunetsukai* or "fox employer." Such people lure the creature into their power by feeding it, then use it as a servant or messenger to carry out their private grudges. The torments caused by *tsukimono* range from bodily aches and pains to apparent possession, in which the "fox" speaks through the victim's mouth. The approved method of cure is through the services of a Buddhist priest or ascetic. In addition to the fox and *tōbyō*, *tsuki-mono* also include dead ancestral spirits who possess a

憑物落とし

憑物につかれた人の身体から悪霊を追い払う各種の方法。日本では、人間にとりついて様々な病や狂気を引き起こす霊的存在には、(1) 粗略に扱われたり冒瀆されて怒った神。(2) 子孫が適切な供養をしないことに腹を立て、不満に思っている先祖の魂。(3) 狐や蛇、あるいは四国地方の犬神のような魔の動物、があるという。

これらの悪霊を被害者の体内から追い払うには、まず、有能な祈禱師を必要とする。普通、山伏か僧侶である。祈禱師は悪霊と交わるために、(1) 法華経やヒンズー教のマントラのような聖典を声に出して読む（内容はともかく、その音だけでよい）(2) 修験道の蟇目の法のような儀式を行う (3) 憑物自身に強制的にしゃべらせ、名乗らせて不平の原因を言わせ、憑物から離れる条件に同意させる。その方法は2つあり、(1) 憑物を被害者の身体から、通常女性か小児である媒体の身体に移動させ、媒体の口を通して祈禱師の問いに答えさせる。(2) 被害者に、日蓮宗の題目などを長時間繰り返させる事により、無意識状態にしておいて、その口で憑物に話させる。

neglectful descendant and *kami* enraged by profanation of their shrines.

exorcist

(*tsukimono otoshi*). The various methods whereby a malignant spiritual entity is driven out of the body of the person it is possessing. In Japan, the entities believed capable of possessing a human being and thereby causing various kinds of sickness or madness are: (1) a *kami* (Shintō deity) enraged by neglect or sacrilege; (2) a discontented ancestral spirit, angry due to its descendants neglect of the proper cult attention required by the dead; and (3) a witch animal, such as a fox, a snake, or, in the Shikoku area, a dog (*inugami*).

The process by which these entities are persuaded to leave the bodies of their victims first requires a competent exorcist. Such a person is usually a *yamabushi* or a Buddhist priest. The techniques he may employ for communicating with the entity include: (1) recitation of a holy and potent text such as the Lotus Sutra or a mantra (the sound alone of such a text is sometimes sufficient to effect a cure); (2) a ritual such as the Hikime no Hō of the Shugendō; and (3) methods whereby the possessing entity is forced to speak, to name itself, to state its grievance, and to agree to terms whereby it will leave its victim. Such methods fall into two groups: (1) The entity is forced to leave its victim and enter the body of a medium, usually a woman or a small child, through whose mouth it is persuaded to answer the questions of the exorcist. (2) The entity is forced to

　憑物落としは、平安時代の文学作品に広く
見られる。なかでも、もっともあざやかで参
考になるのは、清少納言の『枕草子』297段
で、病気の女性が、少女を媒体に、僧侶に祈
禱してもらう。『紫式部日記』の、多くの祈
禱師が雇われる、中宮彰子の難産の話も有名
である。

狐火

日本の伝説によれば、山野や墓地で見られる
赤桃色の不思議な火は、狐がつけるという。
火は一つではなく、連なっている。点火され
ると前に進み、やがて消えるこの火は、狐の
提灯行列とか狐の嫁入りとも呼ばれる。

狐狗狸<ruby>こっくり</ruby>

通俗占いで、占い板を使うプランシェットや
ウィーシャの日本版。たとえば、なくした物
を見つけるために、霊媒は、ゆるく束ねた三

speak through the mouth of the possessed, who is meanwhile reduced to an unconscious state through long repetition of a sacred formula such as the *daimoku* (holy invocation) of the Nichiren sect.

Descriptions of exorcism can be found throughout Heian-period literature. Among the most vivid and instructive is the account in section 297 of the *Makura no sōshi* (Pillow Book) of Sei Shōnagon, where a sick woman is exorcised by a Buddhist priest who uses a girl as a medium. The account in Murasaki Shikibu's diary of the difficult confinement of the empress Akiko, in which many exorcists were employed, is also well known.

kitsunebi

("fox fires"). Japanese legendary belief that the strange, rosy pink fires sometimes sighted at such places as hills, fields, and graveyards are lit by foxes. These fires, which are often seen in chains rather than alone, moving forward as they appear to be lit and then extinguished, are also referred to as *kitsune no chōchin gyōretsu* (processions of fox lanterns) and *kitsune no yomeiri* (foxes' wedding processions).

kokkuri

(literally, "nodding"). Type of popular divination, the Japanese counterpart of planchette or Ouija. In order to find a lost object, for example, a medium holds the top

本の小竹の上端を持って、1から10までの数字と五十音のかなを書いた板の上に軽くふれる。普通は目隠しをした霊媒が、恍惚状態になると、小竹が文字と数字の上を動いて、次々に文字を指す。狐狗狸とは、霊媒がうたた寝をする人のように、思わず知らずうなずくことをさしている。狐狗狸が盛んになったのは、明治時代中期からである。

招き猫

日本人が手招きする形で、前足をあげて坐っている猫の形をした置物。食堂や飲み屋のような、客商売の店頭によく飾られ、幸運と商売繁盛を「招く」と信じられている。紙粘土か焼き物で作られ、右前足をあげているものと、左前足をあげているものとがある。お寺や神社の中には、初詣の人に、小さな招き猫を護符として配るところがある。

破魔矢と破魔弓

初詣の時に神社で売っている縁起物。「はま」は現在では「悪魔払い」の意味の漢字をあてるが、もとは、「まと」の意味だった。「ゆみ」

of a tripod of loosely tied sticks over a board on which are written the numbers from one to ten and the fifty letters of the Japanese *kana* syllabary. As the medium, usually blindfolded, goes into a trance, the sticks begin to slide over the letters and numbers on the board and, letter by letter, a message appears. The name *kokkuri* refers to the movement of the medium, who nods involuntarily like a person dozing off. *Kokkuri* has been popular since the mid-Meiji period.

manekineko

(literally, "beckoning cat"). Figurine in the shape of a sitting cat with one paw upraised, as though making the customary Japanese gesture used in beckoning to people. It is often displayed prominently at the front of shops and businesses that rely on heavy customer traffic, such as eateries and drinking establishments, and is believed to "beckon" good fortune and business success. Usually constructed of papier-mâché or pottery, *manekineko* sometimes have the right front paw raised and sometimes the left front paw. Some temples and shrines give out miniature copies of *manekineko* as protective amulets (*gofu*) to those making their first shrine or temple visit of the year.

hamaya and hamayumi

Good-luck charms sold at Shintō shrines when Japanese make their first shrine visit of the year (*hatsumōde*). *Hama* is now written with characters meaning "to repel

と「や」は「弓」と「矢」を指す。母方の実家が、男の子の初正月や初節句に、この二品を贈る習わしは、今でも続いている。地方によっては、最近まで、正月に男の子に弓を射させて、秋の収穫を占っていた。

三猿

三匹の猿が、それぞれ手で両目、両耳、口を押さえて、見ざる、聞かざる、言わざるを表している置物。室町時代後期に始まり、庚申の行事の時に使う庚申塔という石の柱にも三猿を刻むようになった。三匹の猿は、天台宗の三諦（諦は真理の意）を表している。天台宗の開祖最澄が、この三諦を猿の形に彫ったといわれる。

松竹梅

冬も緑の松と竹、春一番に花を咲かせる梅は、あわせて希望と幸運の象徴とされてきた。この習慣は中国から伝わり、奈良時代に広がった。そのころから、この三種は寄せ植え、生け花、デザインの図案、新年やその他おめでたい機会に飾りものとして使われた。松竹梅は、日本のレストランで、料理の等級を表すのに使われる。松は特上、竹は上、梅は並である。

evil spirits," although it originally meant "target"; *yumi* and *ya* mean "bow" and "arrow" respectively. It is still fairly common for a mother's family to send these two items to her male child on the occasion of his first New Year's or Children's Day festival. Until recently, in certain areas, young boys held archery competitions at New Year's to predict the next fall's harvest.

three monkeys

Figures of three monkeys who clasp both hands over their eyes, ears, or mouth, thus not seeing (*mizaru*), not hearing (*kikazaru*), or not speaking (*iwazaru*). Beginning in the late Muromachi period, it became customary to carve these figures on *kōshintō,* stone pillars used during the observances of *kōshin.*

The Three Monkeys represent the Santai (Three Truths) advocated by the Tendai sect of Buddhism. The Tendai founder, Saichō, is said to have carved a representation of this ideal in the form of monkeys.

shōchikubai

(pine, bamboo, plum). The pine and bamboo, which stay green throughout the winter, and the plum, the first tree to flower in spring, have been collectively regarded as a symbol of hope and good fortune in Japan since the Nara period, when this notion was imported from China. Since that time, the three have been planted together, combined in flower arrangements, employed as a design motif, and used in decorations for New

絵馬

神社に奉納された絵。二字の漢字が示すように、絵馬の起源は、由緒ある神社に本物の馬に代わるものとして、馬の絵を奉納した儀式にさかのぼる。

　絵馬には、互いに関連はあるものの、はっきりと区別される二つの系列がある。第一の系列は、昔ながらの民間信仰をつぐ小絵馬で、満願御礼、願掛け、厄払いを祈願して奉納するものである。多くは、その神社や寺に祀られている神仏に関係する絵が描かれる。狐（稲荷の使いであり、その象徴）や民間で広く信じられている不動明王等がその例である。供え餅などの供え物、大壺などは、幸運と繁栄を願い、石榴や桃は子宝祈願である。錠は禁煙、禁酒、禁賭博の誓いである。機織りなどの技術、武術、学問や習字（天満宮の象徴の黒牛）の上達祈願もある。多くの絵馬は、日常生活の関心を表している。十分な母乳を願う（女性の胸から乳が流れ出している）、子供の風呂嫌いをなくす（子供がにこにこして風呂桶につかっている）、不幸な結婚を終わらせる（男女が背を向けている）な

Year's and other auspicious occasions. Pine, bamboo, and plum are often used to name different meal combinations in Japanese restaurants, "pine" corresponding to deluxe, "bamboo" to special, and "plum" to regular.

ema

Votive pictures presented as offerings to deities. The term *ema* has its origin in ancient ritual, as is apparent from its two character-components. This combination indicates that these pictures evolved as modest substitutes for the real horses traditionally installed in prestigious Shintō shrines.

Two interrelated but categorically distinct lines are apparent in the evolution of *ema.* One continues the earlier popular religious tradition of works of small size (known as *koema,*) offered by members of the general populace, either in fulfillment of a vow or to entreat a deity for help in achieving an objective or rectifying some unfortunate condition. The great majority show a theme or motif that relates to the deity worshiped at a specific shrine or temple. Thus there are *ema* with representations of foxes (the messenger and symbol of Inari shrines) or popular Buddhist deities, such as Fudō Myōō. Other types, such as those that show ceremonial rice cakes and other offerings or large provision jars, are dedicated in the hope of happiness and prosperity, while subjects like pomegranates and peaches express the desire for progeny. Another category, which often incorporates a depiction of a lock in the design, represents the donor's vow to give up smoking, drinking, or

どである。なかでも、もっとも多いのは、病気にかかわるものであって、眼病（二つの目、「目」や「め」の字）、逆睫（松葉）、関節炎（手と脚）、皮膚病（ナマズ）、痔（アカエイ）、いぼ（たこ）などである。

　第二の系列に属する大絵馬は、サイズが大きく、寺や神社の目立つところに、ときには特別に建てられた絵馬堂に飾られている。現存するものには、近世の有名な画家のサインと日付の入ったものがあり、中には、狩野探幽、北斎、円山応挙などもある。

言霊
ことだま

古代の日本語の文献には、言葉には聖なる力と霊が宿るという信仰が示されている。とくに、祝詞や和歌の形で表現された場合、言葉は人間や神、あるいはこの世の動きにさえ影

gambling. Still others symbolize the hope for increased skill in trades such as weaving (a shuttle), or proficiency in military arts (weapons of various kinds), or scholarly and calligraphic accomplishment (a black bull, symbol of *temmangū* shrines). Many *ema* represent pragmatic daily concerns—the desire for satisfactory production of mother's milk (milk streaming from a woman's breasts), to remedy a child's dislike of baths (a child happily seated in a bathtub), or for an end to an unhappy marriage (a couple facing in opposite directions). The largest group relates to ailments and illnesses —the donor's hope for relief from eye problems (pairs of eyes, or the word *me*), ingrown eyelashes (pine needles), arthritis (hands or legs), skin disorders (a catfish), piles (a stingray), or warts (an octopus).

Ema belonging to the second line (known as *ōema*) are characteristically large in dimension and are usually displayed in conspicuous locations in temples or shrines, often in a separate structure called an *emadō* that is specially erected for this purpose. Among extant pieces are many that have been carefully signed and dated by some of the most prominent names in later Japanese painting, among them Kano Tan'yū, Hokusai, and Maruyama Ōkyo.

kotodama

A belief, reflected in the earliest Japanese sources, that a sacred power or spirit dwells in the traditional Japanese language. Particularly when expressed in forms such as *norito* (ritual prayers) or *waka* poetry, it was believed

響を及ぼすと信じられた。したがって、言葉の力を適切に使うには、よかれあしかれ、十分な注意が必要とされた。

アニミズム

自然物、自然現象、宇宙そのものに霊魂が存在し、人間に影響を与えるという信仰。日本人は、明らかに有史以前から「霊」「神」「霊」と呼ばれる霊を信じていた。その定義ははっきりしないが、自然現象と関係していた。『古事記』と『万葉集』には太陽神「大日孁貴」、月の神「月読」、山の神「山祇」、海の神「海神」が出てくる。また、「木霊」、「言霊」の「霊」への信仰もあった。それぞれ名前と特徴を与えられた神々は、「神」とか「尊」と呼ばれた。これらの神々は、神ほど明確な定義のない霊とともに、自然と人間に対する支配力をもっていると考えられた。このような信仰は、日本人と自然の関係に、精神的特質を与え続けているのである。

that Japanese words could exert a special influence on people, the gods, and even the course of the world. Extreme care thus needed to be taken to utilize the power of words properly, for good or for ill.

animism

(*animizumu*). Belief in the existence of a spiritual life in natural objects, natural phenomena, and the universe itself that is capable of exercising an influence on human beings. The Japanese have apparently believed in spirits called *chi, mi,* or *tama*—which, although not clearly defined, were associated with natural phenomena—since prehistoric times. The *Kojiki* and the *Man'yōshu* both refer to the sun god Ōhirume no Mu*chi,* the moon god Tsukiyo*mi,* the mountain god Yamatsu*mi,* and the ocean god Wadatsu*mi.* There was also a belief in such *tama* as *kodama* (the spirit of the trees) and *kotodama* (the spirit of words). Gods given individual designations and characteristics were called *kami* or *mikoto.* These gods as well as less clearly defined spirits were thought to have control over natural and human phenomena. Such beliefs have continued to endow the Japanese relationship to nature with a particular spiritual quality.

第七章

日本文化と動物

Animals in Japanese Culture

日本文化と動物

植物の場合と同様、一年を通じての動物の生活は、「自然の暦」であり、芸術作品の主題にもなってきた。日本人が動物に抱く印象と思想には、中国文化の影響が明らかに見てとれる。日本人の動物観は、おもに二つの要素に影響を受けている。自然と環境、および伝統文化と外国文化の影響である。

　幸運と長寿を表す鶴亀や、必ず戻ってくる燕等の動物象徴には、中国の古典の影響が見られる。中世（13〜16世紀）後半になると、日本固有の動物の象徴が出てきた。加えて、19世紀終わりまで、日本人の多くは肉を食べず、四つ足の動物を殺さなかった。この思想は、仏教の教えからきたものである。また、日本人の動物観には、古代中国の暦法、十干十二支の果たす役割も見逃せない。十二支にはそれぞれ異なった動物があてられた。今日でも、自分の生年を、グレゴリオ歴と元号に加えて、十二支で表す。

Animals in Japanese Culture

As in the case of plants, the lives of animals through the course of a year have provided a "natural calendar" and offered themselves as subjects for works of art. In the images and ideas the Japanese entertain about animals, there are clear signs of the influence that Chinese culture exercised on the native culture of early Japan. Japanese perspectives on animals have been affected largely by two factors: natural and environmental conditions, and traditional and imported cultural influences.

Such traditional animal symbols as cranes and turtles (for felicity and long life) and swallows (for faithful return) were adopted from the Chinese. It was not until the latter half of the medieval period (13th–16th centuries) that a truly Japanese set of animal symbols evolved. In addition, up until the late 19th century, the vast majority of Japanese did not eat meat or slaughter four-legged animals; they relied chiefly on fish for animal protein. These views derived mainly from Buddhist teachings. Finally, the Japanese view of animals includes the role played by the *jikkan jūnishi*, or the sexagenary cycle of the ancient Chinese calendrical system. The cycle is broken down into subcycles of 12 years, each year of which is represented by an animal. Even today the Japanese think of the date of their birth in terms of the year in the sexagenary cycle ("the year of the dragon," "the year of the tiger," and so forth) in addition to the date according to the Gregorian calendar and the imperial reign date.

猫

日本の文学には、猫を書いた作品が多く、
『今昔物語集』には、猫をこわがる男の話が
ある。夏目漱石の『我輩は猫である』では、
皮肉な言い方をすれば、観察眼の鋭い猫が主
人公と語り手をかねている。日本各地に、猫
は殺されると仇討ちをするという俗信があ
り、「化け猫」物語というジャンルが生まれ
た。招き猫は片方の前脚を、まるで人を差し
招くようにあげていて、店に客を招き、富を
もたらすと言われる。

犬

犬の伝承は、日本全国にあるが、特に山岳地
帯の猟師や農民に顕著である。この、宗教が
かった呪術的な信仰は、狼崇拝と結びついて
いるのかもしれない。日本では狼はよく山犬
と混同され、崇拝の対象も、狼と犬が入れ替
わることがある。後に、これら動物の崇拝は、
農村でところを得、犬や狼の霊は山の神が姿
を変えたもので農作物を野獣から守ってくれ
るという信仰を形成した。これが後に、犬と
狼は、火事、泥棒、難産などを防いでくれる
という信仰につながった。伝統的な犬の玩具
犬張り子は、初め赤子から悪霊を追い払うお
まじないとして使われた。「狐憑き」のとき

cats

(*neko*). There are many stories about cats in Japanese literature, such as the one in the *Konjaku monogatari* about a man who was afraid of cats. An observant, if cynical, cat was made the central character and narrator in *Wagahai wa neko de aru* (*I Am a Cat*) by Natsume Sōseki. As in many other countries in Japan, there is a folk belief that cats when killed will avenge themselves, and a whole subgenre of stories about "monster cats" (*bakeneko*) has sprung up. In folk art, the *manekineko*, a cat figurine with one of its forepaws raised as if to beckon, is believed to draw customers to a shop and bring riches to the owner.

dog

(*inu*). Dog lore has been widespread in Japan, especially among hunters and farmers in mountainous regions. Some of these religious and magical beliefs may be connected with wolf cults. Since the wolf in Japan has often been confused with the feral dog (*yama inu*), the object of the cult also alternated between wolf and dog. Later, the worship of these animals found a place in agricultural society as dog–wolf spirits came to embody a familiar spirit of *yama no kami*, or "mountain god," that could protect crops from wild beasts. This idea was later extended to the belief that they provided protection from fire, theft, or difficult childbirth. It is likely that the traditional dog's toy, *inu hariko,* was originally

には、犬または狼の頭蓋骨が、悪霊を追い出
すと信じられた。こういう信仰の裏返しとし
て、まじないをしたり呪いをかけるときに、
犬神が人に乗り移ることもあった。犬や狼は、
超自然の物語にも登場し、妖怪のような神秘
的な力を発揮する。犬は人を守り優しいとさ
れているが、現実の犬の扱いは必ずしもそれ
にふさわしくない。野良犬が町中をうろつく
ことも多かったし、野卑で臆病なふるまいを、
「犬のような」と軽蔑的に表現することがあ
る。

狐

日本人は、古代から、狐は霊的な力を持って
いて、人間を化かすと考えてきた。それは、
狐がきわめて巧みに危険を逃れる能力を持っ
ているためであろう。狐は、人をだましたり
誘惑する女に化けることのできる気味の悪い
動物として恐れられた。このことは、12世
紀の宮廷の女性、玉藻の前の話に出てくる。
彼女は、実は、為政者をたぶらかすために美
女に化けた老いた雄狐だとされた。女に化け
て男と結婚する狐の話は民話に多い。狐はそ
のほかにも、多くの民話や伝説に出てくるが、
神秘的力を発揮し、きわめて賢い動物とされ
ている。狐は五穀の神の稲荷の使いとされ、
好物は、油揚げだといわれる。

used as a charm to keep evil spirits away from babies. In cases of possession by the fox spirit (*kitsune tsuki*), dog or wolf skulls were often used to drive out the intruding spirits. In an inversion of these beliefs, the *inu-gami* (dog spirit) was sometimes appealed to in voodoolike practices or in order to invoke a curse. Dogs and wolves also figure in supernatural tales, in which they sometimes have a ghostlike, mysterious power. The dog spirit was generally thought of as protective and benevolent, but the treatment of the real animals was more ambivalent. Stray dogs often roamed city streets, and there are derogatory phrases in Japanese referring to vulgar or cowardly behavior as "doglike."

foxes

(*kitsune*). Since ancient times the Japanese have thought foxes had spiritual powers and were capable of bewitching people, perhaps because of the extreme deftness with which they escape danger. The uncanny fox was particularly to be feared because he could turn himself into a beguiling and seductive woman. This is exemplified by the twelfth-century court lady Tamamo no Mae, who was alleged to be really an old fox who had turned himself into a beautiful woman in order to tempt the ruler. The story of a fox marrying a man by assuming the shape of a woman is found in many folktales. Foxes also appear in innumerable other folktales and legends, in which they are described as having various occult powers and as being extremely clever. Foxes are thought to be messenger of Inari, the deity of cereals. Their

馬

馬を神に奉納する宗教的習慣は、古代にまで
さかのぼる。今日でも、神馬といわれる馬を
飼っている神社があり、祭りの行列などに参
加する。中世の武士にとって良い馬は欠かす
ことのできないものであった。軍記物には馬
がよく登場する。武士が馬に乗って弓矢を射
る流鏑馬や笠懸は、鎌倉時代に発達した。平
穏な江戸時代にも、大名たちは馬の育成に励
んだが、南部藩産の馬は、とくに珍重された。
京都の賀茂神社では、競馬の儀式が、中世か
ら今日まで行われている。

猿

日本人にとって、猿はかしこく親しみのもて
るおどけものである。古代神話には、猿田彦
の大神の話が出てくるが、猿を神の使いとす
る神社も少なくない。昔話の猿は敵役になる
ことが多いが、かならずへまをしてばかをみ
る。猿は、馬に病気を近づけないという迷信
から、馬小屋の柱につなぐ習慣ができた。こ
の迷信は近代まで続き、馬小屋の壁に猿の絵
を貼ったり、干した猿の手が馬の病気を治す
という信仰や、猿の頭蓋骨を馬小屋の地下に

favorite food is thought to be fried tōfu (bean curd).

horses

(*uma*). The religious custom of dedicating horses to Shintō gods dates back to ancient times. Even today, horses known as *shimme* (divine horses) are kept by Shintō shrines and paraded on festival days. In medieval times a fine horse was indispensable to a warrior; the horse figures frequently in military chronicles. Military arts such as *yabusame* and *kasagake*, for warriors using bow and arrow on horseback, developed in the Kamakura period. Even in times of peace like the Edo period, *daimyō* were enthusiastic horse breeders. Horses bred in the Nambu domain were particularly sought after. Horse races (*kurabe uma*) of a ceremonial nature have been performed at the Kamo shrines in Kyōto since medieval times.

monkeys

(*saru*). To the Japanese the monkey is a clever and friendly buffoon. Japanese myth contains mention of a monkey deity, Sarutahiko, and some Shintō shrines treat the monkey as a divine messenger. In folktales the monkey often plays the role of an adversary, but invariably blunders and ends the fool. A superstition that monkeys had the power to keep diseases away from horses gave rise to the custom of keeping a monkey tied to a post in stables. This superstition survived until modern times in such forms as a picture of a monkey

埋める習慣などとして、残っている。祈禱師の祈禱と猿の踊りが病気の馬を治すと信じられ、ここから猿回しが発生したといわれる。

兎

兎は古来ずるがしこい動物とされ、民話の中では、ペテン師として登場する。そのもっとも古い例が、『古事記』の「因幡の白兎」である。満月の月面では、兎が餅をついていると信じられている。

鼠

日本人にとって、鼠は両義的な存在である。有害生物としてきらわれる一方で、富を授け守ってくれる七福神の一人、大黒天の使者としてあがめられもするのである。これは、たぶん、家や穀物倉に鼠がいるということは、食料が豊富であるあかしだからであろう。今日でも、子年の年賀状には、鼠は金貨・銀貨および米俵といっしょに描かれる。

狸

狸は超自然の力を持つずるい動物として、狐と比較されてきた。しかし、狐とくらべると、

pasted on stable walls, the belief that the touch of a dried monkey's hand would heal horses' diseases, and the practice of burying a monkey's skull under stables. Faith healers, whose prayers and dancing monkeys were thought to cure ailing horses, are said to have originated monkey shows (*sarumawashi*).

rabbits

(*usagi*). The rabbit has traditionally been regarded as a cunning animal and is a familiar trickster figure in Japanese folktales, the earliest example being the "White Hare of Inaba" in the *Kojiki*. It is believed that a rabbit pounding rice can be seen in the full moon.

rats and mice

(*nezumi*). The *nezumi* has always been viewed ambiguously by the Japanese. Detested as a pest, it has also been held in high esteem as the messenger of Daikokuten, one of the Seven Lucky Gods, who bestows and protects wealth. Perhaps this is because the presence of the *nezumi* in houses and granaries is a sign of abundant provender. Even now, the *nezumi* is depicted together with gold and silver coins and bags of rice on New Year's cards for the Year of the Rat.

tanuki

(raccoon dog). The *tanuki* has long been compared with the fox in Japan as a crafty animal that possesses

恐ろしいというよりも、滑稽な動物とされている。狸は昔話によく出てくるが、なかでも有名なのが、『文福茶釜』で、狸は、罠から救ってくれた人に恩返しをする。日本人は昔から、狸の肉は食用にし、その毛で筆を作った。狸を使った表現も数多い。中には、ずるい人のやりとりを言う「狐と狸の化かしあい」や、悪賢い人を表す「狸親父」とか「古狸」等である。

猪

猪は、日本の野生動物の中で、熊と並んでもっとも獰猛である。その激しく直進する攻撃は、結果を考えない激しい行為のたとえとされている。ひたすら攻めるだけで退却しない武士を「猪武者」とよび、短く太い首を「猪首」という。

鮑

鮑は、日本の文学では数限りないたとえや比喩で、片恋いをその一枚貝にたとえて描写する詩的イメージとして使われた。繰り返し使われるうちに、和歌の常套的な比喩になった。このように、鮑は報われない愛と関連づけられてきたので、現代の諺にもこの観念は反映されている。結婚披露宴では、二枚貝は出さ

supernatural powers, but unlike the fox it is considered amusing rather than fearsome. It appears in many folk songs and tales, the most famous of which is probably the folktale *Bumbuku chagama*, in which a *tanuki*, freed from a trap, repays his liberator's kindness. Since ancient times the Japanese have caught the *tanuki* for its meat and used its fur for brushes. There are many sayings involving the *tanuki*, such as *kitsune to tanuki no bakashi ai* (a fox and a *tanuki* outfoxing each other), referring to dealings between sly persons; and *tanuki oyaji* or *furudanuki*, referring to a crafty person.

wild boar

(*inoshishi*). The *inoshishi* rivals the bear as the most ferocious of Japan's wild animals. Its fierce, direct charge has become a common metaphor for strong action that ignores consequences. Warriors who only attacked and never retreated were once known as *inoshishi musha* (wild-boar *samurai*), and a short, thick neck is described as a "wild boar's neck" (*ikubi*).

abalone

(*awabi*). The *awabi* was pressed into service early as a poetic image in Japanese literature. Countless similes or conceits describe a parallel between one-sided love and the univalve (single) shell of the abalone. Often repeated, this elaborate parallel became a fixed conceit in the practice of the Japanese *waka*. Thus the abalone has long been associated with unrequited love, a notion that is

れるが、鮑は不吉な、あるいは避けるべきものと考えられている。結婚式では避けられるものの、めでたさの象徴として、薄く伸ばし乾燥した鮑を熨斗として神の供物に添える習慣がある。

蟹（かに）

昔から日本人は、蟹は何度も脱皮することや失われた脚が再生することから、蟹には不思議な生命力があると考えた。古代の書物には、蟹は生命力と再生の象徴として、しばしば登場する。沖縄には、蟹の生命力と再生への信仰から、赤ん坊が生まれると、体のうえに蟹を這わせる風習がある。近代以前の日本では、甲羅に人間の顔に似た文様のある蟹は亡霊と考えられた。ラフカディオ・ハーンの『骨董』に出てくる平家蟹は、この信仰の例である。ほかにも似たような伝説は多い。

海老

日本では、鏡餅に御飾海老（おかざりえび）と称するゆでた赤い伊勢海老と橙（だいだい）をのせウラジロと昆布を添えて三宝にのせて、正月の飾り物にした。地方によっては、家の入り口や門に伊勢海老を飾ったが、今でもこの風習を守っている家もあ

still reflected in a current proverb. In marriage customs of early modern Japanese society, clams (bivalved or double shelled) were served at weddings, whereas abalone was considered an inauspicious or taboo food on such occasions. Although *awabi* was shunned at weddings, it has long been an auspicious symbol when used as *noshi*— flattened, dried strips of the flesh fastened to offerings to the gods.

crabs

(*kani*). The early Japanese sensed a mysterious and vital power in the frequent shedding of shells and regeneration of torn-off limbs by the crab, and crabs appear as symbols of the life force and regeneration in many early writings. Until the modern period there was in Okinawa a folk custom of letting a crab crawl on a baby's body at the time of delivery, presumably because of the belief in the crab's life-giving powers. In premodern Japan a crab with a pattern resembling a human face on its shell was thought to be a ghost; the *heikegani* mentioned in Lafcadio Hearn's *Kottō* is an example of this belief, and many similar legends are extant.

shrimps, prawns, and lobsters

(*ebi*). In the premodern period, deep red, boiled rock lobsters called *okazari ebi* ("decoration lobsters") were placed on round rice cakes, and these, along with bitter oranges, ferns, and sea seaweed, would be put on a small wooden stand as a New Year's decoration. In

る。海老を正月や結婚式のおめでたい飾り物とする伝統的な風習は、海老の曲がった腰を老人になぞらえ、長寿を象徴するところからきた。また、海老の定期的な脱皮は生命の再生を象徴した。同じ理由で、成人式に海老を食べる習慣もある。

鶯

日本人は、昔から、哀調に満ちた鶯の鳴き声を愛してきた。その鳴き声を、日本人は、ホーホケキョと発音し、幸運と喜びをもたらすと考えた。鶯の別名、春鳥、春告鳥、初音、花見鳥などは、二月から三月にかけて野や町で鳴き始める鶯が春の季節にいかに重要であるかを示している。文人や画家はとくに「鶯と梅」の組み合わせを珍重したが、これは明らかに中国の影響であった。鶯は、和歌や俳句、あるいは絵に、竹、柳、桜、松などとともにしばしば取り上げられる。

ほかの小鳥が七月には鳴かなくなるのに対し、鶯は九月はじめまで鳴き続ける。清少納言は、「夏の終わりまで老いた声で鳴く」と鶯を非難するが、江戸時代には、八月を過ぎ

some regions, rock lobsters were used to decorate the entrances or gates of homes; this custom is still practiced in some households. The traditional conception of the *ebi* as an auspicious creature on occasions such as the New Year and wedding ceremonies may have derived from the idea that its bent back symbolizes old age and thus a long life, but it may also be due to the *ebi*'s periodic shedding of its shell, which came to symbolize the renewal of life. These beliefs explain the traditional custom of eating shrimp during coming-of-age ceremonies.

bush warbler

(*uguisu*). The Japanese people have long loved the plaintive, whistling song of the *uguisu*, which they pronounce as *hōhokekyo*; to them it signifies good luck and rejoicing. Other names for the *uguisu*, such as "spring bird" (*harudori*), "spring-announcing bird" (*harutsugedori*), "first song" (*hatsune*), and "flower-viewing bird" (*hanamidori*), indicate its seasonal significance when it begins to sing in fields and towns around February or March. In particular, Japanese literati and artists have prized the combination of "warblers and plum blossoms," an aesthetic theme apparently borrowed from China. The bird appears frequently in Japanese poetry and art as a motif paired with bamboo, willows, cherry trees, or pine.

Unlike most other small birds, which stop singing around July, the *uguisu* continues to sing until early September. Sei Shōnagon criticized the bird for "crying in an aging voice until the end of summer," but in the

た季節はずれの鶯の声は優雅であると考えられた。

鶏

古墳時代の動物埴輪(はにわ)には、馬に次いで鶏の形をしたものが多い。現代語では「にわとり」とよぶが、古い呼び名は「かけ」であった。古い文献では、「かけ」には、「庭つ鶏(にわどり)」とか「家つ鶏(いえどり)」という形容語が前につけられていたが、しだいに「かけ」が落ちて形容語が独立していったと思われる。

　鶏は、古代の民間信仰によく登場し、易断や生贄(いけにえ)に供された。「天の岩戸」神話には、太陽神天照大神が、ほかの神々のおどけ声や鶏の鳴き声で、隠れた岩の祠から出てきた様が書かれている。鶏の鳴き声は、日の出、つまり、闇の終わりを知らせるので、鶏が悪霊や不幸を追い払うという信仰にもつながっていった。その結果、葬式でも使われ、古墳時代の埴輪に鶏が多かったことと関係している。

鶴

鶴、とりわけ丹頂鶴は、長い間めでたい鳥と考えられ、「鶴は千年亀は万年」という諺に

poetry of the Edo period, the "out-of-season" song of the *uguisu* after August was considered quite elegant.

chicken

(*niwatori*). Many *haniwa* (a clay figurine) pottery figures from the Kofun period represent chickens; their incidence is second only to that of horse figures among the animal *haniwa*. The current Japanese word for chicken is *niwatori*, but a much older term is *kake*. In many ancient texts, the word *kake* is preceded by an epithet such as *niwatsudori* or *ietsudori*, and it is likely that the former gradually gained independent usage, without the noun *kake*.

Chickens figured prominently in folk beliefs in ancient times, being used for divination or sacrificial purposes. In Japanese mythology, the tale called "Ama no iwato" relates how the sun goddess, Amaterasu, was coaxed out of a cave where she had hidden by the antics of other gods and goddesses and the voices of crowing cocks. Since the crowing of cocks signifies the rising sun—that is, the end of darkness—this led to the belief that chickens could drive away evil spirits or misfortune. They have consequently gained a role in funerals, which may also explain their prominence in the early *haniwa* figures.

cranes

(*tsuru*). Cranes, particularly the *tanchō*, have long been regarded as auspicious birds and are a popular symbol of

証明されているように、長寿の象徴として広く知られてきた。「鶴の一声」は、行き詰まりを打開する、高所からの決定を表している。鶴はまた、家紋、菓子、商標などの文様としても広く使われている。「鶴女房」伝説では、男に助けられた鶴が美しい女に変身し、男の嫁となる。

烏

日本では、烏は神々の使者であると考えられていた。『古事記』には、神武天皇の軍の道案内をつとめる烏が出てくる。名古屋の熱田神宮と滋賀県の多賀神社では、神の使者に対する報酬として烏に餅をそなえる儀式が今も行われている。

雲雀（ひばり）

雲雀の鳴き声は、昔から好まれ、たたえられてきた。雲雀はまた、愛玩用としても珍重され、飼い慣らした雲雀を空に放し、飛びながらどれだけ長時間鳴けるか、どの雲雀が降りて鳥かごに一番早く戻ってくるかを「揚雲雀（あげひばり）」で競った。

longevity, as attested by the saying, "The crane lives for a thousand years and the tortoise for ten thousand." The expression "voice of the crane"' is used to describe a decision from on high that breaks a deadlock. The crane is also a popular decorative motif in family crests, confections, and trademarks. In addition, there is a body of "crane wife" (*Tsuru nyōbō*) legends, in which a captive crane, in return for being freed by a youth, turns into a maiden and marries him.

crows

(*karasu*). The Japanese have long considered the crow a messenger of the gods. In the *Kojiki* there is mention of a crow which served as a guide for the army of the legendary emperor Jimmu. At the Atsuta Shrine (in the city of Nagoya) and the Taga Shrine (in Shiga Prefecture), ceremonies are held in which crows are given offerings of rice cakes, probably as a reward for being couriers of the gods.

larks

(*hibari*). The song of the lark has been loved and celebrated since ancient times in Japan. Larks were also prized as pets, and there was a type of amusement called *agehibari* in which tame larks were released and their owners watched to see how long they would sing in flight and which bird would return first to its cage after descending.

雉

美しい姿とその特徴ある鳴き声で、長年珍重されてきた雉は、第二次世界大戦後、国の鳥に指定された。『古事記』『日本書紀』『万葉集』にも詠まれている。雉は吉兆の鳥とされ、大化6年（西暦650年）に白い雉が朝廷に献上されたとき、年号を白雉と改元した。また、勇気の象徴とみなされ、蛇を食ったり地震を予知すると信じられている。

雀

日本の文学で雀の記述は『古事記』に初めて見られるが、そこではある種の超自然的力を与えられている。清少納言は、雀を愛すべきもののなかに数え、宮廷文学に現れる風物のなかでは、きわめて高い地位を与えられている。人間の親切に宝物で恩返しする有名な昔話「舌切り雀」の原形は、『宇治拾遺物語』に記されている。雀は、小林一茶のような俳人にも好まれている。

pheasants

(*kiji*). Long prized in Japan for its beautiful appearance and its unique call, the *kiji* was designated the national bird after World War II. It appears in poems in the *Kojiki* and *Nihon shoki*, and *Man'yōshu*. It was considered a bird of good omen, as is evidenced in the decision in Taika 6 (A.D. 650) to change the era name to Hakuchi (white pheasant) after a white pheasant (a mutation) was discovered and presented to the imperial court. The pheasant was also regarded as a symbol of courage, being reputed to devour snakes and to be able to foretell earthquakes.

sparrows

(*suzume*). The *suzume* is first mentioned in Japanese literature in the *Kojiki*, in an account that attributes to it certain supernatural powers. Sei Shōnagon categorized the sparrow among things that are lovable and it occupies an especially high place in the fauna of court literature. The familiar folktale *Shitakiri suzume* (The Tongue-Cut Sparrow), about a sparrow which repays kindness with fortune, is found in the *Uji shūi monogatari*. The *suzume* has also been a favorite bird of Japanese poets like the haiku poet Kobayashi Issa.

燕
つばめ

燕は人家に巣を作り、同じつがいが春ごとに同じ家に帰ってくることから、日本人は「聖なる鳥」とあがめるようになった。燕の到来は、命の再生と暖かい春の印として歓迎され、農業の年間のサイクルの大切な区切りとされてきた。日本の美術や文学に燕が取り上げられることは意外に少ないが、日常生活では長年親しまれ、燕が巣を作った家には幸運が訪れると考えられた。燕は、また、母性の象徴とされているが、これは、中国の古典文学からの影響と思われる。

蛙

蛙の鳴き声は、日本人の季節感に合うので、昔から喜ばれている。冬の終わりは、まだ冷たい池や湿地から聞こえてくる蛙の求愛の声によって告げられる。春の水田の殿様蛙の合唱、夏、雨が近づくのを知らせる雨蛙の大きな鳴き声、初秋の河鹿蛙の高い鳴き声などは、それぞれに趣があり、しばしば和歌や俳句に登場する。『古事記』にも出てくる蟇蛙は、後年になると、月を飲み込んで、月食を引き起こす力を持っていると信じられ、「地の守護霊」として知られる。

swallows

(*tsubame*). Because barn swallows have the unusual habit of building their nests in people's houses and because pairs of swallows may return to the same house spring after spring, they came to be revered by the Japanese people as "sacred birds." Their arrival was welcomed as a joyful sign of the rebirth of life and warmth in the spring and constituted an important stage in the annual agricultural cycle. The swallow has appeared relatively infrequently as a theme in Japanese art and literature, but it has long been a familiar bird in daily life, and its taking up residence in a house was considered a sign of good fortune. It has also been a symbol of motherhood, an idea probably borrowed from classical Chinese literature.

frogs

(*kaeru*). The croaking of the frog appeals to the Japanese sense of season and has been much admired since early times. The end of winter is signaled by the frog's mating call, heard from the still chilly ponds and swamps; the chorus of the *tonosamagaeru* bullfrog in the paddy fields in spring, the loud voices of the *amagaeru* heralding the approach of rain in summer, and the higher-pitched voice of the *kajikagaeru* early in autumn are all considered extremely evocative and have been celebrated in innumerable poems. The *hikigaeru* (toad) appears in the *Kojiki* and, in later ages it was believed that this frog had the power to cause a lunar cclipsc by

蛇

蛇は脱皮することから、昔から永遠の生命を
持つとあがめられた。春に現れるので田の神
とされ、秋には冬眠のために山に帰るので、
山の神とされた。また、鼠などを捕るので、
家の守り神ともされた。最近まで、鼠を捕ら
せるため、青大将を住まわせている古い家さ
えあった。後に蛇は嫌われるようになったが、
その理由の一つは、『今昔物語集』にあるよ
うに、蛇が女性を襲うという俗信による。

亀

「鶴は千年、亀は万年」という諺にあるよう
に、亀は幸運の運び手であり、長命の象徴と
考えられてきた。甲羅に藻の生えた海亀はも
っともめでたいとされた。水中にゆらめく藻
は、あごひげを生やした翁、したがって長命
を連想させたのである。海岸に打ち上げられ
た青海亀に酒を飲ませるという習慣が昔から
あったが、これは、その長命をたたえるとと
もに、青海亀が海神の使者と考えられていた
ためである。亀は、日本の昔話によく登場す

swallowing the moon. It was known as the "guardian spirit of the earth."

snakes

(*hebi*). In ancient times, snakes were venerated as beings possessed of eternal life because of their ability to shed an old skin and grow a new one. The snake was regarded as a deity of paddy fields, where it appears in the spring, as a mountain deity, since it returns to the mountains in autumn for hibernation, and also as a guardian deity of houses, probably because it kills vermin. Until recent years the habit of letting the *aodaishō* (blue-green snake) live in old houses to eat rats persisted. Snakes gradually came to be detested in later times for a variety of reasons, one of which was the idea that they could violate women, as was described in the *Konjaku monogatari*.

turtles

(*kame*). As indicated by the proverb "a crane lives a thousand and a turtle ten thousand years," the turtle has traditionally been regarded as a symbol of longevity as well as a bearer of good fortune. Marine turtles with algae growing on their shells were regarded as most auspicious: the algae waving in the water reminded viewers of a bearded old man and, thus, longevity. There persisted the custom of giving drinks of *sake* to *aoumigame* (green turtle) that landed on the seashore, presumably in honor of their supposed great age or because the

るが、その中でも有名なのが『浦島太郎』である。

蝶

『日本書紀』によると、朝廷は、揚羽蝶（あげはちょう）の幼虫が神であるとする道教の俗信を禁止した。平安時代中期になると、清少納言が『枕草子』に書いているように、蝶は「愛すべきもの」とされた。紫式部は『源氏物語』で、源氏の宮殿、六条院を飾る蝶のことを書いている。『堤中納言物語』には、虫めづる姫君の話があるが、その昆虫には蝶も含まれている。室町時代以降、蝶の文様は家具や武具の装飾によく用いられた。

蜻蛉（とんぼ）

『古事記』の神話によると、伊弉諾（いざなぎ）と伊弉冉（いざなみ）の間に日本列島が生まれ、最大の島は、大日本豊秋津洲（おおやまととよあきづしま）と呼ばれた。秋津は「蜻蛉」を意味すると考えられている。この神話は、『日本書紀』に出てくる秋津とともに、蜻蛉が初期大和朝廷の権力とその支配地域の象徴であることを示している。なお、蜻蛉は、稲の霊であり、豊作の前兆とされていた。日本人の蜻蛉好きは、多くの詩歌に表現されているが、

turtle was believed to be a messenger of the sea god. Turtles appear in many Japanese folktales, among which the story *Urashima Tarō* is the most famous.

butterflies

(*chō*). According to the *Nihon shoki*, the government proscribed a popular variant of Taoism that venerated the larva of the swallowtail butterfly as a god. By the middle of the Heian period the butterfly had come to be regarded as "something lovable," as Sei Shōnagon fondly describes it in her *Makura no sōshi*. Her contemporary Murasaki Shikibu, wrote in *The Tale of Genji* of butterflies adorning Genji's palace, Rokujōin. The *Tsutsumi Chūnagon monogatari* contains a story about a young lady of noble birth who loved insects, among them butterflies. From the Muromachi period on, the butterfly became a popular motif in decorating furniture and armor.

dragonflies

(*tombo*). According to Japanese mythology as recorded in the *Kojiki*, the marriage of the deities Izanagi and Izanami resulted in the birth of the Japanese islands, of which the largest island was called Ōyamato Toyo Akizu Shima; the word *akizu* (or *akitsu*) in this name is thought to mean "dragonfly." This myth, together with episodes involving *akizu* in the *Nihon shoki*, suggests that the dragonfly (which was believed to be the spirit of the rice plant and a harbinger of rich harvests) was a symbol

中でももっとも有名なのが、三木露風の『赤とんぼ』である。

蛍

日本では、蛍は、中国の貧しい学者が燈油が買えないので、夏の夜蛍の光で勉強したという伝説と結びつけられている。『万葉集』にも多く詠まれ、蛍は情熱的な愛のたとえに用いられている。清少納言は「おかしきもの」の筆頭に、月のない夏の夜の蛍をあげている。『源氏物語』では、源氏の弟君蛍宮は、蛍の光で初めて玉鬘を見るのである。民間信仰では、生きている人間の魂と死んだ人間の幽霊は蛍の形をしているという。蛍狩りの風習は、江戸時代に盛んになった。

蜘蛛

日本の民話では、蜘蛛は悪者や逃亡者の役回りをするが、これは、洞穴に住んで朝廷に反抗したという伝説の部族土蜘蛛と関連づけて考えたためであろう。この蜘蛛伝説は、さまざまな無気味な物語の材料に使われたり、能や歌舞伎の作品にもなっている。

both of the power of the early Yamato court and of the territory over which its power extended. The fondness of the Japanese for these insects is well expressed in many poems, perhaps the best known of which is "Akatombo" ("Red Dragonflies") by Miki Rofū.

fireflies

(*hotaru*). The *hotaru* has long been associated in Japan with the Chinese legend of a poor scholar who, unable to afford lamp oil, studied by the glow of fireflies in the summer. In numerous poems in the *Man'yōshū*, the *hotaru* is a metaphor for passionate love. At the top of her list of "attractive things," Sei Shōnagon put fireflies on a moonless summer night. In *The Tale of Genji*, Prince Hotaru, Genji's half-brother, catches his first glimpse of Lady Tamakazura by the light of fireflies. According to a folk belief, the spirit of a living person or the ghost of a deceased person assumes the shape of the *hotaru*. Firefly viewing (*hotarugari*) became a popular pastime during the Edo period.

spiders

(*kumo*). Japanese folklore frequently casts the spider in the role of the villain or the pursued, probably because of the association of spiders with a legendary race of cave dwellers known as *tsuchigumo* (literally, "earth spiders"). Such spider legends have been used as material for various macabre tales and are a theme in Nō and *kabuki* plays.

日本文化と植物

Plants in Japanese Culture

文学と植物

花鳥風月という言葉で表される自然の美は、日本文学、とりわけ和歌と俳句では、中心的な主題である。また、この言葉の最初に花がくるのは、偶然ではない。『万葉集』の約四千五百首の歌のうち、ほぼ三分の一が植物を主題とするか、なんらかの形で植物を取り上げている。西暦1000年ごろ書かれ、その卓越した自然描写で知られる『源氏物語』には、百一種類の植物が登場する。樹木や植物をもののたとえによく用いるのが、日本文学の特徴の一つである。

　日本人にとって自然は、鑑賞の対象であるとともに、強い詩的感興を喚起する源でもある。日本人は、花を、その香りや色からよりも、その姿や情緒的意味から愛でてきた。日本人は詩歌の中でとりわけ四季を大切にするが、これは移ろいやすくかつ不変の自然のしるしとしての植物のきめ細かな観察と植物への愛着の表れである。日本人のこの植物に対する態度を理解することは、伝統的日本文学の鑑賞には欠かすことができない。

植物と宗教

古代日本人は、自然を神聖なものと考えた。彼らは、山、川、岩、植物などはすべて霊魂を持っていると考えてそれを崇拝し救いを求

plants in literature

(*bungaku to shokubutsu*). The beauty of nature, embodied in the term *kachō fūgetsu* ("flowers, birds, wind, and moon"), is a principal theme in Japanese literature, especially in *waka* and *haiku*. The fact that flowers have been given first place in this phrase does not seem coincidental: of the approximately 4,500 poems in the *Man'yōshū*, about one-third have plants as their main themes or in some way refer to plants. The *Tale of Genji*, written about the year 1000 and noted for its superb descriptions of nature, makes reference to 101 kinds of plants. Frequent use of trees and plants in similes is a characteristic of Japanese literature.

For the Japanese, nature has been not only an object of aesthetic appreciation but also an agent evoking intense poetic sentiments. They have loved flowers not so much for their fragrance and color as for their form and emotional import. The special significance Japanese have attached to the seasons in their poetry is an expression of their close observation of and affection for plants as signs of the ever-vanishing, ever-perpetuating pattern of nature. An understanding of this attitude is essential to the appreciation of traditional Japanese literature.

plants and religion

The early Japanese worshiped nature as divine. They believed that natural features such as mountains, rivers, stones, and plants all had spirits and they offered prayers

めた。常緑樹には神が住むと考え、宗教儀礼には松や榊を供えた。また獣の肉の代わりに、海産物（海草、魚、貝）や生の野菜が供えられた。神社に神を呼び出して、依代とするための榊を供える風習は、今でも行われている。松は正月の門松として使われるが、年の始めに幸運を運ぶ神の依代とされる。竹と栗が門松に使われることもある。仏教は殺生を禁じたので、仏教の儀式では、花や植物が使われたが、その習慣は今も続いている。

植物と民間伝承

古代農民は、自然災害を恐れた。災害を避けるため、人々は悪魔払い、沐浴、占いなどの宗教儀式を行った。このような神事や自然畏敬から、木や花を聖なるものの象徴とみなすようになった。そのよい例が、ひろく行われた常緑樹崇拝である。古代日本人は、松、杉、檜、楠などの常緑樹を、天から降った神の住み着くところだと信じた。霊は花にも住むとされ、その年の収穫を予想して、「花占い」が行われた。桜、卯の花、躑躅、それに馬酔木がよく咲く年は豊作で、花が早く散ってしまう年は凶作と考えられた。

to and sought salvation from them. For religious festivals, evergreen trees such as pines and *sakaki* were offered because they were thought to be the dwelling places of gods, and marine products (seaweed, fish, and shellfish) and fresh farm vegetables were offered to the deities instead of animal flesh. It is still customary in Shintō rituals to offer *sakaki,* sacred branches to summon and offer habitation (*yorishiro*) for gods. The pine is used as a New Year's *kadomatsu* ("gate pine"), which serves as a dwelling place for the god who brings good luck at the beginning of the year. Bamboo and Japanese chestnut are among other types of tree used in *kadomatsu*. Buddhism banned the destruction of living creatures, so flowers and plants were used for its rituals, a practice that is still followed.

plants and folklore

The early Japanese farmer dreaded natural disasters. In the hope of avoiding them, communities formulated sacred rites of exorcism, ablution, and divination. These mystico-religious activities, and awe of nature in general, led people to see in trees and flowers symbols of the divine. An excellent example is the once widely practiced worship of primeval evergreen trees—pines, cedars (*sugi*), cypresses (*hinoki*), and camphor trees—which the early Japanese believed to be inhabited by deities who descended from heaven. Spirits were also thought to abide in flowers, and "flower divination" was conducted to forecast each year's harvest. When the *sakura* (flowering cherry), *unohana* (deutzia), *tsutsuji* (azalea), and *asebi*

　死者に満開の花を選んで供えるのは、人の魂は花を通過するという民間信仰に基づいている。それが仏教と結びついて、死者の魂を呼びもどす象徴となった。また、疫病を引き起こす神々は、春の花が散るとさまよい歩くと考え、疫病を防ぐために鎮花祭が行われた。桜、椿、山吹、柳などの花を傘に飾り、この花傘の下をくぐると、病気にならないと考えられたのである。鎮花祭は、京都の今宮神社で、今日も行われている。

　花をめぐるもう一つの民俗習慣は花見で、これも古代までさかのぼる。元々は農耕儀礼であったが、後世には純粋な娯楽に変化した。

　近代以前から、春の七草の行事が行われてきたが、春の七草とは、せり、なずな、ごぎょう、はこべ、ほとけのざ、すずな、すずしろである。これに対する秋の七草は、はぎ、すすき、くず、なでしこ、おみなえし、ふじばかま、ききょうである。

(Japanese andromeda) bloomed profusely, people believed it meant a year of abundance; when the blossoms fell early, they believed that the harvest would be poor.

The practice of offering to the dead selected flowers at the height of their bloom was based on the folk belief that the soul can pass through living flowers. Linked to Buddhism, it represented an attempt to call back the soul of the dead. It was also thought that the deities who caused epidemics roamed abroad when spring blossoms fell. In the hope of controlling such epidemics, a rite called Chinkasai (Soothing of the Flowers) was held, including among its the observances the fashioning of parasols from the fallen blossoms of the *sakura, tsubaki* (camellia), *yamabuki* (Japanese rose), and *yanagi* (willow). People were thought to be granted immunity from disease by walking under these parasols. Chinkasai (or Yasurai Matsuri, as it is also known) is still held at Imamiya Shrine in Kyōto.

Another folk custom involving flowers, the flower-viewing party (*hanami*), also dates back to antiquity. Originally an event closely related to agricultural rites, it later became a purely recreational activity.

Since premodern times, people have celebrated the appearance of the *nanakusa* (seven edible herbs of spring): *seri* (Japanese dropwort), *nazuna* (shepherd's purse), *gogyō* (cudweed), *hakobe* (Stellaria media), *hotokenoza* (Lapsana apogonoides), *suzuna* (turnip), and *suzushiro* (radish); and the seven flowering herbs of autumn: *hagi* (Japanese bush clover), *susuki* (eulalia), *kuzu* (kudzu vine), *nadeshiko* (fringed pink), *ominaeshi* (scabiosa), *fujibakama* (Eupatorium fortunci), and *kikyō* (balloon flower).

桜

桜は、日本の文学に現れる植物の筆頭である。清純と簡潔という日本の伝統的価値観は、桜の花の形と色に反映されているという。桜の花の開花期間はきわめて短く、すぐに散ってしまうので、日本の美学の中心をなすはかない美の格好の象徴となっている。

　桜は、日本の花ではもっとも古くから知られている。「桜」の語は『古事記』に見られ、『万葉集』には桜の木や花をたたえる歌が約四十首ある。しかし、当時の日本文化は、強い中国文化の影響下にあり、『万葉集』も漢詩の影響を受けて、桜より梅を詠むことのほうが多い。10世紀の『古今和歌集』の時代になると、和歌の主題として、桜がもっと多く詠まれるようになる。平安時代の「桜」は、花の同義になるほど、多くの人に好まれた。

　桜の花は、日本の文化と密接に結びつけられるようになった。本居宣長は、植物としても愛国心の対象としても桜をたたえて、次のように詠んでいる。

〈敷島の大和心を人間わば朝日ににほふ山さくら花〉

sakura

(flowering cherry). The *sakura* is foremost among the plants mentioned in Japanese literature. The traditional Japanese values of purity and simplicity are thought to be reflected in the form and color of the blossoms. Since the cherry flowers bloom very briefly and then scatter, they have also become a convenient symbol of the ephemeral beauty at the heart of the Japanese aesthetic sense.

The cherry is one of the oldest flowers known in Japan. The word appears in the *Kojiki*, and the *Man'yōshu* contains about forty poems which mention the tree and praise its blossoms. At that time, however, Japanese culture was heavily influenced by China and the *Man'yōshu* followed the traditions of Chinese poetry, mentioning the *ume* (plum) more often than the *sakura*. By the time of the *Kokinshū,* a tenth-century poetry collection, the *sakura* had become the more significant subject in poetry. Popular enthusiasm for cherry blossoms during the Heian period was such that the word *hana* (flower) was understood as a synonym for *sakura*.

The cherry blossom has become intimately identified with Japanese culture. In a poem expressing an appreciation that is both horticultural and chauvinistic, Motoori Norinaga wrote, "If someone wishes to know the essence of the Japanese spirit, it is the fragrant cherry blossom in the early morning."

菊

菊は5世紀に薬用として中国から日本に渡ってきた。朝廷や貴族の庭で菊を栽培したことが平安時代中期の文学作品に見られる。時期を同じくして、旧暦九月九日に重陽の節句が行われるようになった。この日には菊の花びらを浮かせた酒を飲み、前の晩に菊の花にかぶせて水気と香りをしみこませた布で身体を拭いて長寿を願った。菊は尊い花とされ、皇室の紋になっている。

蓮

蓮は『古事記』に初めて出てくるが、蓮の花は仏教では重要な象徴である。泥水の上に咲くところから、蓮は不純の世界から浮き上がって悟りを得ることのできる人間の能力を象徴している。蓮はまた、毘盧遮那仏と浄土の象徴でもある。仏教美術では、蓮の文様は、仏像や仏具によく使われる。浄土をあらわすものとして、境内に蓮池を作っている寺は多い。

chrysanthemum

(*kiku*). Chrysanthemums were introduced to Japan from China in the fifth century for medicinal purposes. Their cultivation in the gardens of the imperial court and by the aristocrats of the capital is described in literary works of the mid–Heian period. Also during this period, a Chrysanthemum Festival (Chōyō no Sekku) was celebrated on 9 September of the lunar calendar, at which chrysanthemum wine was drunk and cotton, which had been placed on a chrysanthemum flower the previous evening to absorb the flower's dew and scent, was used to wipe the body in order to achieve a long life. The chrysanthemum has long been considered a noble flower, and the crest of the imperial household is a stylized representation of a chrysanthemum blossom.

lotus

(*hasu*). The lotus is first mentioned in the *Kojiki*. The lotus flower is an important symbol in the Buddhist tradition. Because it rises above the mud to bloom, the lotus symbolizes the human capacity to rise above the world's impurities and attain enlightenment. It is also the symbol of the world of Vairocana Buddha and of the Pure Land. In Buddhist art, the lotus appears frequently on statues and ritual objects. To represent the Pure Land in miniature, a pond with lotus flowers was frequently created within temple precincts.

松

松は、風景の一部として、日本美術や文化の重要な要素である。風や雨に耐え、一年を通じて緑の松は、古代には聖なる木とされたが、今日でも正月の門松に用いられている。その美しい形と色彩は、芸術家や作家に広く支持されてきた。

　松は薪としても重用され、かがり火やたいまつとして使われた。松を焼いた炭は、早く高温を得られるので、鍛冶屋に好まれ、そのすすは墨や塗料として使われた。

梅

『万葉集』には梅を詠んだ歌が多い。最初に梅に興味を持ったのは文人や貴族であったが、しだいに和歌に好んで詠まれるようになった。梅の花は、装飾文様として、塗り物、織物、家紋などによく使われる。

　松竹梅を組み合わせた文様が祝い事に使われるようになったのは、江戸時代のことである。この組み合わせをめでたいとする一つの理由は、松竹の常緑と梅の紅色との色彩の調和である。しかし、その装飾的価値の中心は、あらゆる花に先駆けて咲き、季節を問わず変わらない香りの実を持つ梅である。

pine

(*matsu*). As a familiar and pleasing feature of the scenery, pines have long been an important part of Japanese art and culture. Hardy in the face of wind and rain, and green the year round, the pine was regarded in ancient times as a sacred tree and is used even today for a New Year's decoration called *kadomatsu*. Its beautiful shape and hue has been widely celebrated by artists and writers.

The pine is also valued as firewood and was once used for making watchfires and torches. Pine charcoal is favored by blacksmiths for its quick and intense heat; the ashes are used for making *sumi* (Chinese ink) and paints.

Japanese plum

(*ume*). There are many poems referring to the *ume* in the *Man'yōshū*. Mostly literati and nobility were interested in the tree at first, and it became a favorite theme in Japanese court poetry (*waka*). The *ume* blossom also appeared as a decorative motif, notably in lacquer ware, textiles, and family crests.

It was during the Edo period that the combined decorative motif known as *shōchikubai* (pine, bamboo, plum) came into use for the celebration of auspicious occasions. One reason for considering this combination auspicious is the color harmony of the evergreen of the pine and bamboo coupled with the red blossoms of the *ume*. But at the heart of its decorative appeal is the *ume*,

米

日本人にとって、米はもっとも大切な食料で
あったので、稲の栽培は、稲の心、稲魂に祈
る一種の宗教的行為とされてきた。神への祈
願は、いろいろな民俗芸能として生き残って
いる。

　米作りの行程に応じ、家単位、ときには村
単位で農耕儀礼が行われる。それぞれの儀礼
は毎年同じ時期に行われるので、それが年中
行事の基礎となった。最初の儀式は、一月十
五日ごろ行われ、まじないを唱える。種まき
の季節になると、水口に躑躅の枝を飾り、田
の神に焼き米を供える。田植えの季節には、
神を迎え、送り出す儀礼が行われ、いろいろ
な精進が行われる。初夏から開花期にかけて
は、儀礼が繰り返される。害虫にやられると
虫送りが行われ、干ばつの年には雨乞いが行
われる。地方によっては台風をさけるために、
風祭を行った。秋になって実り始めると、田
の神に稲の束を供える穂掛祭、そして収穫が
終わった後は、収穫の祭りであった。

earliest blooming of all flowers and bearing fruit whose simple flavor remains the same regardless of the season.

rice

(*kome*). As rice was the most important food for the Japanese, its cultivation was traditionally regarded as a religious act—an invocation of the *inadama* or spirit of the rice plant. Supplications to the deity survive today in various forms of folk performing arts.

Each stage of rice cultivation was marked by a religious rite performed either by the family or by the village as a unit. As the rites were held at the same time every year, they formed a basic calendar of annual observances. The first rite took place around 15 January, when incantations were performed. When the seeding season arrived, azalea branches were placed around the paddy sluice gates and roasted rice was offered to the god of the rice fields. During the season for transplanting seedlings there were rituals to welcome and send off the god, and various abstinences were imposed. From early summer to the inflorescence stage, there were many occasions for prayer. When beset by insect pests, the ritual of *mushi okuri* was performed; in drought years, prayers for rain were said; some areas held wind festivals (*kaza matsuri*) to fend off typhoons. When the grains started maturing in the fall, a few green sheaves were offered to the god of the rice fields at a *hogakematsuri*. Finally, when harvesting was completed, a harvest festival was held.

英語で話す「日本の心」
和英辞典では引けないキーワード197
Keys to the Japanese Heart and Soul

1996年10月18日　第 1 刷発行
2000年12月11日　第12刷発行

編　著　　講談社インターナショナル株式会社

発行者　　野間佐和子

発行所　　講談社インターナショナル株式会社
　　　　　〒112-8652　東京都文京区音羽1-17-14
　　　　　電話：03-3944-6493（編集部）
　　　　　　　　03-3944-6492（業務部・営業部）

印刷所　　大日本印刷株式会社

製本所　　大日本印刷株式会社

Copyright ©1996 by Kodansha International Ltd.
ISBN4-7700-2082-1

11 英語で話す「日本の謎」Q&A 外国人が聞きたがる100のWHY
100 Tough Questions for Japan

板坂 元 監修　　　　　　　　　　　　　248ページ　ISBN 4-7700-2091-0

なぜ、結婚式は教会で、葬式はお寺でなんてことができるの？　なぜ、大人までがマンガを読むの？　なぜ、時間とお金をかけてお茶を飲む練習をするの？──こんな外国人の問いをつきつめてゆくと、日本文化の核心が見えてきます。

12 英語で話す「日本の心」和英辞典では引けないキーワード197
Keys to the Japanese Heart and Soul

英文日本大事典 編　　　　　　　　　　328ページ　ISBN 4-7700-2082-1

一流のジャパノロジスト53人が解説した「日本の心」を知るためのキーワード集。「わび」「さび」「義理人情」「甘え」「根回し」「談合」「みそぎ」など、日本人特有な「心の動き」を外国人に説明するための強力なツールです。

13 アメリカ日常生活のマナー Q&A Do As Americans Do

ジェームス・M・バーダマン, 倫子・バーダマン 著　　264ページ　ISBN 4-7700-2128-3

"How do you do?" に "How do you do?" と答えてはいけないということ、ご存知でしたか？　日本では当たり前と思われていたことがマナー違反だったのです。旅行で、駐在で、留学でアメリカに行く人必携のマナー集。

15 英語で日本料理 100 Recipes from Japanese Cooking

辻調理師専門学校　畑耕一郎, 近藤一樹 著　272ページ(カラー口絵16ページ)　ISBN 4-7700-2079-1

外国の人と親しくなる最高の手段は、日本料理を作ってあげること、そしてその作り方を教えてあげることです。代表的な日本料理100品の作り方を、外国の計量法も入れながら、バイリンガルで分かりやすく説明します。

16 まんが 日本昔ばなし Once Upon a Time in Japan

川内彩友美 編　ラルフ・マッカーシー 訳　　　160ページ　ISBN 4-7700-2173-9

人気テレビシリーズ「まんが日本昔ばなし」から、「桃太郎」「金太郎」「一寸法師」など、より抜きの名作8話をラルフ・マッカーシーの名訳でお届けします。ホームステイなどでも役に立つ一冊です。

17 イラスト 日本まるごと事典 Japan at a Glance

インターナショナル・インターンシップ・プログラムス 著　　256ページ(2色刷)　ISBN 4-7700-2080-5

1000点以上のイラストを使って日本のすべてを紹介──自然、文化、社会はもちろんのこと、折り紙の折り方、着物の着方から、ナベで米を炊く方法や「あっちむいてホイ」の遊び方まで国際交流に必要な知識とノウハウを満載。

19 英語で話す「世界」Q&A Talking About the World Q&A

講談社インターナショナル 編　　　　　　320ページ　ISBN 4-7700-2006-6

今、世界にはいくつの国家があるか、ご存じですか？　対立をはらみながらも、急速に1つの運命共同体になっていく「世界」──外国の人と話すとき知らなければならない「世界」に関する国際人必携の「常識集」です。

20 誤解される日本人 外国人がとまどう41の疑問 The Inscrutable Japanese

メリディアン・リソーシス・アソシエイツ 編　賀川洋 著　　232ページ　ISBN 4-7700-2129-1

あなたのちょっとした仕草や表情が大きな誤解を招いているかもしれません。「日本人はどんなときに誤解を受けるのか？」そのメカニズムを解説し、「どのように外国人に説明すればよいか」最善の解決策を披露します。

21 英語で話す「アメリカ」Q&A Talking About the USA Q&A

賀川洋 著　　　　　　　　　　　　　　312ページ　ISBN 4-7700-2005-8

仕事でも留学でも遊びでも、アメリカ人と交際するとき、知っておくと役に立つ「アメリカ小事典」。アメリカ人の精神と社会システムにポイントをおいた解説により、自然、歴史、政治、文化、そして人をバイリンガルで紹介します。

37 英語で話す国際経済 Q&A 一目で分かるキーワード図解付き
A Bilingual Guide to the World Economy

日興リサーチセンター 著　マーク・ショルツ 訳　　　　320ページ　ISBN 4-7700-2164-X

不安定な要素をかかえて流動する国際経済の複雑なメカニズムを、日本最良のシンクタンクのひとつ、日興リサーチセンターが、最新の情報をおりこみながら初心者にも分かるようにやさしく解説。

39 国際貢献 Q&A 世界で活躍する日本人　Japan's Contribution to the World

外務省大臣官房海外広報課 監修　　　　288ページ　ISBN 4-7700-2192-5

日本は、世界の平和の維持のため、経済の発展のため、地球環境の保護のためなどにさまざまな努力をしています。その全容を紹介する本書は、これらの活動に参加したい人々のための絶好のガイドブック。

40 英語で比べる「世界の常識」　Everyday Customs Around the World

足立恵子 著　　　　304ページ　ISBN 4-7700-2346-4

海外の情報が簡単に手に入るようになった現在でも、日常生活での文化や風習の違いは意外に知られていないもの。世界各国の独特の文化や風習に対する理解を深め比べることで日本の独自性を再確認する本書から、国際交流の本質が見えてきます。

42 英語で話す「アメリカの謎」Q&A　Though Questions About the USA Q&A

リー・ハウエル 著　　　　224ページ　ISBN 4-7700-2349-9

さまざまな分野で日本と深い関わりを持つアメリカ。「なぜ、懲役236年などという長い刑期があるの？」「なぜ、離婚率が高いの？」「なぜ、社長の給料があんなに高いの？」など、近くて遠い国、アメリカのあらゆる「WHY？」に答えます。

43 「英国」おもしろ雑学事典　All You Wanted to Know About the U.K.

ジャイルズ・マリー 著　　　　240ページ　ISBN 4-7700-2487-8

「英国人とアメリカ人はどう違うの？」「英国料理はなぜあんなにマズイの？」など、英国のナゾから大英帝国の盛衰、産業革命についての文化的考察、政治や王室のシステムまで、英国のすべてに迫ります。

44 「ニューズウィーク」で読む日本経済
The Japanese Economy as Reported in *Newsweek*

沢田 博 編訳　　　　224ページ　ISBN 4-7700-2543-2

グローバルな視点と緻密な取材で定評のある『ニューズウィーク』誌の経済記事から日本経済を読み解く、これが本書のテーマです。アメリカの経済アナリストたちや政府高官の辛口の批判や提言から、日本の抱える問題点がはっきりと読みとれます。

45 バイリンガル日本史年表　Chronology of Japanese History

英文日本大事典 編　　　　160ページ（2色刷）　ISBN 4-7700-2453-3

日本の歴史を英語で語る。意外に難しいこの問題を解く鍵は年表です。歴史的事項が簡単に引けてそれに対する英語が一目でわかります。さらにそれぞれの時代の解説や、天皇表・年号表なども収録。日本の歴史を語るキーワード集として活用できます。

47 英語で「ちょっといい話」スピーチにも使える222のエピソード
Bits & Pieces of Happiness

アーサー・F・レネハン 編　足立恵子 訳　　　　208ページ　ISBN 4-7700-2596-3

「逆境」「年齢」「感謝」「ビジネス」「希望」「笑い」「知恵」など47項目のテーマを、短く機知に富んだエッセイ・逸話・ジョーク・ことわざの形式で鋭く描写。意味のある話をしたいときに、スピーチ原稿のヒントに、一日を明るくするために、実用的なアイデアが満載！

49 英語で話す「医療ハンドブック」Getting Medical Aid in English

東京海上記念診療所 監修　黒田基子 著　　　　336ページ　ISBN 4-7700-2345-6

海外で病気になったらどうしよう？——本書では、小児科・内科・婦人科などの科目別に、さまざまな症状を想定した「会話」と「文章」を対訳形式で展開することによって、英語で話さなくても指で指すだけで医者や看護婦とコミュニケーションできるようになっています。

50 辞書では引けない 最新ビジネス・キーワード100
U.S. Business Buzzwords

ロッシェル・カップ 著 224ページ　ISBN 4-7700-2606-4

日米で活躍する異文化ビジネス・コンサルタントの著者が、アメリカ人が頻繁に使う現代ビジネス用語の中から、日本人がその概念を誤解しやすいものを100ワード精選し、日本人のために解説します。国際人には必須のキーワード集。

51 「人を動かす」英語の名言 Inspiring Quotations from Around the World

大内 博、ジャネット大内 著 256ページ　ISBN 4-7700-2518-1

世界中の人々の心に焼きついている名言を、ジョン・F・ケネディ、プリンセス・ダイアナ、マザー・テレサ、アガサ・クリスティ、ウォルト・ディズニー、新渡戸稲造、手塚治虫らを、世界的に有名な現代人を中心に集め、その背景や意義を解説していきます。

52 英語で「いけばな」The Book of Ikebana

川瀬敏郎 著 240ページ（カラー口絵16ページ）　ISBN 4-7700-2529-7

本書では、いけばなの基本技術、基礎知識を中心にした花レッスンで、だれでも花がいけられるようになります。また日常の生活に役立つ化の愉しみ方と贈り方をビジュアルに提案しています。気品に満ちた川瀬敏郎氏の花とともに、「いけばな」がやさしく解説されています。

53 英語で話す「日本の伝統芸能」
The Complete Guide to Traditional Japanese Performing Arts

小玉祥子 著 288ページ　ISBN 4-7700-2607-2

外国人に日本の文化を語るときに、避けて通れないのが「伝統芸能」です。「歌舞伎」「文楽」「能・狂言」をメインに、「日本舞踊」「落語」「講談」「浪曲」「漫才」といった「日本の伝統芸能」についての必要不可欠な基礎知識と、会話を盛りあげるための面白雑学を満載しました。

54 折々のうた ORIORI NO UTA: Poems for All Seasons

大岡信 著 ジャニン・バイチマン 訳 304ページ　ISBN 4-7700-2380-4

『朝日新聞』の名コラム「折々のうた」の中から120余りを選び抜きました。啄木、牧水、白秋による愛誦歌から、堀口大學がコクトーの詩をみごとな日本語に移しかえた訳詩まで。もちろん芭蕉や蕪村や子規の代表作や、現代をうたった詩歌も選ばれています。日本語で、そして英語で、その言葉の宝庫に分け入り、過ぎゆく四季と、心の機微に触れてみませんか。

55 英語で話す皇室Ｑ＆Ａ Talking About the Imperial Family

渡辺みどり 著 アラン・キャンベル 訳 304ページ　ISBN 4-7700-2598-X

外国の人によく聞かれる、日本および日本人についての質問の中でも、トップに位置するのが「皇室はなぜ存在しているのか」「天皇・皇后はどんな役割を果たしているのか」といった問いかけです。皇室ジャーナリストとして長年にわたって活躍してきた著者が、折にふれての皇室の方々のお言葉や、人間性豊かなさまざまなエピソードも盛り込みながら解説をしていきます。

56 英語で楽しむ「スポーツ観戦」実況中継が聞き取れるようになる!
American Sports A–Z

マイク・ドッド 著 堀田佳男 訳 304ページ　ISBN 4-7700-2486-X

大リーグ、アメリカンフットボール、NBA、ゴルフ、アイスホッケー、テニス、ストック・カーレースなど日本でも大人気のアメリカン・スポーツのすべてを網羅。メジャースポーツの基礎知識から、グラウンドやコート場外でのウラ話、専門用語や実況中継の英語表現まで、「スポーツ観戦」を楽しむための情報が満載!　アメリカ人と会話を弾ませる絶好のトピックとなることでしょう。

57 「日本らしさ」を英語にできますか?
Japanese Nuance in Plain English!

松本道弘、ボイエ・デ・メンテ 著 256ページ　ISBN 4-7700-2595-5

多くの日本語には、表面的な意味ではうかがい知れないニュアンスや文化的な陰影がたくさん秘められています。外国の人が、それに気づかなければ、言葉を誤解し、ビジネスや生活で、大きな行違いを生み出しかねません。「ウソも方便」「けじめ」「水に流す」といった日本語を英語にできますか?　そして外国の人たちに、英語でわかりやすく説明できますか?

実用英語の総合シリーズ

・ 旅行・留学からビジネスまで、コミュニケーションの現場で役立つ
　「実用性」
・ ニューヨーク、ロンドンの各拠点での、ネイティブ チェックにより
　保証される「信頼性」
・ 英語の主要ジャンルを網羅し、目的に応じた本選びができる
　「総合性」

46判変型（113 x 188 mm）仮製

1 これを英語で言えますか？　学校で教えてくれない身近な英単語

講談社インターナショナル 編　　　　　　232ページ　ISBN 4-7700-2132-1

「腕立てふせ」、「○×式テスト」、「短縮ダイヤル」、「$a^2+b^3=c^4$」……あなたはこのうちいくつを英語で言えますか？　日本人英語の盲点になっている英単語に、本書は70強のジャンルから迫ります。読んでみれば、「なーんだ、こんなやさしい単語だったのか」「そうか、こう言えば良かったのか」と思いあたる単語や表現がいっぱいです。雑学も満載しましたので、忘れていた単語が生き返ってくるだけでなく、覚えたことが記憶に残ります。弱点克服のボキャビルに最適です。

3 アメリカ旅行「使える」キーワード　場面別想定問答集

アンドリュー・ホルバート 著　　　　　　240ページ　ISBN 4-7700-2481-9

出国から帰国まで、アメリカ旅行のすべてをカバーする一冊。ショッピングや食事、レンタカーの借り方からトラブル対処法まで様々な状況で必要となる決め手のフレーズ。そんな「コトバ」と、初心者でも楽しく旅ができる実用的な「情報」を満載。

4 ダメ！ その英語［ビジネス編］　日本人英語NG集

連東孝子 著　　　　　　　　　　　　　176ページ　ISBN 4-7700-2469-X

社長賞を貰ったアメリカ人の同僚に "You are lucky!" と言ってはダメ!?　ビジネスの場面を中心に、コミュニケーションの行き違い110例を紹介・解説。「この英語、なぜいけないの？」「どうして通じないの？」に答える、日本人英語のウィークポイント攻略本。

5 米語イディオム600　ELTで学ぶ使い分け&言い替え

バーバラ・ゲインズ 著　　　　　　　　208ページ　ISBN 4-7700-2461-4

イディオムを使いこなせるかどうかが英会話上達の決め手！　本書は「勘定を払う」「仕事を探す」など、日常生活に即した80の場面別に600以上の重要イディオムを紹介。ただ機械的に暗記するのではなく、状況に応じた言い替え・使い分けがマスターできる。

6 どこまで使える？ "go" と "come"　かんたん単語55の英会話

田崎清忠 著　　　　　　　　　　　　　208ページ　ISBN 4-7700-2527-0

"come" "take" "leave"など、中学校で習う初歩的な単語も、使い方次第で表現力が大幅アップ！　誰もが知っている簡単な単語55の意味と使い方を、肩の凝らないエッセイを通して紹介。つい見落としがちな、意味と用法の意外なバリエーションが気軽に学べる。

7 アメリカ留学日常語 事典　これがなければ1日も過ごせない！

東照二 著　　　　　　　　　　　　　　192ページ　ISBN 4-7700-2470-3

アメリカのキャンパスには、独特の用語や表現がいっぱいあります。本書は、留学を志す人、アメリカのキャンパスで生活する人が知っていないと困る用語と情報を一挙にまとめ、日本人にわかりやすく解説しました。

8 マナー違反の英会話　英語にだって「敬語」があります

ジェームス・M・バーダマン、森本豊富 共著　　208ページ　ISBN 4-7700-2520-3

英語にだって「敬語」はあります。「アメリカ人はフランクで開放的」と言われていますが、お互いを傷つけないように非常に気配りをしています。しかし親しい仲間うちで丁寧な英語表現ばかりを使っていては、打ち解けられません。英語にだってTPOがあります。

9 英語で「四字熟語」365　英語にするとこんなにカンタン！

松野守峰、N・ミナイ 共著　　272ページ　ISBN 4-7700-2466-5

四字熟語をマスターし、その英語表現によってボキャブラリーも急増する一石二鳥のおトクな1冊！　日常よく使われる365の四字熟語を「努力・忍耐」「チームワーク」「苦境」「性格」「能力」「友情」「恋愛」「宿命」などの意味別に分類し、英語にしました。

10 「英語モード」で英会話　これがネイティブの発想法

脇山怜、佐野キム・マリー 共著　　224ページ　ISBN 4-7700-2522-X

英語でコミュニケーションをするときには、日本語から英語へ、「モード」のスイッチを切り替えましょう。タテ社会の日本では、へりくだって相手を持ち上げることが、人間関係の処世術とされています。ところが、「未経験で何もわかりませんがよろしく」のつもりで "I am inexperienced and I don't know anything." なんて英語で言えば、それはマイナスの自己イメージを投影することになるでしょう。「日本語モード」の英語は誤解のもとです。

11 英語で読む「科学ニュース」　話題の知識を英語でGet!

松野守峰 著　　208ページ　ISBN 4-7700-2456-8

科学に関する知識とことばが同時に身につく、画期的な英語実用書！「ネット恐怖症族」「スマート・マウスパッド」から「デザイナー・ドラッグ」「DNAによる全人類の祖先解明」まで、いま話題の科学情報が英語でスラスラ読めるようになります。

12 CDブック 英会話・ぜったい・音読　頭の中に英語回路を作る本

國弘正雄 編　千田潤一 トレーニング指導

144ページ CD (40分)付　ISBN 4-7700-2459-2

英語を身につけるには、英語の基礎回路を作ることが先決です。家を建てる際、基礎工事をすることなしに、柱を立てたり、屋根を造るなんてことはしないはずです。英語もこれと同じです。基礎回路が出来ていない段階で、単語や構文などをいくら覚えようとしても、ざるで水をすくうようなものです。使える英語を身につける、それには何と言っても音読です。本書には、中学3年生用の文部省検定済み英語教科書7冊から、成人の英語トレーニングに適した12レッスンを厳選して収録しました。だまされたと思って、まずは3ヵ月続けてみてください。確かな身体の変化にきっと驚かれることでしょう。

13 英語のサインを読む　アメリカ生活情報早わかりマニュアル

清地恵美子 著　　240ページ　ISBN 4-7700-2519-X

広告や看板の読み方がわかると、アメリカの英語と暮らしが見えてきます。「スーパーのチラシに$2.99Lb.とあるけど」、「コインランドリーを使いたいのだけれど」。本書では自動販売機の使い方、案内板や利用説明書の読み方など、生活情報入手のコツを紹介します。

14 産直！ ビジネス英語　NY発、朝から夜までの英会話

藤松忠夫 著　　224ページ　ISBN 4-7700-2458-4

英語がペラペラしゃべれるだけでは、NYでビジネスは出来ません。会議を司会する、人事考課の評定を部下に納得させる、ビジネスランチを成功させる、効果的に情報を入手するなど……。これらが英語でちゃんと出来て、あなたは初めて一人前です。それには、アメリカ人の常識・習慣・考え方を知ったうえで適切な英語表現を身につけることが欠かせません。

15 A or B？ ネイティブ英語　日本人の勘違い150パターン

ジェームス・M・バーダマン 著　　　192ページ　ISBN 4-7700-2708-7

日本人英語には共通の「アキレス腱」があります。アメリカ人の筆者が、身近でもっとも頻繁に見聞きする、日本人英語の間違い・勘違いを約150例、一挙にまとめて解説しました。間違いを指摘し、背景を解説するだけでなく、実践的な例文、関連表現も盛り込みましたので、日本人共通の弱点を克服できます。これらの150パターンさえ気をつければ、あなたの英語がグンと通じるようになることでしょう。

16 英語でEメールを書く　ビジネス＆パーソナル「世界基準」の文例集

田中宏昌、ブライアン・アズビョンソン 共著　　　224ページ　ISBN 4-7700-2566-1

英文Eメールは、他の英文ライティングとどう違う？　気を付けなければならないポイントは？など、Eメールのマナーからビジネスでの使いこなし方、さらには個人的な仲間の増やし方やショッピングの仕方まで、様々な場面に使える実例を豊富に掲載しました。

17 「恋する」英会話　もっと素敵な女性になれる本

窪田ひろ子 著　　　224ページ　ISBN 4-7700-2526-2

品のない英語を話したら、せっかくの恋だって逃げてしまいます。あなたが使うコトバにより、あなたの周囲に集まる人が変わってくることでしょう。本書では、センスある話題の選び方や話し方から、イヤな男に誘われた時の断り方まで、あなたを洗練された英語の世界にご案内します。

18 CDブック 英会話・はじめの一言　相手を引きつける出会いのフレーズ

中山幸男 著　　　240ページ CD (60分)付　ISBN 4-7700-2721-4

気の利いた一言がサッと出てくるように「機知の引き出し箱」を用意しました。巷には、いろいろな表現を羅列した英会話の本がたくさんありますが、実際の場面で使ってみて使えると思うフレーズはいくつあるでしょう？　苦しまぎれに無味乾燥な表現ばかり並べても、会話はちっとも弾みません。本書は、たった一言でもキラリと光るフレーズをシチュエーション別にまとめました。例えば、握手しながらお辞儀をしてしまったとき "That's how Japanese say hello." と言えば、相手もクスッとして緊張感もほぐれることでしょう。これからは「はじめの一言」をドンドン投げかけていってください。

19 CDブック 英会話・つなぎの一言　質問すれば会話がはずむ！

浦島 久、クライド・ダブンポート 共著　　　240ページ CD (62分)付　ISBN 4-7700-2728-1

質問は相手の答えを聞き取るための最大のヒント！　初級者（TOEIC350～530点英検3級～準2級）向けの質問例文集。英会話にチャレンジしたものの、相手の英語がまったく理解できなかった、あるいは、会話がつながらなかった、という経験はありませんか？　そんなときは、積極的に質問してみましょう。自分の質問に対する相手の答えは理解できるはずです。本書では、質問しやすい99のテーマに1800の質問文例を用意しました。

20 似ていて違う英単語　コリンズコービルド英語表現使い分け辞典

エドウィン・カーペンター 著　斎藤早苗 訳　　　256ページ　ISBN 4-7700-2484-3

英語には英和辞典を引いても、違いがわからない単語がいくつもあります。そんな一見同じに見える表現にはどんな違いがあるのだろうか。どう使い分ければ良いのだろう。そんな疑問に答えるのが本書です。Collins COBUILDの誇る3億語以上の英語のデータベースの分析から生まれた辞典です。例文も豊富に掲載しました。

まんが日本昔ばなし
Once Upon a Time in Japan

テレビで大人気の「まんが日本昔ばなし」のかわいらしい絵とお話が、完全なバイリンガルになりました。お母さんから子供たちへと語り継がれてきた、遠い昔の日本の心あたたまる物語が、英語と日本語で楽しめる新シリーズです。

● 日本語の原文は総ルビ付き。小さいお子様でも楽しく読めます。
● 英語の語句には丁寧な注釈付き。英語の意味がよくわかります。
● 冒頭に物語についての解説付き。お話の背景が理解できます。

川内彩友美 編　46判（128×188mm）上製　48ページ（各巻とも）

あなたの英語が変わる

ネイティブチェック済

講談社パワー・イングリッシュ

これを英語で言えますか？

学校で教えてくれない身近な英単語

四捨五入する	round off
5^2	five squared
モーニングコール	wake-up call
ホチキス	stapler
改札口	ticket gate
昇進	promotion
協調介入	coordinated intervention
貸し渋り	credit crunch
介護保険	nursing care insurance
花粉症	hay fever
朝飯前だよ	That's a piece of cake!

講談社インターナショナル 編
232ページ
ISBN 4-7700-2132-1

日本人英語の盲点になっている英単語に、78のジャンルから迫ります。読んでみれば、「なーんだ、こんなやさしい単語だったのか」、「そうか、こう言えば良かったのか」と思いあたる単語や表現がいっぱいです。雑学も満載しましたので、忘れていた単語が生き返ってくるだけでなく、覚えたことが記憶に残ります。弱点克服のボキャビルに最適です。